CW00543530

Crypto Confidential

Praise for *Crypto Confidential*

'A front-row seat to the roller-coaster rise and fall of crypto during
the 2020/2021 zeal. A great look from the trenches to understand
the good and bad of cryptocurrency from the inside out'
Reid Hoffman, Co-founder of LinkedIn and Inflection AI

'My only crypto-take is that if you don't find some of it inspiring,
you're not paying attention; and if you don't find a lot of it absurd,
you're not paying attention . . . Every investor should read this book'
Morgan Housel, author of *The Psychology of Money*

'The perfect way to understand the culture of the crypto craze. Fast-paced
and informative, newcomers will be shocked and veterans will feel seen'
Eric Jorgenson, author of The *Almanack of Naval Ravikant*

'A riveting insider's account of the cryptocurrency casino.
It's funny, honest, and moving in equal measure'
Jimmy Soni, author of *The Founders*

'The crypto industry has no shortage of scandal,
and yet the allure of its potential persists for many. Nat Eliason's
book is a riveting, personal account of what happens when
you get sucked in – for good and bad. I couldn't put it down'
Zoë Schiffer, managing editor of *Platformer*, author of *Extremely Hardcore*

'A gripping narrative on the highs, lows, and inner workings
of cryptocurrency. Part thriller and part educational,
I found it hard to put the book down'
Nick Maggiulli, author of *Just Keep Buying*

'As someone who used to work in crypto, Nat's book really resonated with
me – the search for meaning, the questioning, the wondering if things really
can be better . . . and the disappointment when it isn't. The book is soulful
and a beautiful exploration of an industry that should ask more of itself'
Kyla Scanlon, financial educator, author of *In This Economy?*

Crypto Confidential

WINNING AND LOSING MILLIONS IN THE NEW FRONTIER OF FINANCE

Nathaniel Eliason

WH
ALLEN

1

WH Allen, an imprint of Ebury Publishing
20 Vauxhall Bridge Road
London SW1V 2SA

WH Allen is part of the Penguin Random House group of companies
whose addresses can be found at global.penguinrandomhouse.com

First published in the US by Portfolio in 2024
First published in the UK by WH Allen in 2024

www.penguin.co.uk

A CIP catalogue record for this book is available from the British Library

ISBN 9780753561232

Printed and bound in Great Britain by Clays Ltd, Elcograf S.p.A.

The authorised representative in the EEA is Penguin Random House Ireland,
Morrison Chambers, 32 Nassau Street, Dublin D02 YH68

Penguin Random House is committed to a sustainable future
for our business, our readers and our planet. This book is made
from Forest Stewardship Council® certified paper.

For Cosette, Sutton, and Kaia

CONTENTS

AUTHOR'S NOTE

This is a true story.

That said, it required some minor massaging, and names have been changed to protect the innocent—and the not so innocent. I have reconstructed conversations from memory, texts, emails, and chat messages. The dollar amounts, while they might seem exaggerated, are all accurate.

I've tried to keep the technical explanations simple, weaving them throughout the story, but there is also a glossary of key terms in the back of the book for those who need a helping hand.

Finally, none of this is financial advice. Please don't gamble away your life savings. This world is crazy, and it can easily chew you up and spit you out if you aren't careful.

Crypto Confidential

Prologue

JANUARY 2022

I was flying out of my bedroom before I even finished reading the message. This couldn't be real. This guy was screwing with me.

My wife, Cosette, called after me. "Honey . . . ?"

"Uh, it's fine. I gotta . . . fix something."

I could hardly form the words. My mouth wasn't working. My heart hammered in my ears, and pins and needles burned my hands and feet. I squeezed my fists as hard as I could to get them to stop hurting as I stumbled into my office and fumbled through my laptop password, pulling up the message that had thrown me out of bed:

"Nat, someone found a way to hack us. It sounds bad. All of our funds might be at risk."

This was the absolute worst-case scenario. The one I'd pushed to the back of my mind. The one I'd pretended was impossible so I could sleep at night. I had always accepted the risk that I could lose all of *my* money. But if I lost $100 million of other people's money . . .

I couldn't let myself think about that right now.

I started running through every possible scenario. Whoever was reaching out might be trying to scam us, trying to trick us into doing something that would enable them to hack us. Maybe they had already hacked us and had other demands. Or, maybe, just maybe, they were actually a trustworthy person and wanted to help us out?

Doubtful.

Just then, crying broke out in the next room. Cosette sighed and said, "I'll get her." I could hear the frustration in her steps to the nursery, Morse code that she wasn't buying my "it's fine," another thing I couldn't think about now. I slipped on my headphones and hunkered down.

Checking the code, everything seemed fine. Everyone's money was still there. Whatever the potential hack was, it hadn't happened yet. Maybe there was still time.

I looked at how much of my own money was at risk: just over $10 million. I desperately wanted to sell whatever I could. But this was crypto. Everything was public, everyone could see what I was doing, and more than a few were already watching me. They'd notice if I pulled my money. They'd get scared and start asking questions. Or they'd assume I knew something was up and preemptively sell everything. A bank run would be almost as bad as a hack.

The hammering in my ears continued. My hands burned.

I joined a chat room with the hacker, whose name was Paul. He asked if I was the programmer in charge of the crypto code in which he'd found the vulnerability. The truth was, I'd hesitate to even call myself a programmer. I'd thrown that code together in two weeks. It was a freelance gig to get my feet wet, not something I thought people would put $100 million into. What I told Paul was:

"Yes, that's me. How can I help you?"

As Paul started typing his reply, I noticed a flurry of notifications coming from the public chat. *Fuck*. He'd sent a message to the entire community of thousands of people whose money was now at risk saying there was a security risk and asking if any team members were online. People were starting to freak out and demand answers. What could I do? I tried to sound reassuring. I said everything was fine and we were on top of it. It's not like I was going to tell everyone they might be about to lose all of their money.

Meanwhile, on the private chat, Paul said he would need to do a couple things to verify that I was the owner. "Obviously, I can't risk giving this information to anyone," he said. "In the wrong hands it could lead to a massive financial loss."

Yeah, I thought, *like your hands, asshole.*

I knew that whatever he was about to ask me to do could be part of a hack. The best way to get the gates of Troy open was to make us think he was trying to help us *prevent* a theft.

"If you could," he continued, "please send a small payment of a few cents from your account to the following account." He pasted in his crypto address. Sending a simple payment should be safe enough, but I wasn't an expert. I'd never dealt with a hacker, but there was no time to find and hire someone more experienced.

If I played along and got us hacked, I'd be ruined. But if I didn't play along, and we got hacked, well, I'd be screwed then, too. A year earlier, I never could have dreamed of making this kind of money. My entire life had changed. I'd secured my family's financial future. I'd ensured the life for my daughter that I was so desperate to give her. And now, it was all about to get taken away. Just like that. Back to start. Do not pass Go. Do not collect $200.

I dug my elbows into my desk and fell forward onto my hands, which were trying to rub the terror and fatigue out of my eyes.

This might be the worst day of my life.

What the hell am I supposed to do?

1

Is Everyone Getting Rich without Me?

APRIL 2021:
NINE MONTHS EARLIER

Getting rich is a long, slow, steady process: get a job, do your work, get promoted, invest in your 401(k). With a few good promotions, maybe a strategic job switch or two, and years of diligent saving, hopefully, someday, you will "make it" and earn the retirement of your dreams.

But what if there were a faster way?

Five months earlier, I had quit my marketing job to find work I was more passionate about. Now, I was running out of time. I had a popular blog that earned me some money, and I would have loved to have found a way to write full time. But our daughter was due in six months, and I was unemployed. I needed to figure something out fast.

I was learning to code, and programming jobs paid well, so that was the obvious answer. But it felt like, everywhere I looked, young people were cirvumventing the system to amass huge amounts of money, enough to live off for years, even decades. Some of these self-made millionaires had built businesses or created new technologies, but a shocking number seemed to have found an easier path: they'd gambled on crypto.

·ɃɃɃ·

I finished the last of that day's coding classes and went inside to make more coffee. After first diving down the programming rabbit hole a few months earlier, I started spending twelve hours a day indoors, hunched over a screen. It was taking a toll on my sanity, so I dragged my desk outside onto my deck, where a towering old oak tree offered enough protection from Austin's heat to survive. I might have looked silly sitting out there for half the day chugging ice water, but I loved it.

While the coffee brewed, I pulled my phone out to check the crypto-trading app Coinbase. Between coding sessions, I had started day-trading Dogecoin (DOGE), a cryptocurrency created in 2013 based on Bitcoin. Dogecoin was never meant to be a serious financial asset. Even the founders said it was a joke. But when the price of Bitcoin started climbing at the end of 2020, and people looked for the next hot cryptocurrency to bet on, Doge-coin started climbing as well.

For most of the currency's eight years in existence, one DOGE was worth a fraction of a cent. Then, in February 2021, the price reached a new high of five cents. Now, at the start of April, it was rising past six cents. I had bought some in January, when it started taking off, and had been holding it ever since. So far, it was the only thing I'd done that year that had made me any money.

Every day, when I woke up and saw that it had gone up, or at least not gone down by much, I had to answer the same question: *Do I sell this, or do I keep holding on to it?* I was up a few thousand dollars by then, and it was tempting to sell, but the pain of missing out on more money might be worse than the joy of cashing in on what I'd already made.

"Are you ready to go?" Cosette's voice brought me back to the present. She must have come downstairs while I was buried in my phone.

"Yeah, sorry, let's do it," I said and started leashing up the dogs. Co-sette was a real estate agent and didn't need to leave to start showing houses until nine, giving us an hour to grab coffee. Our favorite spot, Velocity, was only a couple of blocks away and run by Johnny, one of our closest friends.

Once we left the house, Cosette asked, "Were you looking at your doggy coin again?"

"Maybe . . ." I smirked. "We're up again."

"So, you're gonna sell it?"

"Well, no, I didn't say that."

She laughed. "I don't know how you do that."

"Do what?"

"See it go up and not sell it. I'd be terrible at this. I'd want to sell as soon as I saw I made money." We stopped at the intersection, waiting to cross. "Are you excited for this afternoon?"

"Yeah," I said, stepping into the street. "I can't wait to see her."

"I bet she's a cute little tadpole," said Cosette.

"*Our* cute little tadpole," I said. "I can't believe it's already been three months."

We rounded the corner to Velocity and froze. Johnny was on his hands and knees crawling around on the ground in front of the order window, while Rose, his partner, paced back and forth on her phone, clearly agitated.

"Johnny, what happened?" I yelled as we started jogging towards the trailer.

"Keep the dogs back," Johnny called out. He had shards of glass carefully balanced in his hands, and I saw there was a larger pile on the steps in front of the shop below the shattered window of his café door.

"Again?" I asked him.

"Yeah," said Johnny. "Again." He tossed the glass in the trash and scanned the front steps for any remaining pieces. "I think you're good."

Cosette kept the dogs outside with Rose, and I followed Johnny inside the trailer to survey the damage.

"Lucky they left the prototypes," I said. Johnny was a mechanical engineer at heart and had spent the last year designing the best travel espresso maker money could buy. At $1,500, it seemed like an insane investment to me, but he had hundreds of coffee aficionados who had already preordered it and were eagerly awaiting its release.

"Yeah, probably too hard to pawn. They took all the tablets though."

"Think it was the same guy?"

Johnny nodded. He opened in 2019 and built a thriving community around the café. Then the COVID-19 pandemic nearly put him out of business. His online sales of coffee beans and espresso tools were doing well, but the café was barely scraping by. Worse yet, someone in the area had been breaking in every few weeks. He couldn't easily afford a surprise bill for new tablet computers.

"What're you gonna do?" I asked. "You can't keep letting this guy steal from you."

"I know," said Johnny, inspecting an espresso machine for damage, "but what I can do?"

"What about putting in more security? Or a gate? Booby traps?"

Johnny laughed, "Yeah, a gate and more security would be great, but I can't afford that."

"You could sell your DOGE," I said.

"Yeah . . . but I wanna let that ride," said Johnny. He'd been much more aggressive than me with his DOGE investment. I knew he was up almost $20,000. He was making more from holding a joke cryptocurrency than he was from all his hard work at the café.

"We need to find the next Dogecoin," I said.

"Yeah, well, if you find any more free money, please let me know," Johnny said. "I don't know how much longer I can do this." He stared at his espresso machines. "Anyway, what can I get you?"

₿₿₿

On the walk home, I couldn't get the idea of "the next Dogecoin" out of my head. Would other cryptocurrencies follow Dogecoin's meteoric growth the way Dogecoin was following Bitcoin?

It had happened before. When Bitcoin launched in 2009, very few people cared. For the first few years, one bitcoin (BTC) was worth almost nothing. In 2010, someone spent ten thousand bitcoins on two Papa John's pizzas. Curiosity grew, though, and eventually peaked with the first crypto mania in 2013–14, when Bitcoin hit $1,100 per BTC and spawned tons of copycats who wanted to cash in on its success.

If you caught the wave of that mania early, you could have made a fortune by finding out when a new cryptocurrency was going to launch, buying it early, then selling it as it took off. People made millions speculating on the Bitcoin copycats.

By the end of 2014, though, the mania was over. Bitcoin fell to a low of $172, most of the copycat cryptocurrencies died, and the public consensus was that the Bitcoin story was over.

But it came back. In 2017, the market took off again, this time sending Bitcoin to a peak price just shy of $20,000. Once again, as the fervor around Bitcoin increased, people started launching copycats.

The second wave of mania was even bigger and crazier than the first, but it, too, eventually died down. By the end of 2018, Bitcoin had lost 85 percent of its value from the peak and crashed to a low of around $3,000. Most of the copycats died off, and, once again, the popular sentiment was that crypto was dead, but for *real* this time.

Clearly crypto wasn't dead, though. Today, the ten thousand bitcoins spent on those two pizzas in 2010 are worth more than $300 million. In April 2021, Bitcoin was hitting new highs, and Dogecoin and the rest of the market was following suit. Tons of new cryptocurrencies were launching, and some were taking off. If the pattern continued from 2013 and 2017, I had a chance to make much more money. The trick was to find good information on what was launching.

"₿₿₿."

We got back home, and Cosette left for work. I grabbed my laptop and walked out to my desk. What I needed was "alpha," insider knowledge about what was launching before it went public. I had no alpha, but I had a couple of ideas about where to get it.

I opened Twitter and clicked through to the accounts of friends I knew were involved in crypto. The first hadn't tweeted in two years. That made sense. He'd made millions and probably didn't want to use social media anymore.

Another, Caleb, had been working in marketing at the same time as me. We'd shared a few clients, and I'd even hired him for one project, so we knew each other, but I wasn't close with him. He was tweeting nonstop about crypto, but his tweets were mostly indecipherable jargon. He did seem to be making a significant amount of money, though.

Then I noticed he had a few tweets replying to a mutual friend, Quinn, another regular at Velocity. We'd known each other for years, and she had mentioned something about getting more involved in crypto the previous year during the drudgery of COVID lockdowns. At the time, I'd written it off as day-trading and too risky to explore. Now, that seemed like a mistake. I mentally kicked myself for ignoring her for the last year. But maybe she'd be willing to help me now.

"Hey, Quinn," I texted her, "did you hear about Johnny?"

"Yeah, awful," she texted back. "He really needs a gate."

"Agreed. Listen, I wanna ask you about something else, too. You're involved in crypto stuff right?"

"Yeah, why?"

"Can I ask you about it sometime? Baby is coming in six months, and I'm trying to make some money before then." I bit my tongue and waited. I was basically asking her to tell me how to find free money.

"Sure, tomorrow morning at Velocity?"

"Done. See you at 9."

Finally, some good news. If Quinn knew how this new wave of crypto mania was working, this could be an incredible opportunity.

₿₿₿

A few hours later, Cosette and I arrived at our ultrasound appointment. The technician rubbed the jelly on Cosette's stomach and started searching for our daughter, while we waited, squeezing each other's hands, hoping for the best.

Then we saw it . . . a tiny heartbeat appeared on the screen.

"Looks like you have a healthy baby girl," said the technician.

Cosette sniffled and squeezed my hand, and I leaned over to kiss her on the shoulder. Suddenly, it felt more real than ever. Our daughter was healthy, growing, and we had six months to get ready for her.

I really hoped Quinn had the alpha I needed.

BITCOIN 101

Before the speculative mania in cryptocurrency in 2021–22, there was the dot-com bubble of the late nineties and early 2000s. When that bubble burst, plenty of people said the internet was a fad, but they were wrong; the internet is a pretty big deal. Each time a cryptocurrency bubble has popped, crypto has been the subject of the same skepticism. The common assessment of crypto on the news or in books is that it is all one big, dumb fad, or a grift, and it's never going to turn into anything useful. But what if that's wrong? What if crypto is more than a manic casino?

Let's start with Bitcoin.

Bitcoin was launched in 2009 to create a "peer-to-peer electronic cash system," per the subtitle of the white paper attributed to Satoshi Nakamoto. The goal, according to the white paper, was to make it possible for anyone in the world to send money to anyone else without needing to go through a bank, money-transfer service, or even using a particular country's currency. If you live in a more developed nation and mostly send and receive money with other people in your country, you might think, "So what?" But cross-border money transfers had historically been extremely expensive and slow, making it hard for, say, an immigrant to send money back to their family.

It's worth lingering for a moment on that. Before Bitcoin, there was no way to move money around the world using the internet without going through a financial institution. You could give cash or gold to someone in person if you didn't want to use credit cards and bank transfers, but there was no way to make a similar kind of transaction digitally.

The store-of-value aspect of Bitcoin was initially more of a side benefit. The total number of bitcoins that can ever exist is capped at twenty-one million, so, as more people started using it as a way to move money and store some of their wealth, individual bitcoins went up in value due to scarcity. If your government routinely devalues your savings by printing money, a store of wealth with a fixed supply suddenly becomes very attractive, especially if you can store that currency digitally and easily access it anywhere in the world.

So, Bitcoin provides two compelling use cases besides speculation: It offers a digitally native currency you can send anywhere in the world without going through a financial institution, and it offers a way to store your wealth digitally in a form that, like gold, can't have its value destroyed by currency manipulation. The only way Bitcoin *could* have its value destroyed by currency manipulation is if the majority of people who own Bitcoin and maintain the Bitcoin network agreed to change the twenty-one million cap. So, a simple thought exercise should demonstrate why this hasn't and won't happen: If you could vote on the inflation rate for your currency, would you ask for more inflation?

However, what truly set Bitcoin apart was the innovative "blockchain" technology it introduced—a technology that makes it possible to build global, autonomous software powering much more than digital gold. As I'll explain soon, the potential for what we can do with blockchain technology is even more exciting.

2

If You Tell Anyone about This, I'll Kill You

APRIL 2021

Arriving at Velocity the following morning, I saw Johnny had nailed a lattice of two-by-fours over his window to keep out intruders. Inside, I found Quinn waiting at the register. She was a stereotypically nondescript crypto investor. You'd never know how many millions of virtual dollars she was sitting on. She usually wore athleisure, no jewelry, trendy-but-inexpensive shoes, and drove a nice-but-unflashy car.

I walked in, clapped the back of her shoulder, and said, "Good to see you, Quinn."

"Hey, hey, good to see you, too," she said. "Johnny was telling me about his Dogecoin adventures."

"Nat's got some, too, you know," said Johnny, handing Quinn her cold brew.

"Oh yeah?" Quinn raised an eyebrow at me.

"Uh, yeah," I stammered, feeling embarrassed, "a little." I ordered a cold brew and we took our drinks outside to one of the picnic tables.

"You gotta sell that," she said as soon as we sat down.

"Sell what, the DOGE?"

"Yeah, it's going to crash."

I cocked my head to the side, there was no way she could know that. "Why?"

"Everyone is buying it, Nat. It's on the news. Elon is talking about it. It's all over Twitter. It's a dumb-money bonanza. Everyone still holding it or buying it is exit liquidity for the people who got in early."

I felt a sinking feeling in my stomach. "What do you mean, 'exit liquidity'?"

"You might have heard it called 'dumb money,' or 'retail money,' too. It's the people who see the rocket ship taking off and flood in hoping to get rich quick, but instead end up losing everything and making the early speculators rich instead. The only way you make money quickly in a speculative mania like this is by getting in early and selling as it becomes mainstream. The market cap on it is already, what, $10 billion? The time to buy was when it was under $1. Not now."

"Like a year ago, when you said you were getting into crypto?"

She sighed. "Yeah, like a year ago. Major coins like that, you gotta buy when the market is dead. If you rush in when crypto is in another hype cycle like this, you're the exit liquidity."

Maybe this was a mistake. If Quinn was right that the time to buy was back when the market was dead, then I was already too late. I had missed my chance. I thought the whole idea of making easy money in crypto was too good to be true, but it still stung to hear it.

"So, I'm too late," I said.

Quinn stirred her coffee with her straw. "Well, I didn't say that."

"Come on."

"Okay, okay, look: there's always a way to make money in crypto. Yes, you missed the boat on buying the popular stuff like Dogecoin, but there's always another boat coming. If you had bought Dogecoin when Bitcoin started taking off last fall, you would have done great. And now that Dogecoin is taking off, you need to look at where the money might go next.

Crypto speculators are gamblers. They don't take their money out; they put it into the next thing. Or if they lose money, they try to make it back on the next thing."

"What's the next thing, then?"

"Have you been using Ethereum much?" Quinn asked. Ethereum (ETH) was the number-two cryptocurrency behind Bitcoin. But unlike the Bitcoin copycats, Ethereum was launched to provide a different kind of crypto product.

The Bitcoin network, or "blockchain," was built specifically for sending money back and forth between people, but the Ethereum blockchain was designed so that other internet applications could be built on top of it. Theoretically, you could build anything, from a stock-trading platform like TD Ameritrade to a photo-sharing app like Instagram, using Ethereum. But no one had built anything like that yet, and I still didn't understand why anyone would *want* to, or how that would even work in practice. It seemed like Ethereum was just another cryptocurrency that people liked to speculate on.

"You should check it out," said Quinn. "It's like the financial Wild West right now; the amount of money you can make farming is insane."

"Farming?"

"New way to launch cryptocurrencies. It's kind of hard to explain without being in front of a laptop to demonstrate. Why don't you watch some YouTube videos on it then text me once you think you get it."

"Okay, will do," I said. "That group you joined last year, when you were getting into all of this, with Caleb and Galt and the other guys I see making all this crypto money on Twitter, can I still join that?"

Quinn bit the side of her lip, "Well, you *can*."

"But?"

"But it costs a bitcoin to join," she said.

"You paid $50,000 to join a *group chat*?"

"No, I told you, you should have joined a year ago. It was free. Then Galt decided he only wanted serious people, so everyone had to donate a bitcoin to charity to stay in. We'd already made so much more than that, so it was no big deal."

I rubbed my temple. I couldn't believe what I was hearing. They'd made so much money in the year since I'd written it off that a $50,000 donation was no big deal.

Quinn could tell I was getting frustrated. She continued, "Look, I wish I could share some of the stuff from the group with you, but it's a strict no-leaking policy. If they found out, I'd get kicked out."

I sighed. "I get it. It's all good." We sat in silence staring past each other for a moment.

Finally, Quinn asked, "When's the baby due?"

"October," I said.

Quinn nodded. She looked like she was debating something. "Well, look, maybe I'll find something that I can share with you," she said. "I'm trying to start my own group, too. No promises, though."

I felt a glimmer of hope. If Quinn started her own alpha group and included me, I'd have a way in. And it would be much safer than trying to get information from someone I didn't already know and trust.

"Are you going to charge a bitcoin?" I asked.

She laughed. "You get the new-parent discount."

When I got back home, I went out to my desk to start researching. I'd seen farming mentioned in passing online, but I'd never dug into what it meant. I got the sense it might represent an advantage similar to learning about how to buy new crypto launches before the broader public knew about them back in 2013 or '17. If you did, and you bought into the right ones, you made a killing. It was like Quinn said, people were always looking for the next big thing to speculate on.

Most of the popular videos on crypto farming looked scammy, with influencers who had animated dollar signs in their eyes screaming at their computer. Not exactly professorial. But after a bit of skimming, I found one channel that looked promising called Finematics, which had a long video that went in-depth on farming. I watched it a couple of times and took notes. By the end, I felt like I had a good grasp on what was going on.

During the 2013 and '17 manias, when companies launched new cryptocurrencies, also often called *coins* or *tokens*, they would first try to get their new coins listed on a major crypto exchange such as Coinbase. But if Coinbase wasn't willing, or the company didn't want to wait for their coins to be accepted, they would sell them directly to speculators in exchange for other cryptocurrency.

The problem was that, after the crash in 2018, the US Securities and Exchange Commission started suing the companies that sold their cryptocurrencies directly to consumers, claiming it was akin to selling an unregistered security. This should not have come as a surprise, since the companies called these sales ICOs, short for Initial Coin Offerings. In the wake of those lawsuits, crypto companies were less cavalier about selling their coins directly to the public. The quick influx of cash wasn't worth the potential legal ramifications.

Companies still wanted to launch new cryptocurrencies, though. Coins are a great way to raise money quickly, so they figured out a nonintuitive alternative: instead of selling their coins, they gave them away.

Imagine if every time you posted a picture to Instagram you got some Meta stock. The more you used Instagram, the more stock you got. That was effectively what the new crypto projects were doing. They were telling people: *Hey, we launched this new app, and, if you use it, we'll give you some of our coins for free!* It got their coins into the hands of the public in a way that seemed less legally risky, and it gave people an incentive to try whatever products the companies were launching their cryptocurrencies to support.

"Farming" was the process of finding these new launches, figuring out how they were giving the coins away, and then trying to get as many coins as possible as quickly as possible. As the applications got more popular, and more people wanted to buy the coins, you could sell the ones you had already farmed at a profit.

At least, that's what seemed to be going on. It didn't make sense, though. Weren't they giving away money? Why would anyone want to buy these coins? What were these weird apps that were "built on Ethereum"? But this was apparently what Galt's group was doing. They were getting free coins by farming, and then selling those coins to the broader public as the currencies got more popular.

But making money farming still required being early. You still needed alpha. Most projects released a fixed number of tokens each day, so the fewer people participating, the more tokens each individual would get. In-fluencers posting about projects they were "excited" about on Twitter had probably already been farming them for days, had gathered a huge number of tokens, and were posting to get people like me to come in and buy them. They weren't sharing information to be helpful. They were sharing infor-mation to attract exit liquidity.

I texted Quinn about what I'd figured out so far. I tried to put the over-view of farming in my own words, but I still had a few questions.

"One thing I don't get," I messaged, "is why they would be giving you free tokens to use their app. Aren't they losing tons of money if they do that?"

"Not really, no."

"How?"

"Well, they're creating these tokens out of thin air. It doesn't cost any-thing to give them away."

"Sure, but why not keep the tokens for themselves and find some other way to drive adoption?"

"Everyone uses free money to drive adoption. How many of the new, venture-capital-backed food-delivery apps have you tried? They gave away tons of money to hook new users, and it worked for some of them. This is basically the same thing, but, instead of free burritos, you get free tokens."

It still felt weird, like they were leaving money on the table. I texted Quinn again, "How do the people working on the apps make money, though?"

"Well, they don't give all of their coins away, usually only 10 or 20 percent.

Then, as more people get interested in the application and start trying to buy coins to invest or speculate, the team can start selling."

"Seems like we should launch a project then," I said.

"Hey, if you wanna learn how to code crypto applications, go crazy. It's probably the most valuable skill in the world right now."

"Alright, well, I'm gonna go try to find some projects to farm." I didn't want to ask outright and seem desperate, but maybe I'd get lucky and she'd point me toward one.

"Have fun!"

No luck. *Oh well*, back to researching.

₿₿₿

I was looking at who Quinn followed on Twitter to try to find leads when Cosette poked her head out of the back door of the house and waved at me. "I'm going to film a tour of that house on Henninger. Want to join me?" I said sure and packed up my desk.

Most of Cosette's clients were in their late twenties or early thirties, young professionals new to Austin who were buying their first house. A number of them were wealthier, too, so shopping for them was also fun, aspirational shopping for ourselves. We knew we'd have to move in the next few months, or shortly after our baby was born, as it would be awfully cozy with two work-from-home adults, two dogs, and a baby crammed into a thousand square feet. We might not be able to afford the kinds of houses she was touring for her clients yet, but maybe someday.

In April 2021, Austin real estate was taking off nearly as fast as crypto. It seemed like everyone wanted to cash out some of their crypto winnings, or their tech-stock winnings, to buy a piece of it. Houses were starting to go for 5 to 10 percent above their asking prices, and usually sold within a week or two of a house hitting the market. Cosette's mentors said it was the craziest year they'd seen in Austin, and it showed no signs of slowing down. It was an incredible time to get into the business, but also incredibly overwhelming. Now it was a question of how many transactions she could complete before taking maternity leave in October.

We got to the house, and I helped her film the walkthrough while I filled her in on what Quinn and I talked about and what I'd learned since. I was trying not to think about it too much, but there was a small part of me that saw this crypto pot of gold as a potential ticket to early retirement. Quinn and the other people in her group had clearly made a ludicrous amount of money in the last year. If I had that kind cash to fall back on, I could focus on work I loved, like writing, work less than forty hours a week, and spend more time with my kids. It was a wild dream, especially on a six-month timeline, but crazier things had happened—especially in crypto.

Over dinner, I tried not to think too much about Quinn, the alpha groups, and crypto. I didn't do a very good job. As soon as we got home, I opened up Coinbase and looked at my DOGE again. If Quinn was right, I needed to take my winnings now before it tanked. Then I'd have some funds to farm with, if I ever found a good place to do it.

I hated the feeling of being on the outside looking in, knowing there was all this money being made by the people who were "in the know." Now that I knew what exit liquidity was, I couldn't shake the feeling that it's what I had been to that point to smarter people in the market, their exit liquidity. I clicked Sell on Coinbase and converted all of my DOGE to ETH. Then I opened a bottle of wine and slowly melted into the couch next to Cosette. These ten-to-twelve-hour days of researching and coding had been taking their toll. I was spent.

As I got up to pour myself another glass, I saw my phone light up on the dining table. It was a message from Quinn.

"Screw it, are you by your computer?"

"Yeah, why?"

"Get online. If you tell anyone about this, I'll kill you."

WHAT'S SPECIAL ABOUT BLOCKCHAINS?

Like I said, aside from the currency and store-of-value aspects, what made Bitcoin cool was the network on which it was built, i.e., the blockchain.

The Bitcoin blockchain is the information network that makes it possible to own, send, and receive bitcoins. It is maintained by hundreds of thousands of computers spread around the world, all connected to one another and working together to accurately execute transactions.

Whenever you send someone Bitcoin, that transaction is broadcasted to the network. Every ten minutes or so, every computer maintaining the network submits the list of transactions that they recorded since the last submission. Each computer is submitting the complete list of transactions, so they should all be submitting the same data. If one computer tries to submit a fake transaction, say, to send itself everyone else's bitcoins, the other computers maintaining the network will notice that the transaction from the bad actor doesn't match up with what everyone else is reporting, and they'll ignore it. The batch of transactions submitted by the majority of the computers maintaining the network becomes official, and that block of transactions gets added to the existing historic record of all transactions. That historic record is a "chain" of all the previous "blocks," thus, *blockchain*. This process, whereby everyone maintaining the network agrees on the record of transactions, is what makes Bitcoin a *decentralized* network. There's no one party in control.

Early on, some prescient Bitcoiners saw that they could use this process of digital consensus using blockchain technology for much more than money transfers and storing wealth. That realization eventually led to the launch of Ethereum, which aimed to use blockchain technology to create a decentralized computing network.

Whether you're aware of it or not, most of your life likely runs on software provided by companies like Google, Microsoft, Apple, and Amazon. Your bank account, your email, your documents, your photos, your home security, your car, all of these are controlled, directly or indirectly, by companies that can arbitrarily decide to alter them or take them away from you. Before blockchains, we didn't have any alternative. Gaining access to the incredible services provided by those companies meant giving them control over parts of our lives. It's alarming to imagine a Kodak employee busting into your living room and seizing all your family photo albums, but that's what Google can do to your pictures on Google Photos, if they want to.

With blockchains and the decentralized computing they provide, it's possible to rebuild many of the services we rely on today in a decentralized manner. You could build a photo-hosting and -sharing application on Ethereum where you could back up all your photos online, and no one could take them away from you, restrict your access to them, or delete them, because there is no company maintaining that database. It's automatically maintained by the network using a more advanced form of the same blockchain technology powering money transfers on Bitcoin.

For years after its launch in July 2015, no one used the decentralized global computing network on Ethereum for much other than launching more cryptocurrencies. In early 2021, that started to change.

3
Click Button, Get Money

MAY 2021

I felt my heart rate spike as I reread Quinn's text. I quickly messaged back.

"Did you find something?"

"New launch I'm getting in on tonight yeah. Think of it as a gift for your baby's college fund."

I laughed. I wasn't sure if she was breaking the rules of her group, but I wasn't going to complain.

Cosette looked up from the couch. "Everything all right?"

"Better," I said, "Quinn's sharing some new launch with me." I paused. We'd been planning to watch a movie together when I got the message. "Is it okay if . . . ?"

"It's fine," Cosette said. "Have fun."

"Okay," I messaged Quinn, "what do I do?"

"Go here and start farming." She sent me a link to a project called HawkDex. It was a sterile, single-page website with almost no information on it other than the name and a logo that looked like it was thrown together in Microsoft Paint by a middle schooler. A little further down the page was a box where I could supposedly deposit ETH to earn their HAWK tokens.

The HAWK farm: scam or magic money machine?

Every alarm bell in my head saying *scam* started going off. It was the most suspicious site I'd seen since I started exploring crypto. There was no way Quinn was putting money into this.

"Uh, Quinn, what is this?"

"It's a farm."

"Yeah but . . . what are people farming these HAWK tokens for? Is there some kind of application you use them in?"

"Oh there's no app, it's just a farm. Maybe they'll build one, maybe not, doesn't matter, you can still farm it."

My stomach started knotting; this wasn't what I had imagined. I had assumed we were doing some form of crypto-angel investing, finding great projects and getting in early so that, when they did become popular, we had already bought in. This felt more like one of those video games where you click buttons to earn "gold" or "gems" as fast as possible. The amount it said you could earn didn't even make sense. It said that if you deposited $1,000 of ETH, you'd earn $3,000 of HAWK over a year.

"Quinn, this seems like some kind of scam."

"It's fine, you wanted to know about farming, this is farming."

"Okay, but can't we farm tokens that are for real projects?"

"Sure, if you want to get rich slowly you can try to find the next ETH and wait ten years. But there will be hundreds of these kinds of farms in the meantime. It doesn't need to be either or. Hold the big popular coins for actual crypto projects, and make some money on these shitcoin farms in the meantime."

"But why would anyone want these HAWK tokens?" I asked. Even if this was safe, the only way these tokens would be worth anything was if someone was buying them. I didn't understand why anyone would buy tokens for an app that didn't exist and which didn't appear to have any plans to exist.

"You can farm faster if you use their tokens."

"Wait, what?"

"Yeah, look at the top farm." I looked at the farms again, and Quinn was right. The 300 percent interest rate on ETH was ridiculous, but you could earn 10,000 percent on any HAWK you deposited. People were buying HAWK tokens so they could farm more HAWK tokens. Then, I guessed, they would either sell them to other people who wanted to farm or hold on and hope that an app for them would come out eventually.

I sat at the dining table and stared at the site. Normally, projects launch cryptocurrencies to help fund building something, thus the coin has some use. Ethereum raised the money to build Ethereum by selling ETH, and you use ETH on the network to pay for transactions. But this HAWK token, there was no reason for it to exist, no compelling reason to buy it and hold it other than to participate in this little casino HawkDex had built on its site.

Maybe that's all shitcoin farming was. I still wasn't comfortable with how scammy this site looked, but maybe I was being too cautious. According to the site, there was more than $10 million already deposited in the little HawkDex casino. If I was understanding Quinn right, it seemed like most people knew this was some sort of game, more like poker than investing.

While I contemplated what to do, I checked my crypto wallet, an application on my phone where I stored my cryptocurrency for use on sites like HawkDex. I had $5,000 in ETH from selling my DOGE, but I wasn't going to risk all of it. I typed in one hundred dollars' worth of ETH, hit Deposit, then started biting my lip.

Even a simple transaction like that can take uncomfortably long. It was agonizing to watch the loading animation after I initiated the $100 deposit, hoping it would show up as my balance on the farm and not go straight to some scammer's account. I didn't think Quinn would mess with me by sending me to a bad website, but she could be getting scammed, too.

Suddenly, the page refreshed. Next to the ETH deposit button were two new boxes. The first said, "Balance: $100." I let out a sigh of relief, the deposit had worked. The second said, "Earnings: 0 HAWK."

I stared at my screen a moment longer. *Could it be that simple?* If this farm worked the way that was explained in the YouTube videos, then I should be earning HAWK tokens every second based on the amount of ETH I deposited.

A moment later, the page updated. My balance was still $100, but now my earnings said "0.1 HAWK." I tried refreshing the website to see if that forced it to update my balance. It did. When the page refreshed, I'd earned another tiny fraction of a HAWK token. I kept refreshing, and it kept increasing. My nervousness started turning into excitement. It was working.

"Hey, honey, look at this." Cosette stood up from the couch to look over my shoulder as I hit refresh, and another fraction of a HAWK token appeared in my balance.

"Okay . . . so? Are they worth anything?"

"Let's find out." I could feel my heart rate picking up. There was a Trading link at the top of the site, so I claimed the fraction of a HAWK token I'd earned and clicked the link. It took me to a cryptocurrency exchange where anyone could put any token up for sale, even a sketchy one like HAWK. Apparently, this kind of exchange was one example of the kinds of applications people were building on Ethereum.

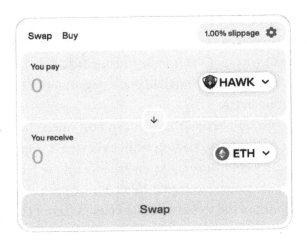

A typical decentralized-exchange interface.

In the Sell box, I selected my fraction of a HAWK token. In the buy box, I selected ETH. A loading icon popped up and spun for a moment. When the icon went away, the exchange said I could get five cents of ETH for my fraction of a HAWK token. I confirmed the trade, another loading animation popped up, and then, a few moments later, my ETH arrived.

"Holy shit, it's real," I said.

"How much did you put in?" Cosette asked.

"One hundred dollars."

"What if you put in more?"

Cosette and I stared at each other for a moment. "I have $5,000 from selling my DOGE," I said. "Should I put it all in?"

"I mean . . . you got that $5,000 for free anyway, right? It's house money? I say go for it."

I squeezed her hand, then deposited the remaining $4,900 of ETH. A few moments later, I refreshed the page again and saw my HAWK balance was climbing much faster. Then another thought occurred to me: If the ETH farm was legitimate, then maybe this 10,000 percent interest HAWK farm was real, too. I asked Quinn if I should be using that one.

"Oh yeah, that's the main one we're farming. I don't recommend throwing all your money in there though," she said. "Instead, take the HAWK you're earning from the ETH pool, and then deposit that in the HAWK pool. You won't have your original funds at risk and you'll be compounding your earnings much faster."

It reminded me of a briefly popular computer and mobile game called Cookie Clicker. At the beginning of the game, all you did was click on a giant cookie. When you clicked on the cookie, you earned a cookie. Eventually, you could spend the cookies you earned to buy Grandmas and Cookie Farms, which would earn more cookies for you. The more cookies you earned, the more cookies you could spend on buying things to earn you more cookies. It was a silly game, but oddly compelling. It was satisfying watching your cookies-per-second increase, even if the only point of getting more cookies was to get more cookies. This farm was basically Cookie Clicker with gambling. Click HawkDex buttons to get more HAWK so you can redeposit it and earn more HAWK. The main difference beween Hawk and Cookie Clicker was that, at some point, I could choose to stop playing and sell all my HAWK for, hopefully, more money than I started with.

I took Quinn's advice and started putting my HAWK tokens back into the farm, refreshing the page every few minutes to compound what I had earned. I opened the exchange in another browser tab so I could keep typing in how many HAWK tokens I'd earned and see how much I could sell them for. It was ludicrous, but, as the night went on, more people kept joining in. The amount of money deposited crept up from $10 million to $20 million.

I kept farming until midnight, and I could feel the fatigue setting in. I had told Cosette I would come to bed "in a bit" two hours earlier. I wanted to keep going, but I needed to get some sleep. I was stuck as to what to do. Should I leave my HAWK in the farm overnight to amass extra rewards? Or should I convert it all to ETH so I can sleep a little better? If I left it in, I risked the HAWK price tanking overnight and wiping out all of my gains. But I could potentially earn another $1,000 while sleeping if it stayed steady.

Quinn wasn't sure, either. She'd done much more of this than I had, but going to sleep was always one of the biggest risks, especially early in a launch, before there's some price stability. One option she mentioned was to set alarms throughout the night. I could roll over, check the price, then go back to sleep. It seemed absurd, but, if waking up a couple of times overnight meant making a thousand bucks, it might be worth it. I decided I didn't want to do that to Cosette, though.

The other members of Quinn's group were going to leave their money in, but I wasn't feeling that bold yet. So, I pulled my HAWK and sold it for ETH. I'd managed to make a $110 profit off my $5,000 investment in just a few hours. Considering a good year in the stock market might give a 7 percent return, my 2.2 percent return in one evening was amazing.

I curled up in bed, tipsy, elated, and a little bit richer. I'd made some of my first money farming in crypto. Sure, it didn't totally make sense. HawkDex might not be a real product. It might have been a little crypto casino game. But I was making money, and if I could keep this up for the next few months and find some big wins, I might figure out how to make a good chunk of money before our baby was born.

₿₿₿

The first message I saw when I woke up was from Quinn:

"We messed up, you see the HAWK price?"

I checked the price chart and swore under my breath. HAWK hadn't tanked overnight. If I had left my money in, I would have made another $1,200. I threw on a pair of sweats and went downstairs to try to clear my wine headache.

"Damn, well, lesson learned," I said. "Should have left a little in."

"There's always next time!" Quinn texted back.

"Yeah so where to next?" I asked. The HAWK token price might have held up through the night, but the earnings rate on the farm was dropping fast as more people piled into it. I got the sense that Quinn and her friends didn't stay in these for much longer than a day or two.

"Next?"

"Where are we farming next? When's the next launch?" There must have been more of these launches. Based on how low-effort HawkDex seemed, I couldn't imagine a launch like that only happening every week or two.

"Sorry man, special situation," she said. "I can't leak group secrets. If you find anything interesting, we can talk about that though."

It was annoying, but I understood.

At least I had somewhere new to search, though. The night before, Quinn had sent me a link to another site called VFAT. It was a minimalist, text-only tool that plugged into all the farms and showed you exactly how much you had deposited, how much interest you were earning, and what your expected return on investment (ROI) would be for the day, week, and year. And it had a list of *every* farm that was already running. There were dozens of other sites like HawkDex out there. If I could find the right ones to invest in, I could have multiple days each week with HawkDex-level earnings. I could double my money in a matter of months, maybe weeks.

I opened VFAT again and saw two new farms had appeared since last night. Two more chances to make some money. One looked even more lucrative than HawkDex.

I sent Johnny a text: "What are you doing? Are you at the shop?"

"Yeah why?"

"I have something I need to show you. I'll be there in 10."

WHAT ARE ETHEREUM "APPS"?

For the first couple years of Ethereum's existence, people only used its decentralized computing capabilities to launch more cryptocurrencies. Launching a token on Ethereum only took a few lines of code and didn't require creating an entirely new blockchain, so if you wanted to raise a bunch of money quickly, that was a great way to do it.

In 2017, the first big Ethereum-native applications started to appear, focusing on decentralized finance, or DeFi. The idea was that blockchains were already great for sending and receiving money, so maybe they could also be used to replace other, more complicated parts of our financial lives.

Among the first of those DeFi apps were decentralized exchanges, or DEXes, like the one I traded my HAWK tokens on. Before DEXes, if you wanted to swap from one cryptocurrency to another, you had to use a centralized exchange like Coinbase. This meant signing up for an account, submitting all your identification information, waiting a few days for the exchange to activate your account, then waiting a few more days for your money to transfer in before you could trade among cryptocurrencies. Even so, if Coinbase ever wanted to, they could shut down your account and lock you out of your money. And if you launched a new cryptocurrency, you had to convince Coinbase to list it so other people could buy it.

The creator of Uniswap, the first major DEX, figured out that you could create a program called a *smart contract* that would run on Ethereum and let people swap between any two cryptocurrencies by interacting with the smart contract. Suddenly, anyone who wanted to create a cryptocurrency and make it tradeable just had to add it to a DEX, and anyone in the world could instantly buy and sell cryptocurrency on the Ethereum network.

Other kinds of applications soon followed, like smart-contract-based lending protocols, where you could deposit your ETH and borrow other tokens against it, or streaming payments, which allowed you to receive your salary in tiny chunks every minute directly in your crypto wallet instead of waiting two weeks for a check. *Stablecoins*, cryptocurrencies pegged to the US dollar and other fiat currencies, quickly became a godsend for people living in countries with less-reliable currencies as they allowed them to store their money in digital currencies less volatile than Bitcoin. Argentinians worried about the government zeroing out their savings via inflation could simply buy the dollar-pegged stablecoin USDC with every paycheck, park it in one of the lending apps to earn some interest, and instantly have access to the currency stability, and many of the same financial services, of a US citizen.

Then there were all the nonfinancial applications, like NFTs (nonfungible tokens), which we're going to explore later in this book, and decentralized social-media networks, which didn't require you to hand over your social life and audience data the way a company like Meta does. But for each innovative new application built on Ethereum, there were hundreds of scammy, casino-esque launches like HawkDex.

The die-hard crypto skeptics like to pretend these real use cases don't exist, but they do. The crypto true believers might try to pretend that the seedy underbelly of the industry doesn't exist, but it does. The challenge for a newcomer is being able to tell them apart.

4
We Are Gonna Make It

MAY 2021

When I got to Velocity, I settled onto one of the picnic benches outside, set up my hotspot, and pulled up VFAT. To show Johnny how to get started, I needed to find a new launch to farm. HawkDex wasn't looking nearly as attractive anymore. Despite its having been live for only a day, there was more than $100 million already deposited into farming the token. How there could be that much money moved overnight into this somewhat-sketchy, single-page site without any sign of a product was beyond me, but I guess that was crypto. It doesn't need to make sense for you to make money. VFAT listed farms in the order they launched, so HawkDex was near the bottom, but now there were two newer sites below it: Dragon and Polycat.

Dragon's site looked the same as HawkDex's, almost suspiciously similar: a low-budget logo, some generic tagline about the "future of finance," and a collection of farms paying out huge annual percentage rates, with the highest being their Dragon Token (DT). Dragon appeared to have launched a few hours earlier and already had more than $10 million invested.

Dragon was tempting, but Polycat showed more promise. It had the same types of farms, but it also appeared to have a product behind it. On a separate page from its farms was its exchange, where its creators apparently had built their own DEX to let you trade any cryptocurrency, including theirs. Uniswap charged a 0.3 percent fee on each trade for every token people added to their platform, so the more new tokens that launched, and the more people traded them, the more money Uniswap made. Naturally, other people wanted to launch their own exchanges to make passive income from trading fees, and it looked like that's what Polycat was doing. They didn't launch a casino game like HawkDex. They had their token, FISH, and their farms, but they also had this decentralized exchange. It occurred to me that investors who held FISH tokens might someday get a share of all the fees the Polycat DEX generated. It wasn't exactly a new product, but it still put them far above HawkDex and Dragon in terms of perceived legitimacy, and it looked like the best place for Johnny and me to start.

I closed my laptop and walked over to the shop to see if Johnny was ready. He was helping out a customer at the register, and the next barista was still getting set up in the back, so I hung out by the entrance and waited. Finally, Johnny poured us a couple of cold brews, and we walked out back to the picnic tables.

"Alright, so, what's up?" he asked.

I walked him through everything that had happened the day before. Farming, HawkDex, the $100 million that was in it now, and how this might be a way for him to make some extra cash to cover all the sudden expenses of the café.

"Wait, you deposit some crypto into these farms, and they just spit out free tokens?" he said, squinting at me. I couldn't tell if it was skepticism or curiosity. Probably both.

"Yeah exactly, then you can double down with the tokens you're getting or sell them to take profits," I said. I could hear myself parroting back what Quinn had told me, only partially understanding it.

"Okay, but why would they give you these tokens?"

I explained that selling tokens directly to the public was risky based on previous lawsuits, so now this was how some crypto companies were getting their tokens out into the market. Farming wasn't necessary to launch a token, but it had become a popular way to do it. And since these new apps, like Polycat's exchange, needed to incentivize people to use them, giving away free money was a great way to do it.

Johnny was still skeptical, so I walked him through the steps on Polycat. I opened their farms, found one where I could deposit ETH, and put in $1,000.

"Alright, ready?" I asked. Johnny nodded. I hit refresh. Almost instantly, I earned a fraction of Polycat's FISH token.

"Whaaat?" Johnny said and started laughing. "This can't be real."

"I know, right?"

I claimed the rewards, went to Polycat's exchange, and swapped the FISH I'd earned for a few cents of ETH. "See? Free money."

Johnny was staring at my laptop, eyes wide, mouth slightly open, but a grin slowly creeping across his face.

"Alright, screw it, I'm in."

He opened his laptop, and I walked him through how to get started. A couple minutes later, he refreshed, and his own reward balance started accumulating. Johnny worked almost exclusively on physical things: coffee, motorcycles, carpentry. However weird this free money game was for me, it was even stranger for him. Making money gambling on DOGE was one thing; clicking buttons to collect FISH coins that other people want to buy from you so they could get more FISH coins was . . . strange to say the least.

We kept running the same cycle I'd been running since the night before. Wait five to ten minutes, collect rewards, deposit, repeat. It was the best video game we'd ever played together.

₿₿₿

After an hour or so, Quinn showed up. Earlier, I'd texted her that I was going to walk Johnny through all the farming stuff and try to find something to throw money into. She said she wanted to join. I figured this was a good time to ask her a question that had been nagging me since last night.

"Hey Quinn," I said, "one thing I still don't get is why these guys can't take our money and run. There's $100 million deposited in HawkDex, aren't people worried about them stealing it?"

"Oh, they can't."

"Why not?"

"Well, you know how you can see every transaction that happens on Ethereum and other blockchains, right? Like, you can see who sent who how much money?"

"Yeah."

"Well, you can also see all the code for these farms. It's all public. Other big-brain farmers will investigate when new projects launch and let the community know if they're safe or not. Sometimes new farms will pay third parties to review their code and publish an audit, too."

"So . . . this is safe then?"

"Eh, I wouldn't say that. Auditors miss stuff. There are other ways things can get hacked. Sometimes the code gets changed after an auditor looks at it. But an outright 'rug,' where someone scams you and takes all your money, is rare."

"Got it, thanks."

As we packed up our bags to leave, Quinn said, "I decided I am going to start putting that farming group together. Do you guys want to join?"

I was interested, but I didn't want to pay an absurd price. "How much?" I asked.

"Free for you two," she said. "I'm gonna charge the other people and coach them, but if you guys want to hang out in the chat and farm with us, that would be fun."

Johnny and I exchanged looks.

"Definitely."

Quinn finished zipping up her backpack. "Great, I'll add you two to the group chat this afternoon then. See you guys online."

₿₿₿

I let Polycat run through the day and into the evening, and by the time I was about to go to bed I'd made $310. I had no idea how much Quinn had made, probably thousands.

Making $310 in a day for playing around in this weird new DeFi video game felt too good to be true. I knew there would be farms on which I lost money or made very little, but the potential for quick wins was intoxicating. Now that Quinn was setting up a group where we could share what we were finding with other farmers, the opportunities would only increase.

Quinn had shared a piece of crypto lingo with us while we were at Velocity: WAGMI. It stood for "We Are Gonna Make It," as in "we're all gonna get super rich together." I was starting to feel like it was true.

WAGMI.

HOW TO TELL REAL PROJECTS FROM RISKY ONES

As long as you recognize the game that you're playing, there's nothing wrong with dabbling in the high-risk crypto casino. There are constantly new things launching that you can speculate on for the chance to get rich quick. You'll probably lose money, but hey, you might get lucky.

What's important is knowing how to tell the difference between the casino and the real projects. You don't want to be one of those luddites who dismisses the entire space because you can't tell the difference between Bitcoin and something like FreeMoneySuperSafeNotAScamCoin. Like I said, there are real, interesting pieces of technology being built . . . and there's plenty of dogshit. Here's how to tell them apart:

The first consideration is originality. Is this project using the blockchain-based technology in some kind of new and interesting way? Or is it doing what another project is doing, just "faster and cheaper." Given the easily copyable nature of blockchain code, it is extremely easy to launch a "cheaper" version of an existing app. Copy Ethereum's code, and your copy will simply be cheaper because it's new and no one is using it. "New and improved" is often a warning sign. None of the "new Bitcoins" have upset the original's dominance in the fourteen years since it launched, nor have any of the "new Ethereums." The same is true for other smart-contract-based blockchain apps. There have been a few successful DEXes that started by copying Uniswap, but not many. You'll see the same pattern repeat when we get around to NFTs. The first movers in the space are often the safest bets. The more copycats proliferate, the riskier and lower quality they become.

In addition to originality, there also has to be some utility. Does this new blockchain or new smart-contract application give people a better way to do something they already do? When Uniswap launched, it made sense because of its utility. The same went for lending apps like Aave. There's a real-world application for exchanging cryptocurrencies and for borrowing against assets. If the only "utility" you can come up with for some new cryptocurrency existing is speculation, then it's probably a risky investment. Again, if you want to speculate, have fun. Just remember, it's eventually going to zero.

5
I'm Putting a Team Together

MAY 2021

I decided to take a little risk and let Polycat continue running overnight. By the next morning, I'd made another $250. It wasn't much in the grand scheme of things, but it was something. Polycat was slowing down, though, so I needed to look for the next farm.

Quinn had added me to her new farming group chat on an app called Discord, which is similar to the online work-chat apps like Slack and Teams but with a techy, gamer flair to it. It was the chat app that most crypto projects used, so if you wanted to learn more about a project before you invested in it, you could join their Discord and read the public discussion or ask questions of the team. Aside from Johnny, Quinn, and myself, there were ten other people in the group, all of them Quinn's students. I would rather have been in a group filled with pros like Quinn, but that could come later. In the meantime, we already had a good system down with VFAT.

I threw on some clothes and walked downstairs to make coffee while I introduced myself in the group. One of Quinn's students, Ryan, had already gone through the new farms on VFAT for the day and picked one we should try to go after, PolyBull. I pushed him for an explanation. I wasn't ready to trust someone else's research yet.

"Well the farm opens in an hour, there's already 10m deposited, and they got a basic audit done," he said. "Seems like an ideal setup."

I pulled up the PolyBull site on my phone, and he was right. It was the first farm I'd seen with an "audited" certification on it.

Audits were professional code reviews that currencies could hire third-party teams to perform. The auditors would look through the code and certify that it wasn't malicious or vulnerable to some kind of hack. Quinn had told me it was rare for these kinds of fast-paced farms to have audits, since they weren't often serious products. If PolyBull had one, it might do even better than HawkDex and Polycat.

"Sounds good to me," I said.

"Me, too," said Johnny, joining the conversation.

"I'm gonna deposit my funds now and go do some more research in the meantime," I said. The fear of putting money into random bits of crypto code had disappeared shockingly fast. Now, I barely thought twice before depositing $2,000 into some random farm.

I set a timer on my phone for forty minutes. That's when the farm would open up, and I could start cycling my rewards into more tokens. In the meantime, I wanted to see if I could find any other good sources of alpha besides VFAT.

Galt's $50,000 group was clearly the one to get into if I wanted the best alpha, but I might be able to find indications as to what they were looking at without joining. During the HawkDex night, there was a collection of crypto people on Twitter—including Galt, Quinn, and Caleb—who were tweeting cryptic references to the HawkDex farm. They wouldn't name it explicitly, probably because they didn't want their rewards diluted, but they left little breadcrumbs for the other people who already knew about it.

I opened Galt and Caleb's Twitter profiles and looked through the accounts they had most recently followed to see if any stood out. No luck. The only account that looked remotely interesting was something Caleb was following called the Bored Ape Yacht Club, which was selling pictures of primates as NFTs, a new kind of crypto token that was usually used for art. They didn't look very artistic, though.

My alarm went off, and I went back to the farm. I saw it had refreshed to show a Claim Rewards button and had the annual percentage rates listed.

I messaged the group: "Only 800% APR?"

Eight hundred percent would seem insane in any other context, but it was considerably lower than the rate we had been earning on HawkDex and Polycat.

"Get out," said Quinn. "It must be oversaturated. People won't buy the token with that low of an APR. It's gonna crash."

"Shit." I scrambled to pull my tokens out. By the time I sold them, the value had dropped to $1,600. It stung, but I couldn't expect to win every time.

Another member of the group, Mitch, messaged asking if there was any way we could have known before investing.

"No, not really," Quinn said. "It all depends on how high the creators of the farm set the token rewards. They got greedy and set the rewards too low, probably to try to keep more for themselves. But it's going to end up hurting them in the end. Watch."

I opened a token tracker, found the BULL token, and immediately saw Quinn was right. It wasn't the slow and steady growth I saw with Polycat, and it wasn't even the slow, gentle decline that happened with HawkDex. It looked like it fell off a cliff. If I had waited another few minutes to pull my funds, I might have lost my entire investment.

I breathed a sigh of relief. Losing money was painful, but it could have gone much worse. It was a good reminder that this wasn't just a money printer. I had to stay smart about it.

"So . . . what next?" asked Johnny.

I snorted out a laugh. I loved his optimism.

"We look for the next thing!" Quinn said. "Don't beat yourself up, Ryan, your research was good, the team botched the landing."

"Alright, thanks," Ryan said. "I'll get back to researching."

"Hey guys," Mitch said. "I think I found something . . ."

The next two weeks were a blur. From the moment I woke up to the moment I fell asleep, my days were consumed by DeFi farming. My laptop came to the gym, to dinners, to happy hours, everywhere. I even started checking in the middle of the night. Each extra *cycle*—that sequence of collecting rewards, converting them to liquidity, and depositing them back into the farm—meant making more money faster. I didn't want to miss out on any potential earnings.

We didn't always get it right, but our evaluations were getting better each time. Velocity's picnic tables were our office, and we'd congregate every time we knew a farm was launching. In the evenings, I'd have a few glasses of wine and watch the internet coins roll in while scanning Twitter for any useful alpha. Sometimes there were three or four coins launching in a single day, and we had to pick and choose which ones to toss some money into. Working together, we settled into a daily rhythm. Every morning, we checked VFAT for the new farms that were starting and then divided and conquered to evaluate them and decide if they were good or bad opportunities.

One morning, I was reviewing the potential farms for the day on my phone while walking to Velocity with Cosette when she asked me how my programming was going.

"I feel like I don't hear you talk about programming stuff as much anymore."

"Oh, yeah, uh . . ." I paused, ashamed to admit that I hadn't made any progress on learning coding while I'd been deep in farming. "It's fine. Slow, but fine."

"Have you built anything new?"

"No, but I've made a few grand farming."

Cosette didn't say anything. We arrived at Velocity and split up, Cosette to hang out with Rose while I caught up with Johnny. I set up my laptop on one of the picnic tables, and Johnny walked over a few minutes later bearing drinks.

"Thanks man, I need it."

"Late night?"

"Yeah, doing research. This 24-7 farming is starting to mess with me."

"Yeah," Johnny sighed. "I'm up to four coffees a day."

"Heh, I'm right there with you. Good newborn practice, at least. But I think I found a way to make this easier." I turned my laptop around to show Johnny what I had been researching the night before. "Check this out. It's called an autocompounder. Instead of constantly having to claim our rewards and redeposit them, it handles compounding them for us."

Johnny started clicking around the site on my computer. "What's the catch?"

"They take a cut," I said. "The biggest ones take 20 percent. But, look." I clicked on another window on my laptop. "There are new ones launching like the farms, and this new one called Pounder only takes 2 percent."

"Wait," Johnny said. "So we can put our tokens in here, we don't have to do any more clicky clicky—and we only lose 2 percent of the profit?"

"Exactly. Contracts are verified and everything. It looks like they even got a mini audit done. And, I mean, look at this, this is so cool . . ." I refreshed the page. The balance at the top of the screen went up by a few dollars. I refreshed the page again, and the balance increased again.

"Well, that seems like a no-brainer," said Johnny. He logged into his laptop and brought up the Pounder site. A few minutes later, he had moved all of his tokens over. "Wow, this is magical," he continued as he refreshed the page and watched his balance go up and up. "I can't believe we were doing this manually."

"Seriously."

Johnny started laughing. "What do we do with all our time now? I got so used to collecting rewards all day." He looked down at his watch. "Oh, isn't DFYN launching?"

"Oh yeah, good call," I said and brought up their site. I bought $2,000 of their tokens and deposited them into Pounder to compound. "I . . . guess . . . that's . . . it?"

Johnny finished his own deposit. "Yeah, I guess so. This is less exciting than when we were clicking buttons all day."

"No kidding," I said. "I'm going to try to make some progress learning how to code these farms for myself. I still think that's where the real money is."

Johnny nodded. "I'm going to look into this NFT stuff that's going on. I keep hearing bits of news about it. I think there's something there."

"Cool, let me know what you find," I said. "Oh, hey, what's going on with the espresso maker?"

Johnny paused. "Huh, good question," he said. "I sent the manufacturer the money for the production run but haven't heard anything. It's been a few weeks, but I completely forgot with all the farming stuff."

"Hey, I totally get it."

We said our goodbyes, and then Johnny returned to the shop, and I packed up my things to head home. If I wanted to get any focused work done, I needed to be alone.

Discovering the autocompounders had renewed my excitement about learning crypto programming. One of the most popular autocompounders, Yearn, was autocompounding three billion dollars' worth of crypto. If tokens were earning around 10 percent interest, on average, by taking a 20 percent fee, Yearn was making $60 million a year completely passively.

That was where I could start. Let Pounder earn me a little farming income while I researched how these smart contracts worked. Then, maybe I'd be able to launch my own.

₿₿₿

I spent three days reading through the code of autocompounders and farms to try to get a sense of how they worked. It was still confusing, but I was starting to notice a few patterns, and that was making me feel a little more optimistic about the possibility of learning to make one. Cosette and

I were on the way to a midwife appointment, and I was explaining some of what I'd learned to her. The more I dug into the code behind these different projects, the more I realized how much they were all the same. People would see one good idea and then copy it hundreds of times, and the copies seemed to get slowly scammier.

"I think I need to find a real project to work with," I said, finally. "That would be better than trying to make money off of these questionable farms."

Cosette smiled and squeezed my hand. "I'd feel better about that," she said. She told me the farms made her feel icky. I knew her instinct was correct. Something did feel icky about all these copied-and-pasted, casino-esque launches. But understanding them would at least give me a foundation for working on something more real later.

I opened Pounder on my phone to check my balance and see if they were listing any new farms. At the top of the screen was an announcement about some new upgrade they had launched. I texted Johnny: "Hey, looks like Pounder updated their contracts. Some sort of autocompounding optimization boost."

"Do we need to do anything?"

"Just click a few buttons to turn it on. I'm gonna do it when I get home."

"Cool, doing it now! See you tomorrow."

·₿₿₿·

The following morning, Cosette and I met up with Johnny and Rose for pickleball. This was the first time in weeks that Johnny and I had met without our laptops. I felt like I was starting to get a little bit of my brain back, the part that had been dedicated to constant clicking and VFAT searching. I needed it, too. I'd been a zombie the last few weeks; it felt like I was living more in the crypto world than the physical world.

Between games, I told Johnny about what I'd been learning. I was impressed by how readable some people had made their contracts, like it was a point of pride not just to deploy functional contracts, but beautiful, easy-to-read ones. It made sense given the transparent nature of crypto. If you knew people would be hesitant to deposit money into your code, making it look more organized couldn't hurt. I still didn't know what was going on most of the time, but I was starting to piece some things together.

Johnny picked up his phone, probably to check a token price, then I saw his mouth drop open a bit. He looked up at me and asked, "Hey, any idea what's going on in Discord?"

I hadn't checked on it at all that morning. "No, why?"

Johnny handed me his phone. There was a message in one of our group chats saying that the Pounder site was down and asking if anyone knew what was up.

I gave the phone back to Johnny and shrugged. "I'm sure it's fine, sites go down for maintenance and such."

"Yeah, I guess," said Johnny. He put his phone down, and we went back to playing, but, the second the game was over, he made a beeline for his phone. He immediately popped his head up and stared at me. No confusion this time. Just fear.

I felt my stomach drop.

"We gotta go!" Johnny started throwing his gear into his backpack. I grabbed my phone and pulled up the group chat. I saw what Johnny had read, and the blood drained from my face.

"Johnny, what's wrong?" Rose asked.

"We gotta go, we gotta go, we gotta go." Johnny was jogging towards the car, struggling to zip up his bag.

"Nat." Cosette was suddenly standing next to me with her hand on my back. "What's going on? Are we okay?"

"We need to get home," I said. "Right now."

CRYPTO'S COPYCAT PROBLEM

You'll often hear crypto skeptics or detractors say something along the lines of "99 percent of everything in crypto is a scam!" Unfortunately, they're somewhat correct. Despite the interesting potential of blockchain technology and networks like Bitcoin and Ethereum, there are many, *many* more unserious cryptocurrency projects that range from get-rich-quick speculative assets to straight-up scams and Ponzi schemes. The problem with crypto is how easy it is to copy everything. Since all of the code powering most blockchains and smart contracts is public, there's a massive amount of copying and pasting of crypto projects that goes on behind the scenes. Anyone can copy anything, and, as soon as some new idea starts to become popular, people start copying it to try to make money.

The inclination to copy a successful existing business is nothing new. If you're walking down the beach and notice someone selling beers out of a cooler with a line that's dozens of drunk, scantily clad spring breakers long, you might think to yourself, *I should go buy a cooler.* Businesses do this all the time. Some chains base their franchise locations on where McDonald's and Starbucks already have stores. Gas stations often open across the street from other gas stations. Bird launched the first electric-scooter-sharing app back in 2017, and, within a few years, we had Spin, Lime, Jump, Skip, Scoot, and Grin all doing the exact same thing.

Copying a successful business is often good business. Sometimes the copycat, or "fast follower," ends up winning, like Facebook eclipsing Myspace and Friendster. But copying a successful business is usually a challenging endeavor. If you see a successful store in your neighborhood, you can't just walk into the building next door, paste up a sign, and compete with them. You need a lease, insurance, employees, inventory, branding, and, most of all, capital. Even in the simple beach-cooler example, it would take you a while to go buy the cooler and drinks and make a nice sign. The same is true for online businesses. You could copy the look and feel of Facebook fairly easily—the front-end code that makes the website look the way it does is mostly public—but you can't copy the code and algorithms working under the hood—that part is mostly secret. Making a fully functional copy of Facebook would be expensive and challenging, even though there's no physical "stuff" to buy. Typically, the more valuable a business is, the harder it is to copy. The guy selling beers on the beach is easy to rival. Facebook and Walmart are infinitely harder.

Crypto applications break the mold. The front-end code that makes the site look pretty is completely public, but so is the back-end blockchain code. A core tenet of most crypto applications is being *legible*, meaning anyone can inspect them to make sure they aren't acting nefariously. You can see every single transaction that happens on Bitcoin, Ethereum, and most popular blockchains. On Ethereum and other smart-contract chains, you can also see what's going on under the hood of every single smart-contract application. That's extremely useful for making sure you aren't getting scammed and that the products are doing what they say they will do. But it's also extremely useful if you want to copy something successful yourself.

Uniswap is one of the most popular smart-contract applications on Ethereum. At the point in 2023 when I wrote this, more than a billion dollars' worth of swaps were happening every day on the platform. That's comparable to the amount of trading happening on Coinbase, one of the largest centralized exchanges. If you wanted to create a copy of Coinbase, it would be as hard or harder than copying Facebook. You'd have all the same challenges of copying another major tech company combined with additional regulatory and financial hurdles. It would be a massive undertaking, which explains why there are so few centralized exchanges. But if you want to copy Uniswap, you can do it from your laptop in one day, maybe within hours. Copy their smart contracts, which are public, copy their website, which is also mostly public, use an artificial-intelligence art tool to generate a new logo, and ta-da! You're live! You now have, functionally, the same product as Uniswap. You won't have their perceived legitimacy, their community, or their team, but you'll have much of the same product. Now, all you need to do is set up some aggressive farms like HawkDex and Polycat to attract money. Once you do that, speculative farmers will move their money over to start collecting your tokens, and, as the mania drives your prices higher, you can sell the tokens you set aside for yourself. It might not last—maybe the farmers will move on after a day or two and your token price will crater—but it won't matter; you can spin up another copy and play the game again.

Imagine if, within twenty-four hours, you could create a clone of Facebook, take it public, and start selling your shares. It took Facebook about eight years to get to an initial public offering. In crypto, you can do it in a day. It's not called an IPO, sure, and it's not *actually* stock that you're selling, but it will attract speculators nonetheless.

So you can see why there are so many copycats and so many low-effort cash grabs or outright scams. For every one good idea, there are probably thousands of copies of it trying to draft off its success. Ninety-nine percent of everything in crypto probably *does* fall somewhere between bullshit and a scam, but that's mostly because it is so easy to make a copy of something legitimate and try to cash in on its success. If anyone could quickly clone Uber, do an IPO, and start selling the stock, you can bet that they would do that, too.

One of the most important things to recognize in crypto is the extent of this copycat problem, and the high likelihood that almost everything drafting off the success of a major innovation will die. Not everything will, of course, there are some very successful copycats, but the vast majority of the copycats are cash grabs that are going to zero.

Rugged

MAY 2021

I dug through the messages on Discord to try to figure out what was going on. It looked like Pounder had pulled a switcheroo on us and swapped out the safe, trustworthy code we'd been using all week for a new, malicious application that stole everyone's money.

My money was likely gone, but there was a small chance I'd be able to withdraw it—if I was quick enough.

Johnny had beaten me home. "Did you get your tokens out?" he messaged me.

"I don't know yet," I said. "Almost home."

"Mine are gone, everything I started with," he said. "Back to zero."

Fuck. I didn't realize he had put that much in there. I couldn't help feeling guilty for introducing him to this DeFi stuff in the first place.

The group chat was blowing up. Others had also lost everything. So far, it was looking like no one had been able to get their money back out. Cosette pulled into the driveway, and I sprinted out of the car and inside the house, straight to the dining table. I threw open my laptop.

When a new crypto project launches, there are two parts to it. There's the cosmetic front end that you interact with, the *user interface*, which is familiar to everyone. When you go to Facebook, you're using the Facebook UI. When you visit a crypto app's website, you're using their UI. The big difference between crypto applications and normal web apps like Facebook is that crypto applications also let you read the *back end*. You can look up the exact code being run on the blockchain to execute your transactions. You can even run those transactions yourself without using the UI at all, which is like being able to continue posting to Facebook even if site goes down.

I found a link to Pounder's smart contracts, scrolled down the list of actions, and found one called "check balance." I connected my wallet, hit enter, and it showed that I still had a balance.

My money was still there.

But that didn't mean I'd be able to withdraw it. The funds could have been sitting there waiting for the scammer to take them. They had probably started with the larger deposits, after all. There were millions of dollars sitting in Pounder. I scrolled further and found the withdraw function. I typed in my full balance amount and hit enter.

When a crypto network is congested, transactions can take a few seconds, even minutes, to confirm. Until they're confirmed, you don't know if they worked or not. If my funds were locked, the transaction would be rejected, and I'd get an error message saying the withdrawal was blocked.

I could see my transaction pending and waited, watching the spinner, praying that it would go through.

Five seconds went by—

Ten—

Fifteen—

I kept refreshing the page. My heart was hammering. My leg bounced frantically under the table. *Please, please, please* . . .

And then, there it was:

Confirmed.

I got back all $20,000 I had deposited. Nothing was lost. I let out a huge sigh and slid back in my chair.

"We're okay," I called to Cosette. "I got it all back." I let out a laugh and wiped the sweat off my palms as the terror flushed out of my system. "That was way too close."

"Yeah, please don't scare me like that again."

"I know. I'm sorry."

I felt awful that I almost lost so much money. Even though it hadn't happened, it was a brutal morning that Cosette shouldn't have had to endure. "Let me see if I can help anyone else in the group."

I messaged the chat. "I don't know how, but I got it out." No one else had been able to pull their money. I made a quick video explaining the process I went through and sent it to everyone, but it didn't work for anyone else. Why did it work for me?

Mitch was the first to figure out what was going on. When Pounder launched the boost contract the day before, they said a code audit was "in progress." No one questioned it, because they had been acting honestly to that point. That should have been a big red flag, but we were excited and didn't think twice about it. Executing the boost was a two-step process, though, and I only completed the first step. I must have gotten distracted and forgotten to complete the second step, which meant I never moved my funds from the safe, verified contract to the malicious one. Everyone else did, so their funds were gone for good. And they weren't the only ones. We could see how much money the Pounder creators had stolen. Based on our napkin math, it was between $2 million and $3 million.

Johnny hadn't sent anything since I got out of the car, so I sent him another message. "Hey, how are you holding up?"

He responded almost immediately, "I don't know. Everything I made so far, it's just . . . gone. Everything I made from DOGE. All the money I thought was going to help get me out of the shop."

"I'm sorry man," I messaged him. "I feel like this is my fault. I shouldn't have gotten you started on the DeFi stuff." I felt awful for dragging him into this world. He would have been better off selling his DOGE and never messing around with DeFi in the first place.

"No, not your fault," he said. "We all got too cocky. You never think it will be you who gets rugged."

"No, I guess not. How much do you have left?"

"0.5 ETH lol."

I was crushed, Johnny had been up to $30,000 at one point. He was truly out of the game. "Jesus . . . What're you going to tell Rose?"

"I don't know, trying not to think about it right now. I'll text you later."

"Alright, I'm here if you want to talk."

I felt relieved that I had avoided being wiped out, but I was devastated by what had happened to Johnny and everyone else. It could not have been a closer call, and the message was clear: We were too comfortable taking risks. We had been dancing on a cliff all along.

As I tried to fall asleep, I couldn't ignore the gnawing anxiety. My adventures in DeFi had been profitable so far, but the few farms that were launching were even scammier than usual, and I was worried about getting trapped by another rug like Pounder. I had to accept that I might not be able to make the kind of life-changing money I had hoped for from farming, that I might have missed the boat on being able to invest early and make a crazy return.

But I kept coming back to that short exchange I'd had with Quinn a few weeks earlier. The people who knew how to write smart contracts using Ethereum's programming language, Solidity, were still in high demand. Every crypto project I checked out on Discord was trying to hire Solidity programmers, and they were offering multiple six-figure salaries, plus tokens. If farming wasn't my ticket, maybe programming was.

₿₿₿

The next morning, I was out at my desk at seven a.m., filled with a renewed determination to figure out crypto programming. If I could spend the next few months learning Solidity, maybe I could land a spot on a team. I was tired of speculating on farms and praying the price would go up. Building something would be more satisfying. It would give me a better chance of making good money, too.

My approach to learning these kinds of skills was always to get to a very basic threshold of competence, then start doing it in the wild to find out where the gaps in my knowledge were. If you spend all your time taking courses or reading books, then you're just collecting random pieces of information that don't fit together into a cohesive web of knowledge. You need experience and practice to tie the information together. The sooner you start getting that experience, the sooner you fill those gaps and build your web.

I figured that if I could figure out the basic building blocks for coding contracts, I could put together a self-directed curriculum by reproducing things that already existed. The code was all public, but I had already tried looking at contract code, and it barely made any sense to me. I needed *some* initial way to learn.

I found one of the only online courses for learning Solidity, and into the lectures I went. The next two days were a blur of scrubbing through videos, working through code exercises, and trying to get a grip on the basics. The course said it was sixty hours long, but the instructor talked slowly and spent a painful amount of time on review and preamble. The coding portions only took twelve hours to devour.

At the end of those twelve hours, I felt more optimistic. Solidity wasn't as challenging to learn as I thought it would be. It was just, well, scary. Scary because you could release a smart contract into the wild, people could deposit millions of dollars into it, then some malicious hacker could discover a bug and steal everyone's money. Unless you found that flaw first, there would be nothing you could do about it. Those kinds of exploitations happened all the time, even to big, established teams with professional auditors. It's why I'd been so nervous about putting my money into some of the DeFi farms the previous month.

If I tried writing contracts from scratch, I'd either have to pay auditors tens of thousands of dollars to review my code or roll the dice and hope I got it perfectly right on the first try. No pressure. The job's stakes were one reason why Solidity developers were so rare and so highly paid. It couldn't be easy to sleep at night if your code was protecting millions of dollars of other people's money.

At the end of the basics section of the course was the first assignment:

an "allowance" contract that allowed you to deposit money, designate someone who could borrow the money, and then allow the borrower to connect
their wallet and withdraw the amount they had been authorized to withdraw. The contract was simple, fewer than a hundred lines of code, and I felt
rather proud of myself for having completed it. I was having fun with it,
too, so I took a break from the course and built a simple website that could
house the contract so I could practice putting something out into the wild.

I sent the "activate" command for the contract, waited a few seconds for
the network to confirm it, and it was live. In a few days, I'd gone from not
knowing any Solidity to deploying my first contract and a web app for it. I knew
I had a long way to go before I could build anything useful, but this was a
huge first step. Not many people had gotten this far in their Solidity journey.
There were supposedly fewer than ten thousand Solidity programmers.

I now also had the first piece of a crypto résumé. If I reached out to a
team to work with them, their first question would be, "what have you already built?" Now, I could show them I had at least some basic idea of what
I was doing. The more of these little sites I built, the stronger my résumé
would be. I uploaded all the code for my contract to GitHub, a site programmers use to share and edit code, and made it public. One piece of my crypto
résumé was done.

That seemed as good an excuse as any to take the rest of the day off, so
I changed into exercise clothes and went to the gym. I'd run the Austin
Marathon the previous year, but I probably couldn't have made it more than
a few miles at this point. My new life in crypto-land was starting to take a
toll on my body. It had been barely a month, but I could tell I was slowly
gaining weight. I felt weak. The only use my muscles were getting was
walking downstairs to make coffee and clicking buttons to harvest and reinvest DeFi rewards.

Later, Cosette met me back home after her house showings, and I
showed her the app I'd finished building. I felt a little like a kid showing
off his art project. I was running into an error, so I couldn't show her all of
it, but she was excited for me. I suggested we go out to dinner.

We talked about baby names and real estate while we waited for our food. We already knew the first name we were going to use for a girl but hadn't decided on a middle name yet. While I'd been busy learning programming, Cosette had been running all around Austin meeting with new clients. The housing market had only been getting wilder in the last month, and she could barely keep up with her growing client list.

"I know I've been busy," she said, "it's getting exhausting, and I feel like we barely see each other. I don't know how agents do this with kids." She was talking half to me and half to herself.

"I can't imagine it's always like this, right? This market seems insane."

"Yeah, hopefully. I'd be fine with it slowing down for a bit."

"Well, I'm sorry I've been so absent, too." I knew I hadn't been fully present the last month while being obsessed with DeFi, and then this week while on my coding binge. "This is nice, though. I'm glad we snuck a little dinner in."

"Me, too," she said. We held hands over the table. "We've both been so heads down, but it's for a season. And hopefully it means we can take it easy when she's here."

"Yeah, I'm looking forward to it."

We finished our food, treated ourselves to some dessert, then drove back home. When we got in, Cosette said, "I need to finish up an offer from earlier, that fine?"

"Totally, I'm gonna try to fix that error I was running into."

We sat down at the dining table across from each other, and I opened up my laptop. The allowance contract had worked fine earlier. I didn't understand what could have changed.

I looked at the error again; it said "Transaction failed: insufficient funds." That didn't make any sense. That would only happen if I didn't have enough ETH in my wallet to run the basic commands, I should have more than enough. I checked my wallet and froze. It said there was no ETH in it.

Shit. I had to spend some ETH to create the contract, and I must have messed up and spent more than I intended. It was an expensive lesson, but everyone makes mistakes like this in the beginning. Thankfully, I didn't have that much ETH sitting in my wallet; most of it was in farms. I opened my transaction history to read through the details of the contract creation and figure out what happened. Suddenly, all the hairs on the back of my neck stood up.

Something was very, *very* wrong.

NOT YOUR KEYS,
NOT YOUR COINS

Most people who own crypto keep it on an exchange, like Coinbase. You can log in with your email and password, see what your coins are worth, buy and sell them, and even send them to other people.

But when your crypto is on a centralized exchange like Coinbase, you don't *really* own it. Coinbase is holding it for you and keeping a record of how much you own, but if Coinbase gets hacked, or something terrible happens to the exchange, all of your crypto will be gone, and you'll have no way to get it back. One of the main benefits of crypto is not needing to trust a third party with your money, but the majority of crypto investors trust Coinbase or another centralized exchange with their money anyway.

The alternative is to keep your crypto in a *wallet*, a program that lets you control your crypto on your own without having to trust anyone else with it. It might seem like the wallet has control over your crypto, but there's a very important difference between wallets and exchanges. With a wallet, instead of keeping your crypto at the exchange's crypto address, you're keeping it at your own unique crypto address.

A crypto address, also called a *public key*, is a long string of letters and numbers that looks something like this: 0x21e2A5504A414b-

85778296C5824fA154559f595C. The address identifies your account. Let's say your account is on the Ethereum network. If you search for that address on an Ethereum blockchain explorer, like Etherscan, you can see every single transaction that address has ever performed. All of its activities are public, but only you can control it.

The way you control what that address does is with a *private key*. A private key is another long string of numbers and letters that looks like this: ec072a30cda95d49635086479bc517d0547c5bb29b85755f5c-94cec98fe4c68a. Whenever you try to submit a transaction using your address on the network, you have to give the network the private key for your public address. The network runs a couple of math functions on the private key to verify the network owns that address, and then it allows the transaction to go through. If you don't have that proof, you won't be able to submit a transaction. That's why no one can arbitrarily take your ETH or other tokens away from you: They don't have your private key.

But you can easily interact with crypto without ever worrying about private keys at all. That's where the wallet comes in. A wallet, such as MetaMask, lets you store all of your crypto and interact with everything on the blockchain via a nice user interface. It uses something called a *seed phrase*—which looks like this: aspect attend cherry concert dignity doctor fury hammer liquid prefer ribbon sudden—to create, and recover, a theoretically infinite number of private keys and the public addresses that go with them. So, if you want to use a dozen different addresses, you don't need to save a dozen different private keys. You can just save one seed phrase.

There's another big difference between using a wallet and an exchange, though. If you install MetaMask on your computer or phone, it holds all of your private keys on your device, but it never saves them anywhere online. The downside of that is, if you lose your device, and you didn't save your seed phrase or your private keys anywhere else, your money is gone. Permanently. There's no way to get it back. Also, if anyone else gets access to your seed phrase or private keys, they can take all of your money.

Seed phrases, private keys, and public keys are the blessing and the curse of crypto security. The money in your crypto wallet is truly 100 percent untouchable by any force in the world, as long as no one else has your seed phrase or private keys. No government, business, or angry ex-lover can steal your money without those magic words or strings of characters. But that high level of security comes with a price. If you lose your seed phrase or private keys, your crypto is gone. No one can recover it for you. There's no manager you can call, no lawsuit you can file, no insurance check in the mail. It's gone. Thanks for playing.

That's why, for many people, it might not make sense to move all of your crypto to a wallet that you fully control. Yes, you'll be able to trade your ETH for guns and cigarettes if society collapses (assuming the internet works), but you have a *huge* risk of losing all of it if you're not careful with your seed-phrase storage. You'll also have a tricky balance to strike: You can reduce your risk of losing your seed phrase by storing it in more places, but the more places you store it, the easier it will be for someone else to find it.

And that can be quite a painful mistake to make.

7

There's Always Some Way to Make Money

JUNE 2021

I couldn't believe what I was seeing. There were a dozen transactions in my wallet history that I hadn't done, and that had been executed while I was at dinner. And they were sending all of the crypto in my wallet to another address.

I grabbed my phone and called Quinn. "Hey, are you at your computer?" I said, my voice choked with panic. "I need your wallet address *right now*. I need to send you all of my crypto."

"What? Why? What's going on?"

"Someone's hacked me," I stammered. "They're taking everything!"

If what I was seeing was correct, someone had broken into my wallet and was slowly sending themself all of my money.

"Uh . . . Nat?" Cosette was giving me a terrified look from across the table.

"Not now," I shot back. "I'll explain once I've handled it." I needed to focus. The ETH in my wallet was gone, but I had stored most of my crypto in farms, and it was still there.

I started to withdraw my tokens from the farms, but when the confirmation window popped up, it had an error message: "Cannot withdraw, insufficient funds."

Fuck. Now I knew why they had taken all the ETH in my wallet first. Everything you do on the network requires paying a small transaction fee, often called a *gas fee*, in ETH. If I didn't have any ETH, I couldn't pay the transaction fees, which meant I couldn't perform any transactions on the network. If I couldn't perform any transactions, I couldn't save my funds.

"Can you send me 0.1 ETH?" I texted Quinn. "They drained my wallet, I can't get anything through."

"No problem, sent," she messaged back. I saw the ETH show up in my wallet, but then, a few seconds later, it was gone.

What the . . . I messaged Quinn: "Did the transaction revert?"

"Nope, it went through fine, what happened?"

"It's gone already."

"Did they take it?" she asked. Sure enough, another transaction appeared showing them immediately taking the 0.1 ETH. They must have had some code running that was watching my wallet and immediately draining any ETH I sent to it.

Any ETH that Quinn sent me would immediately get taken. And if there was no ETH in my wallet, I couldn't rescue any of my other funds from the farms I had them deposited in. I was screwed. If I knew how to code better, I could maybe create something to outrun their transactions and get my funds, but I had no idea how to do that. A moment later, $10,000 of the ETH I had farming was gone. They knew I had caught on and were racing to take everything before I could stop them.

I watched as the transactions continued to roll through. They sent my wallet a tiny fraction of ETH, took another $10,000 from a different farm, then sent it to themselves. Then they took $10,000 of USDC.

I groaned and slid down in my chair.

"Nat . . ." Cosette said. I didn't reply.

Then, in a flurry of transactions, they took all that was left: $5,000 of various tokens I had sitting in my wallet.

"Nat, what do you need?" Quinn messaged me.

"Nothing. It's gone. They took everything," I messaged back.

"What about your Polygon funds?"

My heart jumped. Quinn was right. Some of the farming we were doing was on the Ethereum network, but I had some funds on another network called Polygon, too. The wallet credentials were the same, but the hacker might not have thought to look there.

I checked my balance on Polygon and my pulse sped up more: my funds were still there.

"Holy shit you're right, sending it now," I messaged back.

"Go! Go! Go! Go!"

I queued up the transactions to send her everything, paying ten times the normal transaction fee to force it through faster. As soon as I made the first transaction, it could alert the hacker and they could come take these funds, too. I probably only had one chance.

I hit enter and clenched my jaw, refreshing the page as fast as I could to see if it had gone through.

"Come on . . . come on . . . come on . . ." I muttered.

"Nat?" Cosette asked again.

The page refreshed, and I saw a green "Confirmed" mark next to the transfer. Quinn had the last of my other funds.

"NAT!"

I looked up and made eye contact with Cosette for the first time since the hack had started, and the full weight of what had happened washed over me. Tears started to build up at the corners of my eyes, and I slumped forward onto my laptop.

Cosette came over and knelt by my chair to hug me. "Honey . . . what happened?"

"It's . . . it's gone."

"What's gone?"

I took a deep breath and tried to keep my voice steady. "Thirty-five thousand dollars. Someone stole $35,000 from me."

Cosette got quiet and kept hugging me. She knew she didn't have to say anything. I was completely distraught. Thirty-five thousand dollars could cover our mortgage, cars, and living expenses for four to six months. It was a soul-crushing amount of money to lose.

"I just . . . I don't get it. How did this happen?" I didn't think I had a virus or anything on my computer, but the hacker had clearly gotten hold of my private key, a cryptographic password that gives you control over your wallet. That was the only way they could have executed all these different transactions. I began to realize that it had to have something to do with the contract I deployed. The timing was too close for it to be anything else.

I checked the code of my contract, but nothing stood out that could have given someone access to my wallet. Then I checked the code for the website where the contract was hosted; nothing stood out there, either. I started going through the files on my computer and remembered I had used my private key in the deployment code for the contract. But that was stored on my computer. No one else could have accessed it. Unless . . .

I went to GitHub, found my published contract code, and groaned. I had to use my private key to pay the transaction fees to deploy the contract, but then I forgot I had included it in the code, and I'd published it along with everything else. I'd done the crypto equivalent of posting my banking credentials on an online forum. The only way I could have been more stupid and obvious is if I'd titled the code project PLEASE ROB ME.

What almost certainly had happened was that hackers had automated code running that searched new projects published to Github for certain crypto terms, then checked through the published code to see if there was any mention of private keys. Considering I had labelled it "privateKey," I couldn't have made it easier for them. That automated code then probably sent a notification to whoever was maintaining it with a link to my code, indicating where the private key was published, and they used my private key to access my wallet and take all of my funds.

I could hardly even say I'd been hacked. I basically gave my money away. It was the worst kind of careless error I could have made in all the excitement of publishing my first contract. I'd made some progress on learning, great. But I'd lost months of income in the process, and I felt like a complete fool for making such a massive blunder.

I opened a bottle of wine. Cosette sat with me and tried to help me feel better, but there was only so much she could do. I'd screwed up worse than I could have imagined. Eventually, she went to bed, and I sat drunkenly staring at my reflection in the living room window.

I thought I was going to get rich by day-trading DOGE, and I failed. Then, I thought farming would get me there, and I almost lost everything. Now, I tried building something, and immediately got hacked and lost more money than I'd made since I started. I had been stupid, cocky, delirious. The people who were getting rich were lucky, and, in their wake, was a sprawling graveyard of degenerate gamblers who had lost everything. You never focus on all the people who lose money, because they don't get celebrated on social media or in books and movies. You just focus on those lucky few and think *that could be me!* But I'd learned my lesson. It was dumb to get into this in the first place. I saw a few people getting rich, got FOMO, and gambled away my savings.

I could start looking for a job tomorrow.

₿₿₿

The following morning, I laid on the couch in a hungover fog scrolling Twitter. I'm not sure what weird masochism made me want to see how rich everyone else was getting while I wallowed, but here I was, and seeing crypto influencers posting their wins felt extra awful.

If this was the end of my crypto journey, I could at least try to save anyone else from falling into the same fate. I wasn't the first person to make this kind of mistake, and I wouldn't be the last. If I could put the story out there for other people to learn from, maybe some other budding programmer would be spared from making the same error. Sure, losing that much money was awful, but it wasn't completely life-ruining for me. For some people who staked their whole financial lives on crypto, an error like that would have been much, much worse.

I drafted up a Twitter thread explaining what had happened. I didn't have many followers in crypto, but if a few of them picked it up and shared it, it might get some exposure and help other newbie coders. If nothing else, it might be a little cathartic.

After posting the thread, I decided to take the rest of the day off to decompress. Wear pajamas, lay on the couch, play video games. I was mentally and emotionally exhausted, hungover, and I needed a break. But then I remembered Quinn had scheduled a happy-hour get-together later that day for some of the crypto people she knew in Austin. The last thing I wanted to do was go out and be reminded of how much I'd been failing, but I had said I would go and felt obligated.

If nothing else, there would be alcohol.

₿₿₿

Ah Sing Den had a refreshing vibe for Austin. Intricate glass lanterns hung from the ceiling, the walls were adorned with floral patterns and peacock themes, and the menu featured fusion dishes with a Tex-Mex twist. It was an ideal spot for a hush-hush conversation about cryptocurrency debauchery.

Joining us were Vinay, Mark, and a pseudonymous character I knew from Twitter as Leif. He'd come up in my Twitter research, and Quinn said his calls were unusually good for a day trader. As the cocktails arrived, Vinay talked about how similar the recent crypto events felt to 2017. The market had started dropping over the previous few weeks, and we weren't sure if this was the end or a momentary correction. Vinay thought it was the latter. He didn't think we'd seen enough mania yet, and there would surely be more wildness to come.

His friend, Mark, disagreed. He pointed out that the surge of casual-investor interest had died down, and there wasn't much new money coming into the space. If there was going to be any more mania, it would be among people already in crypto, not from newcomers.

"It doesn't matter," Leif chimed in. "If you need the market to go up to make money, you shouldn't be playing this game."

I asked him what he meant.

"Well," said Leif, "you can short it on the way down, obviously, but there are always new trends emerging within crypto that money moves into. Get ahead of those, and you can do exceptionally well. Like right now, there's this Ethereum-killer trade. Solana has already ripped. Avalanche and Luna seem like they're going to follow. Even if ETH and BTC drop from here, there's always something else to rotate into."

Solana, Avalanche, and Luna were all new blockchain networks trying to compete with Ethereum's dominance as the "world computer." I'd heard them mentioned but hadn't dug into it.

"Okay, so, Ethereum-killers. Are there any other things like that you're watching?"

"Well, NFTs. They're coming back."

"Like the art stuff?"

"No, those are dead. More like profile pictures."

I figured Leif was referring to projects like Bored Apes, the primate headshots I had seen Caleb talking about on Twitter and that Johnny had said he was going to start exploring. Supposedly there were only ten thousand of them, so there was some rarity attached, and by buying one you became part of the community, whatever that meant, but it seemed like a weird thing to speculate on.

"NFTs are this cycle's ICOs," said Vinay, becoming visibly excited. "In 2017, there were all these shitcoins, the dumbest shit possible, but you could make money on it if you got in early and got out early. It was great. Same thing is happening with NFTs."

"Did you make money on those?"

"Hah, sorta. Yes and no. I made a ton, but I didn't prepare for taxes. I rode it all the way up, and all the way back down. I had to sell all of my ETH and other stuff to cover the tax bill. Almost took me back to zero."

"Shit, I need to start calculating my taxes," Quinn said.

"Yeah, me, too." I hadn't even thought about tracking what I was making and losing for taxes. Did getting hacked count as a write-off? I knew what I wanted to ask next but was afraid to embarrass myself in front of the group. Finally, I built up the courage.

"Have any of you guys ever gotten your wallets hacked?"

"Oh god yeah," Leif said, laughing. "One of the first things I did, immediately signed a bad transaction, lost $30,000, only had $5,000 left."

"I did something worse," Vinay said. "I sent $10,000 to the wrong address. It's sitting in limbo. Gone forever. No way to get it back. I go look at it sometimes."

"Not to mention the rugs . . ." Quinn said. "Worse than Pounder. Plus, there were all those early DeFi projects that had bad tokens and went to zero and wiped us out anyway."

"I'm still searching my house for a set of private keys I lost," Vinay said. "Nearly $100,000 of ETH on there. Thought I was being smart by creating a secret wallet I never touched that held my savings account. Then I lost the piece of paper I wrote the private key on. Dumb, dumb, dumb."

I couldn't believe what I was hearing. Everyone in the group had lost tens of thousands of dollars or more to hacks, scams, careless errors, and bad investments. But they were still here. And they were making money.

"I don't get it," I said to the group. "It seems like you have all lost a ton of money doing this at some point. Why did you keep going?"

Leif grinned. "It doesn't matter how often you're right or you're wrong," he said. "What matters is making sure you only lose a little when you're wrong and make a lot when you're right. Crypto is like venture capital on steroids. You can be wrong fifty times and lose a bit of money each time, but that one time you're right, you might get a one-hundred-time return or more."

A thought started to itch at the back of my mind. These guys had all made careless errors, but took them in stride, and kept going. They kept learning. And it seemed like they'd all eventually made back what they lost and more. Could I make it all back, too? I still had the funds I'd rescued from Polygon left to play with, and I was already doing better than Leif was after he got hacked. Maybe I was giving up too soon? I was much smarter now about where *not* to invest. I could make better calls this time.

But how many people try to "make it all back" and end up losing everything? What if I got hacked again? What if I lose all our savings and we have to sell the house?

But also . . . what if I pulled it off?

₿₿₿

Sitting in the back of a car on the way home, still grappling with what to do, I checked Twitter to see if anyone had responded to my thread on the hack. I opened my notifications, and they were filled with a flood of empathy and commiseration from people in the crypto community. My thread had gone viral, with some sharing it to spread the warning about not making the same error, and others sharing it by tagging on their own story about how they had made similar mistakes.

There were a surprising number of professional Solidity programmers who responded sharing that they had done very similar things early in their careers. The founder of Dharma, a major crypto wallet, had done the *exact* same thing as me when he was starting out. So had the founder of a popular NFT project called the Pixel Portraits. There were other traders and investors who also shared their stories about getting hacked or making a stupid mistake and being set back early in their crypto careers.

Clearly, I wasn't special. It sucked, but it was par for the course for anyone getting heavily into crypto. It was a rite of passage, a gauntlet you had to go through. Most people would quit and not touch the space anymore after something like this, but the ones who pushed through and learned from it often turned things around.

I opened Discord and saw I had a message from Caleb, the NFT influencer I knew who Johnny had been following closely the last month.

"Saw your story . . . absolutely brutal," he said. "I had something similar happen when I started in NFTs, I got scammed by a fake launch and lost almost $20,000 on it."

"Wow . . . I guess you didn't quit though?"

"No, painful, but it made me smarter. I ended up making more than that in the month after. I know it sucks now but don't let it get you down too much. Keep going. We need more Solidity programmers!"

"Thanks man, I will."

As I continued scrolling through the responses, I got a text from Quinn.

"Hey, are you free tomorrow morning? I have something I wanna show you."

"Yeah, I can meet up, why?"

"It's a surprise, I think it'll help you feel a little better though."

"Alright, see you then."

I put down the phone and stared at my reflection in the mirror. Determination had taken the place of the self-hatred I'd felt the night before. Everyone who'd had success in crypto had made mistakes. I'd lost $35,000, sure. But another way to think about it is that I paid $35,000 for an extremely important lesson. The loss was my tuition, and I shouldn't let the resulting education go to waste.

I couldn't give up now. And it sounded like Quinn might know the next step I should take.

ETHEREUM-KILLERS AND THE BLOCKCHAIN TRILEMMA

As Ethereum got more popular, the cost to do anything on the network increased, because there is only a finite amount of computing power on the network that can be used each day, and only a limited amount of data that can be stored.

When DeFi was starting to get popular, transactions on Ethereum cost less than $1. There were fewer people using the network and less demand for space on the blockchain (also called *blockspace*), so transactions were cheap. But as the activity on the network heated up through 2021, transactions started costing a few dollars, then tens of dollars, and eventually hundreds of dollars during periods of peak activity. There were even some cases in which people paid *thousands* of dollars to get their transactions through (more on that later).

Clearly there was demand for blockspace, even if most of it was to speculate on shitcoins. But few people could afford to pay $100 per transaction. So, something needed to be done.

Some teams launched competitors to Ethereum, either by copying Ethereum's code and changing some minor variables in it, or by designing entirely new smart-contract-enabled blockchains. These were the Ethereum-killers that Leif was talking about. Some of the big ones at the time were Binance Smart Chain, Solana, Avalanche, and Luna. Most of them had much cheaper transaction fees than Ethereum, but there was a tradeoff. In some cases, the transactions were cheaper simply because the network was being used less, and so, with time, they would run into the same congestion issues as Ethereum. In other cases, the transactions could stay cheaper for longer by centralizing some of the power over the blockchain, thus giving up some of the security the blockchain is supposed to provide.

This problem is called the *blockchain trilemma*. You can't have a fully decentralized, fully secure, inexpensive blockchain. One has to be sacrificed for the other two. You can have a cheap, decentralized one with minimal security; you can have a cheap, secure one that's controlled by one or a few parties; or you can have a secure, decentralized one that's expensive.

One way to get out of the blockchain trilemma is to build additional layers on top of Ethereum. Instead of submitting every transaction one by one and having to pay a huge gas fee, you could use additional blockchains to roll up transactions into batches and submit them all at once, making transactions cheaper, on average, without sacrificing the decentralization and security Ethereum provided. Polygon, where I stashed away some of my funds, was one of the first attempts at a layer 2 network. Since then, many more have launched, such as Optimism, Arbitrum, and Coinbase's Base chain.

It remains to be seen who will win. Ethereum is dominant right now, and, while the layer 2 solutions are taking off, in time there could be a competitor that does it better or finds a new way to solve the blockchain trilemma. Either way, what the rise of layer 2s and competitive blockchains shows is that the demand for blockspace is growing. And as layer 2s and alternative layer 1s drive down the cost of transactions, the possibilities of what we'll be able to do with an always-on, decentralized world computer will keep growing.

8
Rich or Rekt

JUNE 2021

I sat down across from Quinn at Velocity. "All right," I said. "Hit me. What's this new launch you found?"

Quinn turned around her laptop to face me. It was open to the website for something called Iron Finance.

"What is it?"

"New stablecoin project on Polygon."

"So what? We've farmed stablecoin launches before."

"This isn't another farm. This is a real product."

She sent me the link to their site, and I quickly saw that Quinn was right. This was more than a farm. It was the first serious project I had seen since I got into crypto.

Apparently, Iron Finance was creating a new stablecoin on the Polygon network called IRON. In addition to being pegged to the US dollar or another fiat currency, stablecoins are often backed by cash in the bank or other collateral. The two most popular stablecoins were USDT, or Tether, and USDC. Both USDC and USDT were examples of *collateralized* stablecoins. For every one USDC or USDT, there was $1 in a bank account backing it. At least, there was supposed to be. Tether has been investigated and sued multiple times for allegedly not having sufficient assets to collateralize the USDT they've issued.

Iron wanted to make something different: an *algorithmic* stablecoin. One where $1 of the stablecoin was backed by other cryptocurrencies, and the price was maintained by a combination of algorithms, code, and financial incentives.

Iron Finance had two tokens: IRON, which was their stablecoin pegged to the US dollar, and TITAN, their normal token, the price of which would fluctuate, and which you could buy if you wanted to invest in the project. You could create $1 of IRON by depositing seventy-five cents of USDC and twenty-five cents of TITAN into the Iron Finance application. Then, if you wanted to cash out, you could trade in one IRON to receive seventy-five cents of USDC and however much TITAN was equivalent to twenty-five cents US. So, the value of their stablecoin was mostly backed by US dollars using USDC, but it was also partially backed by the value of the project itself via TITAN. Another plus: it was on Polygon, so the transactions to make IRON were extremely cheap.

It was a cool idea for a stablecoin, but what was *cooler* were the farms. If I was looking at it right, I could make 4.5 percent per day on the TITAN token, and 1.5 percent per day on the dollar-pegged stablecoin IRON. Considering most savings accounts were paying less than 1.5 percent per *year* at the time, getting that much in a day was almost unimaginable.

It got even more insane when you calculated how high your returns would be if you collected your rewards and compounded them every day. If you are earning a 4.5 percent return per day, your APR is about 1,640 percent. So $10 today will be worth $164 in a year if you don't touch it. But if you claim the rewards every day and reinvest them, then your return is 926,948,926 percent, and your $10 would turn into $92,694,892.60 after a year. That compounded rate is referred to as APY, for annual percentage yield.

Now, obviously, it's impossible to actually achieve that kind of return long term. But even if you compound 4.5 percent returns every day for a week, you get a 36 percent return. In a month, you get 374 percent. And considering how early we were to finding Iron, it seemed like it could last for at least a week, or more. Even the 1.5 percent daily return on the IRON would turn into a 56 percent return over a month.

I waved Johnny over from the shop and walked him through everything I'd learned. "I think this is it," I said. "This is the one."

He stared at my laptop. I could tell he wasn't sure what to think.

"Look, this is a real project for once," I said, talking faster now, the mix of caffeine and excitement getting to my head. "We missed all of the great DeFi projects last summer and fall. Now there's one we can get in early on. No more sketchy farms. This is our big one. Our shot."

Johnny thought for a moment, then said, "Let's see what the group thinks."

I shared the Iron info in our group chat, and Quinn chimed in and said the people from her group with Galt were already putting their money in it. This was the first time since HAWK that I knew the whole group had been in on something together.

I searched through Twitter and started noticing coded messages among crypto Twitter influencers about Iron. No one was saying "put money into Iron!" But they were sharing coded messages like "Iron > Gold" or "can't wait for the new Titan of DeFi."

"I'm gonna do it," I told Johnny.

I deposited all of the farming money I had left, $20,000, into the IRON farm, and $5,000 into the TITAN farm.

WAGMI.

₿₿₿

The next morning, I rolled over in bed and immediately checked the TITAN price. It was up almost 50 percent and the group was already excited and talking about it. Not only did we earn 5 percent interest in one day, but the value of our deposit was also up. I'd made about $2,000.

I did a quick scan through Twitter to see if there was any obvious chatter about Iron yet. There were a couple coded messages about "algo-stables," clearly intended for people like me who also knew what was going on with Iron, but nothing from people heavily promoting it or encouraging others to jump in. I was an insider this time; it was still under wraps. If I'd learned anything from the last couple months of DeFi adventures, it's that, once something starts getting pushed heavily on Twitter and YouTube, it's time to get out.

I tried, and failed, to get through the day without constantly watching the price and cycling my rewards. It was intoxicating being in this early on such a big launch. The TITAN price kept climbing higher. Everyone else who was finding it must have been buying TITAN to create IRON and farm. It was an extremely effective incentive to get people to check out their launch.

I did start to wonder, though, what would happen when the price stopped going up.

₿₿₿

The following morning, the value of my TITAN had grown from $5,000 to $8,500, and my IRON was worth $20,700. I was up $4,200 in two days.

Johnny and I met up at Velocity and couldn't believe what luck we'd stumbled into. He'd decided to follow me into the farm, despite his previous heavy losses, and was close to making everything back. I was on track to make more this week than I'd made in the last month. I finally understood what got Quinn so hooked last year. If the wins had been this easy, no wonder she'd gotten consumed by the crypto casino.

₿₿₿

Day three: My $5,000 in TITAN had turned into $12,000, and my $20,000 in IRON was worth $22,000.

I'd made $9,000 in three days.

Johnny had already earned back all the money he had lost.

We started debating in the chat about whether now was the right time to get out, or if it would keep going higher. Over $1 billion had been deposited into the TITAN and IRON farms, more than I'd seen in any new project since getting into crypto. A couple people in the group decided to get out while they were ahead. Johnny and I stayed in, though. I wasn't too worried about it crashing. As long as Twitter was quiet, I felt safe.

₿₿₿

Day four: The price of TITAN had dropped by 25 percent overnight.

I texted Johnny, "What are you thinking, ride it back up or get out?"

"Ehhh I might buy more lol," he texted back. It wasn't a bad idea if we thought it would go back up.

"Yeah why not," I said. "Rich or rekt right?"

"Rich or rekt!"

₿₿₿

Day five: The mania was back on track.

The 25 percent drop had only been a blip in TITAN's meteoric rise. I had my laptop outside Velocity with Johnny, and we were trying to decide what to do. I was up $21,000, but, instead of celebrating, I was kicking myself for not buying more. It was a good reminder of an ironclad rule of investing I'd heard from multiple people: You never buy or sell the exact right amount at the exact right time. No matter how well you do, you can always imagine doing better.

We were getting concerned about how long this would last. Everyone knew about Iron now; the mania had completely consumed Twitter. It was being called the future of stablecoins and the main stablecoin for layer 2 networks. Investors, speculators, and gamblers had invested nearly $2 billion into the project now, and it showed no signs of slowing down.

I was scanning through my Discord servers trying to get a pulse on how people felt about it, when Quinn shared an article with the group.

Mark Cuban had been interviewed about crypto, and he had apparently put money into Iron. He was talking about what a cool project it was and how excited he was about the potential for DeFi to change the banking system.

"That's gotta be our sign to get out, right?" I messaged the group. Crypto Twitter was already blowing up with people excited about Iron, but if celebrity billionaire Mark Cuban was talking about it, that was going to bring in a ton of additional excitement and unsophisticated investors and might be the sign the early whales needed to exit their position. All the new capital following Cuban in would be the exit liquidity for people like us who were early.

"Totally, let's call it," Quinn responded. I withdrew my funds from the two farms and sold everything for USDC. What started as $25,000 was now $51,000. I hadn't quite made everything back, but making $26,000 in a week and a half felt incredible.

Still, I couldn't help checking the price on my phone for the rest of the night. It was still slowly creeping up, and now I worried that I pulled my money too early. If it doubled again, I would miss out on another $20,000 gain. Part of me even wondered if I should get back in, but, in the end, I decided against it. It was time for bed.

₿₿₿

"Hoooly shit."

When I looked at my phone the next morning, I saw that TITAN had dropped by nearly 50 percent overnight, then recovered most of the way to where it was the day before.

I stumbled downstairs to open my laptop and make some coffee. I messaged the group chat: "Anyone know what's going on with TITAN?" We had all cashed out, so we didn't have any skin in the game. It was more curiosity than anything. Given how wildly the price had jumped around the night before, it seemed like it could be on the precipice of a big drop.

"I don't know," Quinn replied. "But anyone waking up and seeing last night is probably going to exit. That's a hell of a fluctuation."

As I pulled up one of the price tracking apps so I could watch the token sales happening in real time, Cosette came downstairs and saw me fixated on my laptop.

"Is everything alright?"

"Well, no, but it is for us," I said. "That project we got out of yesterday, something's happening. I think it might be collapsing."

"Like the price is going down?"

"Maybe worse." I had an idea of what might be going on, but I'd never seen it before. "We're fine, though, I got it right. Give me ten minutes, and we can go for our walk."

TITAN was still hovering around the price it was at the day before, but I was more interested in IRON. When you buy a token like TITAN, you know there's some risk that it might go to zero. But when you're holding a stablecoin like IRON that's supposed to always be one US dollar, you treat it differently. You don't imagine there could be any loss there, so you're comfortable putting much more money into it. That's part of why there was more than $1 billion in the IRON farm; it felt risk free.

Except now that "stablecoin" was trading at ninety-eight cents, not so stable after all. If the Iron Finance system worked properly, people would be able to buy IRON on the market for ninety-eight cents and redeem it for one US dollar of value, essentially earning free money. That had happened every time in the past couple weeks that IRON had briefly dipped below $1. Would it happen this time? There wasn't much to do for now other than wait and see.

Cosette and I leashed up the dogs and started walking towards Velocity. I filled her in on what I thought might be going on.

At Velocity, Johnny had his laptop out on a picnic table, staring at it with the same concerned intensity I'd been glaring at my screen with this morning.

"Hey, are you good?" I hoped he hadn't put money back in.

"Oh, yeah. Trying to figure out what's going on. You've seen the IRON price, right?"

"Yeah, it's at ninety-eight cents."

"Down to ninety-six now."

I felt a pang of fear. It had never dropped this low before. Theoretically, you should be able to earn a free 4 percent return if you used their redemption system, so why weren't people doing it? There were probably millions of dollars' worth of tokens you could get a free 4 percent return on sitting out there right now.

I pulled out my laptop to look at the transaction feed, and it seemed like people were trying. They were buying hundreds of thousands of IRON tokens, presumably to take advantage of the arbitrage, but selling even more as they got scared by the decreasing price and raced for the exits. The more people sold instead of redeemed, the faster the IRON token dropped.

The TITAN token was dropping much faster. When people redeemed their IRON tokens, they got back seventy-five cents of USDC and twenty-five cents of TITAN, then they immediately sold the TITAN tokens. People were redeeming and selling so fast that the TITAN token was in free fall.

"So . . . at what price does this become a good deal again?" Johnny asked. I had been thinking the same thing. If the redemption mechanism worked, and the IRON stablecoin restabilized, there might be an incredible buying opportunity here. But only if the mechanism worked.

"I don't think there is one," I said. "This might be going to zero. Besides, we already won." This was the first catastrophic disaster I had seen a DeFi product experience. I'd heard about past ones, but seeing it happen live was completely different. It felt like driving by a car crash. I knew it was bad, but I couldn't look away.

By the afternoon, TITAN had dropped 66 percent from the morning, but IRON was rebounding.

"Hey are you guys seeing this?" I posted in the chat. "IRON is back up to $0.98."

"Shit do we buy TITAN again?" Johnny posted.

"I'm definitely not," I replied. "I just want to watch."

It was a smart call. IRON never went higher than ninety-eight cents.

As soon as the remaining investors holding IRON saw it get close to $1, they withdrew whatever they had left and sold. The immense surge in selling pressure pushed the IRON price even lower, and everyone trying to redeem it for the arbitrage started pushing the TITAN price lower, as well.

By the end of the day, Iron Finance was dead. TITAN had dropped 99.99 percent from where it had started the day. And with TITAN worthless, every IRON was only worth seventy-five cents, the value of the USDC backing it. Thankfully, they hadn't tried to do an algorithmic stablecoin fully backed by the value of TITAN. Then IRON could have gone all the way to zero, and anyone still holding it would have lost everything.

Within a day, the crypto community had agreed on a rough theory of what happened. Iron's redemption mechanism worked by giving you what it thought was twenty-five cents' worth of TITAN along with the seventy-five cents of USDC. But the code had to figure out how much TITAN was worth twenty-five cents, and since prices might fluctuate moment to moment, it used the average price over the previous ten minutes and reported that as the price of the token.

That was fine during normal market conditions, but when investors got spooked and started selling huge amounts of TITAN tokens, the price kept going down. As a result, the average price over the previous ten minutes was slightly higher than the price at any given moment. That meant that, when people tried to redeem their IRON, they got slightly too little TITAN, because the app thought the TITAN was worth more than it actually was. They were only getting back twenty-three cents' or twenty-four cents' worth of TITAN, which naturally led to them freaking out more and selling more tokens, accelerating the death spiral.

A simple design oversight had created a weakness in their model that poured fuel on the bank run as soon as it started. Future teams would hopefully learn from Iron and not make the same mistake, but it was a brutal loss, nonetheless. Thankfully, those affected were mostly people who were heavily into crypto, and there weren't too many unsophisticated people putting money in.

The group and I were elated at our good timing. It was almost hilari-

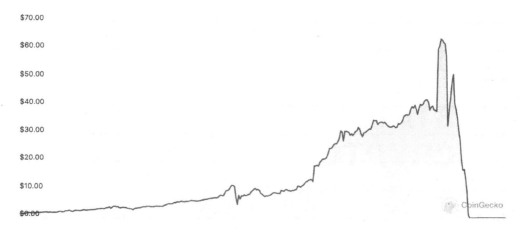

TITAN's meteoric rise and fall

ous; the chat was jovial about how close we'd come to the edge and still got away with all of our winnings. Johnny was made whole again, and it seemed like everyone in the group had enjoyed a big win from it. Our little ragtag team of crypto speculators had turned Mark Cuban into exit liquidity.

Who's the shark now?

STABLECOINS: CRYPTO'S KILLER APP

You might be wondering why stablecoins exist, let alone are such a large percentage of the cryptocurrency market. It does seem strange at first blush: one of the original goals of cryptocurrency was to replace the existing financial systems and what we use as money. So why would the existing financial system have so much presence in the crypto market?

There are two main reasons that stablecoins are extremely useful. First, they benefit the cryptocurrency world by providing a lower-volatility set of tokens. Second, they benefit the traditional financial world by providing an often faster and better way to use digital dollars.

If you want to hold most of your wealth outside of a bank or other financial institution, your options are limited. You could fill a vault with gold and cash, but that would create storage and transportation issues. You could hold Bitcoin and Ethereum, but you might not want your net worth subject to the wild value fluctuations of those major cryptocurrencies. Instead, you can hold USDC. You could put $1 billion of USDC in a crypto wallet on your phone, get on a plane, and go anywhere with it. There are certainly other risks with that (you better not forget your phone at the security line!), but it is possible.

Then there are the ways stablecoins improve how we can use our money. If you reside in one of the many countries in the world subject to rapid inflation or unreliable financial institutions, holding digital dollars on a device you can control is a significant improvement over holding your local currency in a risky banking system. If you're working in one country and sending money to your family in another, stablecoins provide a much faster, more reliable, and nearly free means of doing that.

It also simplifies the merchant process. If I sell you something and want to charge you $5 for it online, I can take that payment via 5 USDC for a tiny fraction of the fee I'd normally have to pay to process a credit card or bank transfer. Crypto payments haven't caught on in a big way in most parts of the world, but with layer 2 networks making the gas fees near zero, they're quickly becoming feasible. Coinbase is in the process of launching (and may have already launched by the time you read this) a point-of-sale integration that allows merchants to accept USDC for payments and pay no transaction fee, instead of the 2 to 3 percent they usually have to pay to accept credit cards.

Stablecoins also enable new ways to transact that aren't an option in our traditional financial system. One example is streaming payments. It's unfair that you typically have to wait two weeks to get paid for work you have already done, sometimes much longer if you're recording hours and sending invoices. Because of how easily we can move stablecoins between wallets, you could receive a streaming payment from your employer that deposits a fraction of your salary into your wallet every day, hour, or even minute. The same is true if you're a business with customers on recurring payments. Those payments could arrive each day instead of each month, at no additional cost to you or your customers.

Even if other parts of the crypto ecosystem, like NFTs, don't catch on, stablecoins seem here to stay given the utility they offer over the existing technology we have for digital money transfers.

9
Million-Dollar Profile Pictures

JUNE 2021

As satisfying as it was, our victory betting on Iron came with a cost. The Iron blowup was so catastrophic, and wiped out so much crypto wealth that it ended much of the wildly speculative farming and gambling we'd done for the previous couple of months. Farms launched slower. Crypto Twitter was less active. And everyone was feeling the pain of so much money being lost.

For a couple of weeks, I had only taken breaks from learning programming for morning walks and meals, but when Johnny texted me one morning saying he had something to show me, I packed up my bag and walked over.

"What're we working on?" I asked.

"Remember all that NFT craziness earlier this year? Like with Beeple?"

I nodded. It had been the first meaningful sign that something was going on in crypto besides people gambling on random tokens like DOGE.

Beeple was a digital artist who had released a piece every single day for more than a decade. He posted most of them online for anyone to look at, but, the previous year, he'd also started releasing each one as an NFT, or non-fungible token.

Fungible means that every unit of something is the same and interchangeable. If you ask me for a dollar and I have three in my pocket, it doesn't matter which bill I give you. They're all the same.

Most of the things we own are not fungible, though, or at least not fully fungible. Art is the easiest example. There's a big difference between having a painting and having the Mona Lisa. And there's a big difference between having the original Mona Lisa and having a picture of it from the internet. The original painting is not fungible.

That distinction between an original piece of art and a copy of it had never existed for digital images. If I uploaded a digital photo of Big Ben, and someone else copied the photo and uploaded it themselves, there wouldn't be a way to tell which was the original. The same is true for digital artwork. If I made a piece of art on my computer and uploaded it, anyone could copy and paste it, and it would be impossible to say which one was the original. Thus, there wouldn't be any sense in which someone could "own" that piece of art digitally the way they can own a piece of art physically.

Non-fungible tokens are a way to solve the ownership problem. I can upload that same piece of digital art and create an NFT of it, which I would have in my crypto wallet along with my other tokens, like ETH and USDC. The NFT would be a token, a record on the blockchain, of who uploaded the piece of art, what the piece of art is (like a link to where the image is displayed), and who currently owns it. Anyone could see the image, and they could still copy and paste it, but I would still have the original token signifying that I owned it. An NFT is like the certificate of authenticity for a painting or the title you get with your car. It proves you own the original.

When Beeple started selling NFTs for each piece of artwork he released, they sold for a modest amount of money. But he quickly gained fame for his strange, pop-culture-influenced digital creations, and the daily auctions for his NFTs climbed higher and higher. The mania around his NFTs peaked in March 2021, when a collage of five thousand of his daily pieces was sold at Christie's for a whopping $69.3 million.

"I thought the NFT mania died down," I said. By now I knew the pattern. Each of these manias tended to grow to a major, blow-the-top event, after which the balloon started deflating. Beeple's $69 million sale had been the top of the NFT art market. And then we'd seen the same kind of growing mania and explosion, except in DeFi, that happened leading up to Iron Finance.

"Welllllll," Johnny said, "the art stuff is quiet now, but profile pictures are taking off."

"Profile pictures?"

"Yeah, the little headshot NFTs, like CryptoPunks."

CryptoPunks were pixelated headshots of animated, punk-rocker-type characters that rich crypto investors sometimes used as their profile pictures on Twitter. They launched in 2017, and, at the time, you could buy one for 0.07 ETH, around $70. Now, the rarest were trading for more than a million bucks. A CryptoPunk profile picture was the ultimate crypto status symbol. Not only was it a sign that you were an insider who knew the industry, but also that you were rich enough to have a tiny picture worth more than many people's homes.

"So, you're buying CryptoPunks?" I asked. "Where are you getting the money?"

"Oh, hell no." Johnny laughed and shook his head. "There's new stuff, new projects launching that are copying them and the Bored Apes. Did you see how high the apes have gotten?"

"No, what're they at?"

"Nearly two ETH."

"Jesus," I said. When Bored Apes launched, you could buy one for 0.07 ETH. Now, they were up nearly thirty times that in a month. This was wildly more lucrative than anything we'd done in DeFi besides Iron. "Did you buy one?"

"No, I missed it," said Johnny, "but there are more. It's like the DeFi farms again. Are you following Caleb on Twitter?"

"Yeah, not closely though."

"He has a whole schedule of upcoming NFT drops. He's some sort of influencer in the space now. Check it out." Johnny turned his laptop around to show me. "Look at all the drops coming up soon."

I looked through the list, and there were new drops happening every day. It would be a full-time job staying on top of them but potentially extremely profitable. "Are you doing this?" I asked.

"Oh yeah." Johnny laughed and filled me in on his NFT adventures over the previous couple of weeks.

First, a project called SuperYeti had launched earlier in the month with 3D-animated abominable snowmen you could supposedly use in a future YetiVerse. Johnny had bought fifty and made a few ETH off of them.

Then, he'd heard about a project called My Fucking Pickle. It was a lower-effort project with ten thousand animated pickles with various traits and rarities, but they were only charging 0.01 ETH for the initial purchase, called the *mint*. Johnny had minted four hundred of them. They'd jumped to 0.15 ETH, and he was selling a few every day and was already up multiples on his initial investment.

Then, while he was driving through Arizona with his brother, another project called Wicked Craniums had launched. It was profile pictures again, but with punk-rocker- or biker-gang-looking skeletons. Johnny had bought eighty at mint for 5.6 ETH, total, and had sold all of them for two to three times that price over the course of a day. That was his biggest win yet, nearly $20,000 in profit in an afternoon of driving around with his brother.

Then the MetaBots. And DystoPunks. And more Pickles. Johnny was on fire.

"Oh, and I got you something," he said. "What's your wallet address?" I texted it to him from my computer. "Sent!" he said.

I refreshed my wallet on my computer, and, a moment later, an NFT showed up. It was a headshot of a striped cat in a red flannel shirt that looked stoned out of its mind.

"Uh, Johnny, what did you send me?"

"It's a Gutter Cat!" he said with pride. "They launched earlier this month, and I got one for you as a thank-you for helping me learn all of the DeFi stuff. I got it for 0.07 ETH. Check the price."

I went to the main NFT marketplace, called OpenSea, looked up Gutter Cats, and let out a low whistle. "Wow, good work, dude." The average sale was already 0.7 ETH, ten times what he had paid.

"Thanks, I saved two for myself," he said. "Anyway, there's something I think you should check out." His face was lit up with excitement now. "Have you looked at Axie at all?"

I shook my head. "I've heard the name, but no, not really. It's a video game, right?"

Johnny smiled. "Yeah, it's a video game, but you earn crypto and NFTs from playing it."

That caught my attention. The crypto community had long been excited about the potential for crypto-native video games, and it was an area I had been meaning to explore for months. I'd played obsessive amounts of RuneScape, World of Warcraft, and Dota 2 at various times over the previous two decades, and, in all three games, there were exceedingly rare items that people were willing to pay huge amounts of real-world money for, purely to have the item as status symbols. NFTs were the perfect technology for trading status symbols and other items within and across different video games. Someone just needed to figure out how to do it. And if you could also convert the in-game currencies you earned, like Gold in World of Warcraft, into cryptocurrency and take that money out of the game, then you could start earning an income by playing video games.

"Have you played it at all?" I asked. Before we got into crypto, Johnny and I had been playing the game Fortnite together most afternoons. If we could play this together and make money, it could be the best of both worlds.

"No, but apparently some people are making tens of thousands of dollars a month off it."

"Tens of *thousands*?" Tens of thousands of dollars a month wouldn't have been impressive in DeFi, or speculating on shitcoins, but for playing a video game it seemed unreal.

Johnny nodded. "Yeah, it's wild. I'm focused on these profile-picture launches, but you should check Axie out. There might be something there."

"Will do." I paused for a moment, staring at my coffee. "Hey, question: Do you think it's still a good idea to buy an ape?"

"Hmmmm," Johnny said, pinching his eyebrows together. "Well, the cheapest CryptoPunks are, what, twenty ETH? And apes are around three to four. So, even if they get to half the value of a punk, you're looking at more than doubling your money." He looked like there was something he wasn't telling me.

"You seem unsure," I said.

"Well," he continued, "you could make a much better return minting and flipping like I've been doing."

"But then I'd have to do this full time. I just wanna hold something."

Johnny nodded. "Then, yeah, an ape is probably a good bet. It's like if we held ETH instead of doing all the DeFi stuff. It's the safe, easy bet."

"Great, that's what I was thinking." With how excited Johnny was about NFTs, and how fast they were moving, it did seem like they were the next wave of mania. But I'd learned from our DeFi adventures that it was often better to buy and hold the first mover than to try to pick a winner that was competing against them. If I had left my money in Polycat instead of chasing every new farm on Polygon, I would have done much better. Maybe there was a similar opportunity in buying one of the first movers in NFTs.

Johnny went back into the shop to help serve customers, while I packed up my bag and started heading home. On the way, I looked up the Twitter profile of a friend, Sam, who I'd seen posting about NFTs and gaming. Sam and I both had popular blogs, and we had interacted at various times over the previous few years, responding to each other's pieces or sharing them on social media. He had started talking about crypto around the same time I did, and he had shifted his focus more towards gaming in the last couple of months.

As I scrolled through his Twitter feed, it was clear he was printing money doing something in the Axie universe. He kept posting pictures of the rare characters he was selling for outrageous prices. I did some quick math as I scrolled and realized he wasn't making tens of thousands of dollars a *month*. He might have been making that each *week*.

I sent him a text: "Hey, I've been following some of your Axie stuff on Twitter, you mind if I ask you a few questions about it sometime?"

As I waited for him to respond, I started looking through Bored Apes on OpenSea. It would be a massive investment, but if I was right, it could pay off handsomely. If I bought one of the cheapest "floor" apes (as in: on the price floor), and it caught up to the cheapest CryptoPunks, I would earn a 500 percent return. It was hard to imagine making 16 ETH on one trade, but I'd seen weirder things happen.

I just needed to figure out which one to buy. There were ten thousand different Bored Apes, and the collection of traits an individual ape had determined its rarity and its value relative to the other apes. There were some obvious things you could charge more for—like an astronaut suit, laser eyes, or golden fur—but there were other, subtler things to look for, too. For example, some apes had six or seven traits, but the rarest only had four. An ape with only four traits, even if those traits were common, was rarer than a six-trait ape that had some rare qualities.

Thankfully, there were tools to help with figuring out how valuable a given ape was. I scrolled through all the apes for sale to look for ones I liked and calculated what they should be worth given their traits on the rarity site. One stood out as slightly undervalued. He had a Russian fur hat and a star-covered stunt jacket, plus a smoker's pipe. It was a hodgepodge of traits, but he was right at the floor price, so I decided I'd found my match. The 3.8 ETH, about $7,600, felt like a huge investment considering how little I understood about NFTs compared to DeFi, but I trusted Johnny. If he was right, I could hold this monkey and wait. Once it arrived in my wallet, I got to do the fun part. I changed my profile picture on Twitter, Discord, even LinkedIn, to my new ape.

I felt some FOMO about what Johnny was up to with the high-paced NFT speculating, but I wanted to investigate Axie. If people were making tens of thousands of dollars a month off a video game, I needed to get in on it.

Just then, Sam responded. "Good timing," he texted. "You're right, it's working insanely well. We're gonna raise some money to juice it further. Are you free this afternoon?"

"Definitely. Two?"

"Talk then."

I didn't necessarily want to invest in someone else playing Axie, but maybe, if I was lucky, Sam would give me some insights into how he was making so much money.

ARE NFTS USEFUL?

NFTs became famous during this period for two primary use cases. One was as a digital representation of ownership of art, like the kinds of images Beeple created for his everydays. The other was as profile-picture collections like the Bored Apes and CryptoPunks. There were others, but these were the two types of uses that most people heard about: digital art and profile pictures. As you'll see in the coming chapters, the profile-picture type, in particular, eventually became as wild, speculative, and low-effort as the DeFi farms Johnny and I were playing in. If all you saw of NFTs was people spending hundreds of thousands of dollars on a picture of an ape, you couldn't be blamed for wondering if NFTs had any use besides being a new tool for speculation.

The actual non-fungible token is a blockchain record of which address owns a certain digital object. If you own an NFT, that means you can go to the NFT's smart contract, plug in your address, and see a number representing the NFT that you own. Then you can plug that number into the contract and see a link to what that NFT represents, like an image. That's all it is on the back end, a record that your address owns that number, and what that number represents. If you have the private key that controls the address that owns a certain NFT, you can do things with it, like transfer it to someone else, if you want to sell it or give it away.

Normal, fungible tokens, like USDC and DOGE, are a way to create digital proof that you own a certain amount of something that many people own different amounts of, like dollars or video-game credits. But non-fungible tokens are a way to create digital proof that you own a specific asset not owned by anyone else. Artwork is just one example of such an asset, but the tech could be used as the standard for digital ownership of any kind of asset.

One example that has yet to fully catch on but seems inevitable is tickets. Instead of buying concert tickets through a site like Ticketmaster, which takes a huge cut of the sale and charges exorbitant fees, you could buy concert tickets directly from the artist as NFTs in an NFT marketplace. The best part of this model, aside from avoiding the marketplace fees, is that if you change your mind and decide to resell the ticket, the artist could get a cut of that resale price.

Another is various forms of digital real estate. You might balk at the idea of metaverse "land" ever being worth anything, but there is already one form of digital real estate that people spend billions of dollars on every year: domain names. To whatever extent other forms of digital real estate catch on in the future, NFTs can provide a way to prove ownership of those forms outside of any specific domain registrar or other third party. Even if you don't believe metaverse land will ever have any value, there are already billions of dollars spent each year on land, cosmetics, and other in-game items in games like Fortnite, Roblox, and Eve Online. But, once again, you typically cannot resell those items or bring them to other games or parts of the internet.

Finally, NFTs offer some new forms of fundraising and community participation for artists. Some musicians have already experimented with selling NFTs of their songs, with the NFT entitling you to a share of the royalties generated by the track as a form of easily tradeable digital copyright with instant royalty distributions. The same could be done

for books, movies, and even entire online brands, such as a YouTube channel.

While NFTs may look silly based on what caught the public eye during this first surge in their popularity, the potential for what they can be used for goes well beyond pictures of apes.

10
Play to Earn
JUNE 2021

My call with Sam about Axie Infinity wasn't until two p.m., so I had a few hours to learn as much as possible about the game.

Axie was a digital card game in which you collected "monsters," called Axies, and then sent them into battle in teams of three against other players' Axies. Each Axie was an NFT and had various traits that affected its rarity and effectiveness in battle. You could also "breed" your Axies together to get new Axies, and those new Axies might have different traits from their parents.

In order to breed your Axies, you needed an Axie cryptocurrency called Smooth Love Potion, or SLP. The only way to get SLP was by playing the game, and the better you did, the more SLP you earned. The more you earned, the more you could breed your Axies to sell them. Or you could sell your SLP directly for ETH or USDC. The reason you could do that was there were people out there, like Sam, buying SLP so they could breed their Axies without having to spend time playing the game.

The Axie ecosystem was described as *play to earn*, since you could, quite literally, get paid to play video games. Some people were making well above minimum wage playing. For players in developing countries with much lower wages, it was among the best jobs available.

But the real money wasn't in playing; it was in breeding. Rare Axies were selling for upwards of $1,000 each, and you could breed your Axies together up to seven times, creating exponential growth in your team and, hopefully, your money. By playing the game full time, you could make a few hundred dollars a day. By breeding full time, you could make thousands, assuming you had the capital to fund it. That must have been what Sam was doing, and why he needed more money.

Sam called me at two o'clock, and I started walking laps around the backyard while we talked. He explained that he had hundreds of Axies and bred them based on a calculator he'd designed to determine the optimal breeding pairings and maximize his chances of getting rare Axies. Sam was spending thousands of dollars buying SLP to breed his Axies, but he also had dozens of employees in the Philippines earning SLP more cheaply by playing the game for him using his Axies. That allowed Sam to do even more breeding. Then he'd sell some of those Axies, hire more gamers to play with the rest of them, and let their Axie collection grow week after week. Best of all, he could pay his army of SLP farmers by simply giving them a cut of the SLP they earned. Sam said that if I invested $10,000 in his fund, I'd probably get $40,000 back in a month, assuming he could keep the strategy going.

But as Sam was talking, a thought occurred to me. This was just farming with extra steps. The game was barely a game, and there were thousands of free mobile games with much richer gameplay. The game was an obfuscated way to farm SLP. Instead of depositing your tokens and then clicking a button to get free tokens, you had to click a few buttons to make your Axies jump around, and *then* you got free tokens. Breeding was the second part of the farm, where, instead of depositing your crypto and earning tokens over time, you instead had to click some buttons to multiply your assets.

Breeding should have been driving the price of Axies down, because it was massively increasing the supply. But as long as everyone kept holding their characters and kept breeding them, the price would keep going up, and more people would rush in to try to buy characters and get their share of the gold rush. On paper, you might have tens or hundreds of thousands of dollars' worth of characters, but if everyone decided the game was over and started selling, the market would implode as quickly as Iron.

Sam may have been making money over the last couple of months, but it seemed clear that Axie was in some sort of mania. You can't double your money every two weeks for very long, especially at the levels he was talking about. There wasn't much reason other than speculation for the characters to be worth anything. People were only buying Axies because they wanted to breed them to get more Axies because they heard people were getting rich from "playing" the game.

Sam's offer was tempting, but I felt like I was slightly too late. The market cap of Axie's token was already half a billion dollars, and breeding experts like Sam were flooding the market and taking all the profit. There were hundreds of thousands of full-time Axie players in East Asia battling around the clock to earn SLP for breeding or to dump on the market. If I had found it six months earlier, it would have been an incredible investment. But it didn't feel that way anymore.

It did give me a glimmer of hope, though. If Axie was the market leader for gaming, like punks and apes were for NFTs, then there would surely be a host of games trying to draft off its success. As soon as something works, it gets copied to the point of maximum stupidity. If I could find a game that was following in its footsteps and which showed potential, it might be an incredible investment, especially if we saw a mania in gaming similar to what we were seeing in broader NFTs.

₿₿₿

Cosette was home between showings, so I asked her if we could go for a walk. I filled her in on Johnny's NFT adventures and what I'd been looking at in gaming, and she agreed that it seemed like a perfect combination of my lifelong interest in gaming and the new crypto and NFT mania. Something was clearly on her mind, though, so I asked her what was wrong.

"I think we need to move," she said.

I stopped walking. I couldn't believe what I was hearing. We were having a baby in three months. I was the busiest I'd ever been with work in my life. She was the busiest she'd ever been. I was still figuring out how to make money. And I adored our house, especially my backyard office oasis.

"Okay . . . why?"

"I'm looking at all the baby stuff, and it'll be tight. We can do it in this house, of course, but I think we'll all be much more comfortable if we have a little extra space." She had a point. As much as I loved our house, it was cozy. The second bedroom could be turned into a nursery, but then we'd have no workspace. We'd discussed this lightly before and kept putting it off, but she was right. If it was possible to move, then we needed to consider it. Even an extra couple hundred square feet would make a big difference.

Thankfully, while I had been figuring out crypto, Cosette's career was soaring. She had sold four million dollars' worth of houses already this year and looked like she might do as much, if not more than that, the rest of the year. It was a huge boon to our family finances that neither of us had been expecting, and it did shift the odds a little in our favor if we wanted to make the move.

I told her I needed to think about it. I still hadn't found a paying gig yet, and I definitely didn't want to rely on farming for a mortgage payment.

₿₿₿

Returning from our walk, I went outside to my desk and messaged Johnny to fill him in on my conversation with Sam. I asked him if he had found any other crypto games besides Axie. He wasn't as into gaming as I was, but all crypto games started as NFT projects, selling NFTs first to raise money, then using the money to build the game. Well, some did. Others ran away with the funds.

Johnny said he hadn't found any, but he'd keep an eye out. I found more crypto-gaming influencers on Twitter to follow and crossed my fingers that someone would eventually mention something worth investigating. Thankfully, I didn't have to wait very long.

A few days later, Johnny directed me to a project called CryptoCraft that he'd heard about from Caleb, who had been talking about it on his NFT podcast. CryptoCraft was trying to build a classic dungeon-crawling role-playing game in which the characters, gear, and currency were all crypto assets. It looked like CryptoCraft was just getting started, too. They were still in the process of releasing their first batch of ten thousand characters. Johnny said that if I joined the Discord, I could buy ten for 0.1 ETH. They were launching them cheaply to help bring people into the game. They didn't want everyone to get priced out, like they might on other games, such as Axie—at least, not yet.

I hopped onto their Discord to see if I could grab some characters. They had posted an announcement saying they were going to release the remaining seventy-five hundred characters on OpenSea at the same prices they were selling them on Discord. I made a note in my calendar to get on OpenSea at six p.m. that night, which was when they planned to release them. Above their announcement of the auction, though, was another announcement. They were looking for a "Solidity or Web3 Engineer" to help them with their token launch and the "tokenomics" behind it.

Tokenomics was a new crypto discipline focused on designing the game theory and logistics behind a token launch. Since tokens were typically released over time and had to be distributed among the founders, employees, investors, the company itself, and the public or users of the application, there was quite a bit of thought and design that went into creating a good token launch. A great project with a poorly thought-out token strategy could sink itself before it ever got started.

I knew some basic tokenomics from the writing I'd been doing about crypto, but I primarily knew it in a DeFi context. But there weren't any gaming-tokenomics experts yet, since Axie was the only major player. So maybe I could be helpful with figuring out CryptoCraft's token launch. As for the other part of the job, the Web3 or Solidity engineer, I thought maybe I could be helpful there, as well. I could definitely assist on the Web3 side, all the JavaScript that wires the smart contracts together into the site. But I didn't feel confident about my Solidity abilities yet. Especially not confident enough to run a whole token launch. That would be a significant amount of responsibility, and if I got it wrong, I could seriously wreck the project. It's one thing to screw up and lose your own money. It's another to screw up and lose everyone else's.

The person in charge on the Discord was "Leeroy Jenkins," a pseudonym in honor of a famous World of Warcraft player. He was online, so I sent him a message.

"Hey man, I found CryptoCraft and absolutely love it. I've been looking for a project like this. I write a weekly newsletter to about 30,000 people, cool if I mention CR next week?"

A few minutes later, he responded. "Maybe in a month or two once we start breeding and have more characters? I don't want too many people to come in now and get priced out." That made sense. If a couple thousand people came in and bought characters, they could dramatically constrict the supply and make the game more expensive than Leeroy seemed to want at this point.

"Sounds good," I sent back. "So excited about this project."

"Thanks man, we are, too."

Not a particularly deep conversation, but I at least opened the door so he knew who I was now.

But then he kept typing: "The idea for the in-game currency is to create some sort of profitable balancing loop. We control how much gold drops in a dungeon, we also control how much gold a dungeon costs. We can use those levers to control inflation and make the game profitable to play."

It was a weird segue. I didn't even tell him I wanted to work on the tokens. But hey, I could talk about video games all day. "Yeah that makes sense," I wrote back, "you're gonna have three different inflation paces to manage I guess: gold, characters, items. Crafting in-game items that are worth real-world money will be wild."

"Yeah, exactly. And then the materials you use for in game crafting like wood and iron can be crypto tokens as well."

Interesting, so it would have all the normal video-game elements, but also have crypto-farming elements. It was a good way to attract money into the system and to build on the hype started by Axie. I texted back: "Ooh that's cool. This is an exciting roadmap."

"It's going to come down to execution at the end of the day. Hey shot in the dark, but Caleb said some good things about you. We need a real winner and someone we can trust to build the token for the game. If you're interested or know someone who has the know-how, let us know and we can explore further."

I stared at my computer in shock. Unless I was completely missing something, this stranger I had met online was offering me a dream job. It didn't make any sense. How could he even know I might be interested in it? Quinn knew I had been spending most of my time learning Solidity, and she was close with Caleb, so maybe she told Caleb, and Caleb told Leeroy? Caleb had encouraged me to keep learning, too, so maybe he was keeping tabs? It felt like a stretch, but here we were. Caleb must have been working with the team closely. He was listed as a senior member of the team on Discord, and it would explain why he was promoting it so much on social media. It must be even harder than I thought to find a good Solidity engineer. Offering a job on one of the most important parts of your business to the first stranger who wanders onto your Discord is not a normal hiring practice.

I thought about it for a moment and decided I shouldn't oversell myself. "It's something I'd love to help on, but I wouldn't feel comfortable taking on the token building yet. I'm still earlier in my Solidity journey. Very down to help think things through or help on any marketing and website stuff though. I can see if I come across anyone, too. It's a tough hiring market for Solidity devs man, such a short supply."

"Literally, Solidity devs are rarer than an endangered animal. Impossible to find one that has an ounce of creativity, isn't doing their own projects, is for hire, and doesn't want 30%."

"Yup, exactly," I said. "That's why I started learning."

"Totally, my cofounder Excalibur is a very experienced dev, new to Solidity, but picking it up on the fly. We would rather work with someone we can trust with less experience, than someone we can't trust with more experience. So let me know if you think you can help or know anyone who can."

"Will do."

We kept talking about game mechanics and immediately hit it off. It sounded like they were thinking of doing most of the things I'd been excited about as potential opportunities for a crypto game, and they were doing it in the niche that I loved and knew the best. The more we talked, the more I wanted to join the team. Farming in the DeFi casino was so dissatisfying, because so few of the apps were actually building anything. If I was being honest, it felt like most NFT projects weren't building anything, either, other than something to speculate on. But this was a *real game*, something people could play with their friends and on which they could potentially make money. It was one of the most compelling uses for NFTs and tokens that I could think of given how much people already spent on games like this *without* the potential to make money.

But I wasn't sure if my skills were remotely good enough. It was a big undertaking, and our interaction still felt completely surreal. I didn't understand why Caleb would have mentioned me to Leeroy, or why he'd be willing to take a risk on someone with so little experience. You'd only imagine that kind of trust from a friend or someone you'd worked with before, but I didn't even know this guy's real name.

Working with pseudonymous characters like Leeroy was strange, and I felt like I had a big informational disadvantage. He could look up anything he wanted to know about me. I had no way to research him. The "Leeroy Jenkins" pseudonym didn't appear to exist on Twitter or anywhere else before he started working on CryptoCraft. I could understand him wanting to maintain his privacy, especially if the game took off the way Axie did.

But it must have made it harder to hire people or find people to invest in his project. He could be scamming people, and if he did, no one would be able to track down who committed the crime. I knew I might have to work with pseudonymous people like this if I joined a crypto project, but it still felt off.

Even so, I couldn't deny how exciting it all was. This might be another piece of crypto weirdness I had to accept. Getting a ridiculous job, without qualifications, from an anonymous internet character seemed ludicrous, but hey, this was crypto. It doesn't have to make sense.

₿₿₿

I brought the opportunity up with Cosette over dinner that night. "Somehow this guy already knows who I am through a mutual connection," I said, "and he hinted that they might be interested in hiring me to do some smart-contract work for them."

She cocked an eyebrow. "Do you know how to do what they need you to do?"

"No, not really. Maybe I could figure it out, but it's a big leap. And if I mess it up like I did with my first contract, I could kill their project."

"Is there any way you could try to figure out how to do what they need you to do before they hire you? Then you'd have a better idea of how hard it actually is."

My mind started racing. I *could* try building it before committing to anything and see how hard it was. Maybe it would be easier than I thought. I'd already looked at some code for tokens, and it didn't seem *that* complicated. So much of this world was copy and paste, after all.

Cosette smiled. She could tell my brain was somewhere else. "Do you wanna go look now?" she asked. She didn't look annoyed. It was more like she was excited for me.

"Yeah, let me go give it a quick look." I grabbed my laptop and took it to the couch with my dinner. Leeroy had sent me a link to another game that had launched recently, CryptoBlades.

Looking at a smart contract now compared to a month ago, when I started, was like night and day. What previously seemed like an impenetrable mess of spaghetti was starting to make sense. The whole token contract was only two hundred and fifty lines, and I knew what most of it meant now, too.

It also seemed oddly familiar, like I'd seen it before. I knew there was an open-source Solidity library of free code called "OpenZeppelin," so I compared the CryptoBlades code with the OpenZeppelin code and saw they were almost identical. I had assumed teams put more effort into their tokens, but maybe I was wrong. I checked the code for a few other tokens. They all did the same thing, some even more explicitly than Blades did. That's all anyone was doing for launching a token. Copy, paste, ship. It was so easy. No wonder there were so many. I could probably get this token done in a day. That explained why these farms could launch so fast, too. Not only were the user experiences copy and pasted, the tokens and the smart contracts were, too. You could launch a farm in a matter of hours if you knew what code to copy and how to deploy it.

I barely slept that night. I felt like there was a newfound power coursing through my veins, like I had discovered this huge industry secret. I could do this. I could launch their token, and I could charge them for it. And if it went well, I could help other teams do the same thing. Solidity was scary if you didn't know what you were doing, but I felt like I'd made it through the fog and now I could see how simple most of it was. If you weren't pushing the frontiers of new innovations in the space, all you had to do was find the right people to copy. Then, the frenzy for new things to speculate on would send the herd your way.

Whoever this Leeroy guy was, his game might be my ticket.

THE SHOCKINGLY LARGE WORLD OF DIGITAL LUXURY GOODS

A CryptoPunk or Bored Ape being worth tens of thousands of dollars seems irrational. The only explanation that most people will accept for valuing a digital image so highly is rampant speculation: gamblers buying coveted assets in the hopes they can sell them to some greater fool for even more money. There was plenty of that going on in the NFT boom, but dismissing the price of these assets as purely mania-driven speculation misses a real phenomenon that started decades ago and is only now starting to pick up steam: the rise in digital status symbols.

We're already familiar and comfortable with status symbols in the physical world. Someone spending $4,000 on a Celine bag might seem ridiculous—it's not *that* much more functional than a plastic bag, after all—but many people still do it. An expensive bag provides a variety of benefits besides schlepping things. It shows people you're wealthy. It demonstrates something about your fashion sense. It suggests you're a member of a certain group or class of people. For those reasons and others, owning one makes some people feel good.

Status-signaling luxury goods are a massive market. According to Statista, the global revenue for luxury-goods companies in 2023 was approximately $354 billion. Not all luxury goods serve purely to signal status, but status signaling is undeniably a part of the value of luxury products. We humans love signaling our status, but, until recently, there hasn't been a great way to do that online. You can post photos of your physical luxury goods, like putting car and outfit pictures on Instagram, but there aren't many digitally native luxury goods. That is, unless you are into video games. As soon as video games started offering online, multiplayer experiences, markets for rare items within the games started to pop up. There were a few examples in the late 1990s of unofficial item markets starting to pop up for video games like Diablo and Ultima Online, but they took off with a game called RuneScape in the early 2000s.

RuneScape was a massively multiplayer online role-playing game, or MMORPG, in which you could run around in a digital world with thousands of other players and could outfit your character with various weapons and types of armor to improve their stats. RuneScape launched in 1998, but in 2001, they held a Christmas event during which you could find party hats in various colors around the world of the game. At first, the party hats were fun novelty items, but as the game got more popular, and more people started playing, the party hats became rarer and rarer, eventually selling for thousands of real-world dollars.

As other online games became popular, their rare items also started selling for thousands or tens of thousands of dollars. A World of Warcraft account was once sold for $9,500. A sword in the game Age of Wushu was sold for $16,000. A recreation of the city of Amsterdam within the game Second Life was sold for $50,000. A planet in the game Entropia Universe was sold for $6 million. (I know, I barely believe that last one, too.)

But the problem with all of these in-game items is that they're stuck in the game. Fortnite players spend $2 billion a year on cosmetics, but those cosmetics can't be brought to any other game. If you spend $38,000 on the pink Ethereal-Flame War Dog in Dota 2, the only people you can show it off to are the other Dota 2 players.

What NFTs enable are a way to create digital status symbols that are cross-platform. If you have a Bored Ape, you can show that off anywhere, and people can verify that you own it if they don't believe you. So, if a rare item that you can only use in one game can be sold for $10,000, maybe it isn't so irrational that a rare primate illustration you can show off everywhere could be sold for $100,000, especially as people spend more and more of their time online.

If your goal is to signal wealth and status, a digital status symbol conveys that status more broadly than a physical one. So, perhaps it isn't all speculative mania. Video games may have predicted a future in which everyone covets digital status symbols, and NFTs demonstrated one of the first ways those status symbols might come into existence.

11

You Can't Eat Tokens

JULY 2021

I got up at six a.m., made coffee, and got out to my desk as fast as possible. I needed to see if I was right. I needed to know if it was truly this easy to create new internet money.

I followed the OpenZeppelin guide and wrote a basic version of what I thought would be a working token contract. The first couple of tests didn't work, and I had to solve a few bugs, but then, on the third try, it ran with no issues. I had made a token. I checked the time on my computer: it wasn't even seven yet.

It can't be that easy, I thought. But I couldn't find anything wrong with it. I could send tokens back and forth between addresses, see my balances, create more tokens, destroy tokens, everything Leeroy would need to do for a video-game currency that's also a crypto token. Everything I would need to do for a token for *anything*. Anyone posting on Twitter about their wacky new NFTs-for-Dogs idea who needed a token, I could help them out, and charge a meaningful sum for it, too.

I wanted to send the contract to Leeroy, but I knew I could impress him even more. So, I started building a basic website where you could manage how many tokens there were, send them to different people, and destroy some of them, if you needed to—a kind of central bank for this new digital currency I had created. I worked on it for the rest of the day, through the next morning, and by two p.m., it was ready. I sent Leeroy the contract and the site and told him to check it out.

He messaged me back a few minutes later. "Dude this is legendary. So in 48 hours you went from, 'I don't think I'm qualified to build you a token' to 'Hey I built you a token check it out.'"

"LOL yeah. Turns out I knew more than I thought."

"We need to get you involved in CryptoCraft. Excalibur and my other cofounder Tyrael are the only guys working on this with me right now, I'll put out feelers to them if you're interested."

"I would love that man. All my years of playing World of Warcraft finally paying off."

I pushed back from my desk and stared at my computer screen. I did it. I got a crypto gig working on a video game. It was a dream job, one of the first times I'd ever felt like the thirteen-year-old me would be ecstatic and proud of what I was working on. And I'd had a ridiculous amount of fun in the last forty-eight hours figuring all this out. That experience was like its own new video game. And unlike farming, it was a crypto video game in which I wasn't in constant peril of losing all my money.

Leeroy messaged: "How do you want to get paid for this?"

I hadn't thought about that yet. I knew Solidity developers could charge tons of money, but I was pretty junior. I would have been happy with a modest payment to get my feet wet, but I knew how valuable this skillset was. Plus, it's always better to anchor your negotiations with a high number and let them try to bring it down from there.

"How about 2 ETH a week as a retainer for any Solidity stuff you guys need till the platform token launches, then we can reevaluate?" I knew I was pushing it by asking for 2 ETH, about $4,000, a week, but he could always negotiate.

"Ok for the token we can give you a percent of launch, and some per-cent of fees for recurring work. Something like that if that's interesting to you."

That made sense, but he was dodging the request. Who knew if and when these guys would actually launch anything. Leeroy and I had hit it off, sure, but I had to keep in mind I'd only met him two days ago. I couldn't do a ton of free work and hope they'd give me some of the token when it launched. I also didn't have any reason to assume the token would be worth anything. This was a brand-new project, and most projects flop. Getting some percent of a worthless token was no way to get paid.

"Definitely," I said, "but what about until then?" I couldn't do all this for free.

Silence. Leeroy stopped responding. *Shit.* He had the code for the to-ken contract. Maybe he decided to run off with it and that they'd do it on their own. I might have overplayed my hand. Maybe sending him every-thing before figuring this out was a mistake. I could see the little green bubble that meant he was online. He was clearly ignoring me. *Damnit.*

I could reach out to Caleb, he had put in a good word for me, but we didn't know each other that well. I didn't want to seem whiny by running to him to fix my problem. But if these guys did take my code and launch with it, I'd have to say something. I could at least blast them on Twitter, not that it would do very much. God, I was going to feel so stupid if they launched this thing and made a ton of money off it.

I took a deep breath. Leeroy had the token code, true, but that was the easiest part of a token launch. Instead of whining to Caleb or getting pissed off, I should start working on the harder part and keep bugging him. If I made it clear that I was committed to doing this, then he'd be an idiot not to hire me.

The biggest challenge wasn't how to make the token, it was how to make it easy for anyone to buy and sell the new CRAFT tokens. They would use a decentralized exchange to list it, but there was a big catch to adding your token to a DEX: you also needed to add ETH, or USDC, or whatever you wanted people to trade your token for, and you needed to add a lot of it.

If Leeroy had millions of dollars to invest, he could provide all the trading funds himself. But considering the CryptoCraft website looked slapped together, the art on the NFTs wasn't anything impressive, and he'd run away when I asked for 2 ETH a week, I doubted he had that kind of money.

Thankfully, there was another option. Leeroy and his partners didn't necessarily need to provide all of the trading funds themselves. One of the special features of a decentralized exchange is that *anyone* can deposit tokens to get a share of the trading fees. Instead of adding millions of dollars themselves, Leeroy and his team could add some smaller initial amount, then incentivize other people to add more by giving them CRAFT tokens in return. For it to work, I would need to figure out how to build a farm that could pay people for adding trading funds to a DEX. I knew those kinds of farms existed; I'd used them during the Pounder and Iron Finance days. I just had to find a good one to copy.

After a few hours, I found a simple one to start with. By the end of the day, I got an extremely basic version working. That was the second of the three pieces they needed.

The third was the tokenomics: the plan for what the tokens would be used for, how fast the token would be released, and how many would be reserved for the team and the community. I wrote up a basic outline of my thoughts on how the token could be launched and distributed, took some screenshots of the basic farming contract I had put together, and sent it over to Leeroy.

Then I took a break to grab lunch with Cosette. We got in the car and turned out of the driveway, and I started telling her how annoyed I was getting about the Leeroy situation. Rain was battering the windshield, and we could barely see more than a few feet ahead of us.

"I don't get how he could be so excited a few days ago and now not be responding at all," I said.

"You're sure he's online and not out of office or something?"

"Yeah, I can see him responding to other people in the public chat. It's infuriating."

"Well, is there anyone else you could ask?"

"I don't think so," I said. "I don't know the other guys on the team."

Cosette didn't say anything. We drove on in silence, while I glared out the window.

As soon as we returned home, I checked Discord and, sure enough, still nothing. I knew I was getting desperate and negotiating against myself, but I really wanted this gig, so I messaged Leeroy again:

"Hey I'm fine holding off on payment till we get the token launched, seems like that's better for you guys and then we can focus on shipping. Let me know what you think of the tokenomics plan."

He wasn't online, for once, but maybe he'd respond in the morning. I made a few more little improvements to the code, then tried to relax the rest of the evening without checking for a message from him every ten minutes. I didn't want to seem too desperate, but the more I worked on this, the more it felt like it could turn into an incredibly lucrative project.

I just needed him to say yes.

THE WEIRD LAND OF INCENTIVIZED LIQUIDITY

Before we dive in, a quick disclaimer: This is probably the most challenging concept in this book to grasp. If it doesn't make sense, don't worry, it's not essential. If you want to learn more about it, check out some YouTube videos on "decentralized exchanges," "liquidity pooling," and "impermanent loss."

Alright, ready? Here we go . . .

When you buy or sell a cryptocurrency on a centralized exchange like Coinbase, there's another person on the other end of the trade. I say, *I want to buy one ETH for $2,000*, and Coinbase finds someone selling one ETH for $2,000. Or I say, *I want to buy one ETH*, and Coinbase finds me the best price it can based on everyone selling. That's how most stock exchanges and trading apps work, too.

DEXes work differently. When you trade on a DEX, you're not trading with another person. You're buying or selling the token *with the exchange* based on an automatically calculated price. The price is determined by the number of tokens in the DEX at that time. To allow the community to purchase CRAFT with USDC, Leeroy needed to add CRAFT and USDC to the exchange, creating a *liquidity pool* for his tokens. The trading price is determined by the ratio between the tokens deposited. For instance, if Leeroy deposits 100,000 USDC and 10,000 CRAFT tokens, one CRAFT will cost 10 USDC:

$$\frac{100,000}{10,000} = \frac{10}{1}$$

However, when someone makes a trade, the pool balance and price change. If someone buys 1,000 CRAFT for 10,000 USDC, the pool now has 110,000 USDC and 9,000 CRAFT tokens, making one CRAFT cost 12.22 USDC:

$$\frac{110,000}{9,000} = \frac{12.22}{1}$$

The more liquidity you add, the more stable the price is, allowing larger trades without causing massive price swings. So, you want your token to be as liquid as possible, and the only way to do that is to have a pile of money to start with, or to incentivize other people to add liquidity to your token.

Anyone can add trading liquidity for any token on a DEX, and sometimes it's profitable to do so. If you deposited enough ETH and USDC to equal 10 percent of the trading liquidity for those two currencies, then you'll get 10 percent of all the trading fees generated when people swap between ETH and USDC. But a new token like CRAFT probably wouldn't have a high-enough trading fee to sufficiently incentivize people to add liquidity, so you have to offer them a bonus incentive.

When you add funds to a DEX, the DEX gives you a receipt for your deposit in the form of a token called a *liquidity token*. You could trade that liquidity token back to the DEX at any time to get your share of the funds in the liquidity pool based on how many tokens you added and how their prices changed since your deposit, plus any trading fees you've earned. Since that liquidity token was proof that you had contributed a certain amount of trading liquidity to the DEX, though, teams would often create smart-contract-based farms that would give you free tokens simply for leaving your liquidity in the DEX. This was usually referred to as *incentivized liquidity*, and almost every DeFi farm offered it, as it was the main way they made their token tradeable. It meant anyone could spin up a token and attract millions of dollars of trading liquidity for it without needing much money of their own, because people were incentivized to add liquidity to earn more tokens to add more liquidity. You get the idea.

So, here's how it would work in CRAFT's case:

1. You add 1,000 CRAFT tokens and 10,000 USDC to the DEX to help make CRAFT more liquid.

2. The DEX gives you a liquidity token signifying that you added that much liquidity.

3. You go to the CRAFT site and deposit that liquidity token into a farm.

4. The farm gives you a steady stream of CRAFT tokens as long as you leave your liquidity deposited.

There is, however, a big downside to this way of procuring liquidity for your token: Other people own all your trading liquidity, and they could pull it at any time.

But that would never happen, right?

12

Just F*%$#%@ Ship It

JULY 2021

I woke up to an early response from Leeroy saying that my plan sounded great, I could work on the token launch, and they would pay me a share of the tokens. Maybe I was going to do all this work for nothing, but at least I would learn something. I had my first gig.

I threw on my clothes and went outside to my desk to bring up our chat. Leeroy wanted to understand some of the recommendations, so I walked him through my thinking around how they should break the economy into two tokens: one, for use in the game, called GOLD with an infinite supply they could control, and one called CRAFT with a fixed supply. People could lock their CRAFT tokens in the farm for three to twelve months to get free GOLD tokens to use in the game, and holding CRAFT would earn them special in-game rewards, like horses and special gear. I'd love to say that I designed this genius plan myself, but I was copying Axie Infinity. This was how their economy was set up, and, since they were worth billions of dollars and supposedly making tens of millions of dollars a month in profit, they seemed like they were on to something.

I proposed launching CRAFT with one hundred million tokens at a fully diluted value (all the tokens that will ever exist multiplied by the price of one token) of $1 million, which meant an initial token price of one cent. People liked owning a whole token instead of a tiny fraction, and one cent felt low enough to be an appealing investment without being so cheap that it looked suspicious. They could launch the in-game currency, GOLD, at the same time, but at a much lower valuation of $100,000. There was no reason to buy GOLD yet, it just needed some liquidity so that, when people started earning it, they could convert it to dollars if they wanted. If the launch worked, the treasury would have hundreds of thousands of dollars' worth of tokens it could sell, as needed, to fund work on the game, the token would have potentially millions of dollars of liquidity provided by the community, and everyone who supported the game early would get a nice little payday. Like the NFTs representing the characters you could play the game with, every token would have a use. It wasn't some speculative shitcoin farm. It was the kind of project I had been dreaming of getting involved in since day one.

"Alright, that makes sense," said Leeroy. "Let's do it your way."

"Great," I said. "When do you wanna launch?" I had a basic farming contract working, but it would need more work to support a real token. Plus, I had to make a site where people could use the contracts. There was a ton of work ahead of me.

"How about a week?"

I groaned. Not responding to me for days and then asking for a token and a farm in a week was infuriating. "Why don't we do ten days," I said. "I have to finish the contracts, get them audited by someone, and get them built into a site people can use. Then we also have to put an announcement together and get some initial investors interested. Even ten days is aggressive."

"Sounds great, how can I help?"

"Well, I assume you don't have hundreds of thousands of dollars to help create the initial liquidity, right?" I knew Leeroy had a CryptoPunk that might be worth close to that much since it was his profile picture, but that was probably his most valuable asset. I didn't imagine he would sell it to gamble all of his crypto money on this launch.

"No."

"Alright, well, you'll need to find at least thirty or forty grand. And then other investors who will join in once we seed the initial amount."

"Okay, I can do that."

"And we need an auditor," I said. This was the part I was more worried about. I could write the contracts, sure, but I couldn't guarantee they would be safe. It was much easier to convince people to put money into a contract that had been audited, as then we'd have an extra layer of security and social insurance if anything went wrong.

"Okay," said Leeroy. "I'll look for them too."

"Thanks," I said. "I'll get to work, talk soon."

I signed off Discord and stared off into the yard past my laptop. It was almost impossible to believe that we'd only started talking a few days ago, and now, here I was, designing the token, tokenomics, and farms for a video game. The math on the token launch was starting to get interesting, too. If they launched it at a $1 million valuation, and people didn't immediately sell all their tokens, I would probably make at least a few thousand dollars. It wasn't quite what I had initially asked for, but it was hardly anything I could complain about given my lack of experience. There were still plenty of ways it could fail, though. Leeroy might not be able to raise the capital. Maybe no one would buy the token. Maybe there would be a bug in the code, and everyone's money would get stolen. Or maybe Leeroy would go AWOL again. Regardless, I knew what I needed to do: get the token, farm, and website done so they could launch it in ten days and hope that Leeroy could find an auditor and raise some capital in the meantime.

The next week was a blur. Every morning, I woke up at seven a.m., was at my desk with coffee by 7:15, and coded until seven or eight p.m., only breaking to get more coffee or grab the Chipotle delivery from the front door. It wasn't sustainable, but hopefully it would only last through that week.

On day five, Leeroy checked in to say he had good and bad news. He explained that professional smart-contract auditing firms were extremely expensive and took weeks to review contracts. It might cost upwards of

$20,000 to $30,000 and take four to six weeks to get ours reviewed. We didn't have that kind of time, or that kind of money, which meant we would need to do a less formal audit from a more experienced Solidity developer. Thankfully, Caleb had found one who could review the contracts for us.

Caleb set up a group chat with me, Leeroy, and the engineer, Kairo, and I showed Kairo the work I'd already done.

"Okay, I see the contracts," Kairo said, "but where are the tests?"

My stomach dropped. I hadn't written any tests. Tests are code that runs other code and makes sure it's working the way you want it to work. They're extremely helpful when you're, say, writing code that might hold millions of dollars of funds, don't know what you're doing, and need to make sure it's as airtight as possible. I knew there were ways to write tests for smart contracts, but I hadn't had time to learn how to do it yet.

"Ahh . . . there are none."

I hoped Leeroy didn't think I was an idiot now and bag the whole thing. He wasn't a programmer, though, so he probably wouldn't realize how embarrassing this was.

"Okay, interesting. I'll start working on my own then," Kairo replied. At least if this guy thought I was an idiot, he was keeping it secret. I appreciated that. He said he needed the rest of the day to test it, and then he'd get back to us with any issues he found.

While waiting for Kairo to come back, I kept chipping away at the website that would house the farming contracts, which they were calling the "bank." He messaged us again only an hour later. Too fast. He must have found something.

"Hey Nat, this contract won't work for you guys," he said. "I tested it and it stops working once you have around 500 people using it." They already had more than five hundred people on the Discord, so that was a dealbreaker. Kairo explained that, the way I'd written my contract, the transaction fees got slightly larger with each additional person who used the farm. According to Kairo's testing, five hundred people was around where the transaction fee would exceed the maximum allowed on the network, the contract would break, and everyone's money would be permanently trapped in the contract.

Not good.

I stared at it for a couple hours and couldn't figure out how to get it to work. I only had a few days left, the bank site still wasn't done, and now the most important contract was broken, too. The deadline was arbitrary, they could always move it, but I really didn't want to let these guys or the community down. The Discord had been getting busier and busier leading up to the launch.

"Honey!" Cosette was standing by the back door of the house, beaming, holding her laptop. "Did you see the house I sent you?" She'd been watching the market like a hawk the last month trying to find the perfect potential move for us. We were slowly getting priced out of everything attractive, but this was the most excited I'd seen her about a house yet.

I pulled up the Zillow link and scrolled through the photos. It looked perfect: fifteen hundred square feet, three bedrooms including a great primary bedroom, great kitchen area, small living room, but we never use that anyway, and it was barely a mile away. We didn't have to change neighborhoods.

I needed a break. My brain felt like it was melting from staring at code all day. "Let's go check it out," I said.

₿₿₿

The house was exactly what we needed: room for a nursery and a workspace, a great layout for hosting friends for dinner, still within walking distance of a coffee shop, and a small yard for the dogs. We'd been looking at everything as it hit the market, and this was the best blend of what we needed and what we could afford that we'd seen. And we were running out of time. I was the pickier one, but I couldn't find any reason to say no.

"So . . . are we doing this?" I asked when we got home.

"I don't know. You tell me. I love it. Do you wanna do it?"

"Hell yeah. Why not?"

Cosette whipped her laptop out of her bag and started writing up the offer. There were a handful of other people seeing it today, and the selling agent had said she expected to receive a few offers, but maybe we'd be able to get it. Hopefully we wouldn't have to offer more than 10 or 15 percent over asking.

While Cosette worked on the house, I went back to my desk to look at the CryptoCraft contract again. I was going to miss sitting out at this desk if we did move, the outdoor workspace was the big thing I was giving up, but if we were going to move into a more expensive house, I felt even more motivated than before to nail this job and finally make some money.

I was out of ideas to try on my own, so I went back to reading other contracts to see what I could copy. I pulled up the original farming contract I'd copied, and the code sections made much more sense now than they had the previous week when I'd started working. That one week of obsessive programming had increased my understanding of these contracts enough that some parts of the code, which seemed opaque before, were suddenly crystal clear. I wrote up my version of its method in our contract, re-ran the tests that our auditor had sent over, and . . .

They were working.

Roughly half of all the websites, apps, or pieces of code you've interacted with have been slapped together by a programmer on deadline who stitched together whatever code they found from a Google search. Apparently crypto code was the same. The stakes were just higher once you went live.

I sent the updated version back to Kairo and kept chugging away on the website. The next day, he got back to say he couldn't find any other issues with it. Since I wasn't able to, either, it seemed like we might be in the clear. He'd also looked at it for only a day, and he wasn't a professional auditor, but no amount of testing could make us 100 percent positive there were no vulnerabilities. It was simply impossible. Contracts had run perfectly fine in the wild for a year and then been exploited and lost all their funds. We could spend weeks auditing ours and find nothing, and we'd still be un-sure if we were safe or not.

It was Wednesday, and the team wanted to launch the token Sunday. Caleb, Leeroy, Excalibur, Tyrael, and I were all going back and forth in the chat trying to decide what to do about the contract risk. Do we launch this thing, even though there's some risk of a vulnerability, or do we delay, try to raise some money to pay for a professional auditing team, and make sure it's as buttoned up as humanly possible? None of us were sure what the right answer was, so Caleb said he'd ask Galt. Galt had seen more launches than any of us and had helped other teams with theirs too. A few minutes later, Caleb sent Galt's reply:

"Just fucking ship it, it's crypto. Shit gets hacked. People lose money. Who cares. You know what you're getting into with these insane APRs. If you get hacked you just apologize, relaunch, and move on. Stop being a bitch and ship it."

I shook my head. Galt texted just as aggressively as he tweeted, and, as brash and careless as he came across, there was a kernel of truth to what he was saying. People this deep in crypto *did* know there was some chance their money would go poof and disappear. Hacks and mistakes *did* happen all the time, and the victims often forgave the developers because they knew it was the Wild West and you could never be completely sure something was safe. There was a nicer way to phrase it, but Galt had a point. Eventually, you did have to accept the risk and hit go.

"So . . . what do you think Leeroy?" I asked. "Do you want to ship it?"

Leeroy's response was almost immediate: "Let's do it, WAGMI."

That settled it. We were launching a token on Sunday.

CAN I PAY YOU IN TOKENS?

*C*rypto introduced a new form of money and a new way to transfer currency, but it also introduced a new way to get paid: entirely in the currency of the project you're working on.

Companies, especially tech companies, have always had some form of stock-based compensation. If you work at Google as a software engineer, you might earn $250,000 in cash and then another $100,000 in the form of Google stock. Sometimes, the highest-ranking members of a company elect to get paid entirely in stock. Stock-based compensation has long been an appealing option to companies, because it's a way for them to pay their employees without having to give up too much of their cash. Google can do more with $100,000 of cash than with $100,000 of its own stock. So, even though it's giving up some of its ownership with stock-based compensation, the company is improving its cash flow.

Startups will often offer their employees some percentage of their compensation in the form of equity. If a young company is low on cash and can't afford to pay someone what they might be able to command at a more established company, offering them equity is the only way to get them on board. But an employee takes on a big risk with startup equity. The average time from the founding of a company in the US to its

IPO is approximately seven years, and, until the company IPOs, it is very hard for an employee to convert the stock they're earning into cash. Startups might love to offer all-stock compensation to reserve their cash, but if they did that, only their employees who were already wealthy would be able to pay their bills.

This is another area where crypto offers something like the best of both worlds. Since tokens are a way to speculate on the future value of a company, getting paid in the tokens of the company they're working for lets employees share in its potentially massive returns. Meanwhile, since most tokens can be traded for cash at any time, they don't share startup equity's risk of never obtaining a cash value. So, paying employees in tokens can be a win for everyone in a fledgling crypto company. The company saves money by not having to pay a cash salary, and the employees get to decide whether they want to sell their tokens immediately or hold on to them to see how high they go.

But there's one big tradeoff: all crypto transactions are public, so the community supporting a project will be able to see what tokens the employees are selling. If a prominent employee at a crypto company starts selling their tokens, investors might interpret that as a lack of faith and follow suit. As you'll see in a subsequent chapter, the social pressure not to sell your tokens can sometimes turn nasty.

13
Print Money

AUGUST 2021

My eyes felt like they were going to melt out of their sockets, but it was done. The bank site was live. The contracts were plugged in. Everything was set for Sunday's token launch, and it was only Friday. I might even get to have a nice dinner with Cosette. We had a lot to celebrate: My first project was about to go live, and our offer on the house had been accepted. In one month, we would be in our new home.

The piece of the launch I was most excited about was the airdrop. *Airdrops* were a common way to reward early adopters of a crypto project. If you launched a new application but didn't launch the token with it, you could give the token away for free later to the people who had supported you early on. We were giving away 5 percent of the token supply to people who were holding CryptoCraft–character NFTs at the time of launch. That was five million tokens across seventy-five hundred characters, or 667 tokens per character. That was worth only $6.67 based on the launch price, but it was still a nice freebie. And who knew how high the token would go if they held on to it.

Beyond the appeal of free money, I knew CryptoCraft was on to something special. There were no role-playing games with a crypto economy like this on the market. Zero. We'd be the first. And I knew that if we nailed this launch, it could attract a huge amount of excited capital. I wanted to lock in my compensation before that happened, though, so I sent Leeroy a message:

"Hey, before the launch on Sunday, can we agree on my comp? I'd like 1% of the CRAFT supply, vested over a year. That'll be about $10,000 at launch prices which seems fair given all the work I've done on the contracts, site, and now marketing."

He replied almost immediately, "1% is fine, you sure you don't want 2% though? You put in a lot of work and I want to make sure you are incentivized properly."

I laughed. This guy was so unpredictable. First, he avoided paying me. Now, he wanted to pay me more than I was asking for. I would have loved more, but I knew giving more than 1 percent of the token to a contractor for a couple of weeks of work was too much. Even 1 percent was kind of aggressive.

"Well, I'll obviously take more comp, how about 1 percent of CRAFT and 1 percent of GOLD? I appreciate you thinking of me like that. It means a lot. I hope we can keep working on stuff together past the token launch."

"One percent of each sounds great. And yes, definitely. I say we launch this, you keep focused on it for a few days, put out any fires, then we can talk about another project." He was excited. I was excited. Now we would find out if anyone else was excited.

Within minutes of posting the blog entry explaining the token launch on CryptoCraft's site and sharing it on Twitter, I got a message from Leif, the guy I'd met at Quinn's happy hour.

"Launch looks insane man, nice work. Problem though. I wanna buy $100,000. You won't have enough liquidity. I can stagger it, but there's no way to buy that much at that low of a starting price."

My chest tightened up in a confusing mesh of terror and excitement. It was unfathomable to me that someone would be willing to throw $100,000 into the launch of a video-game token built by an anonymous team and a guy who'd started coding a few months ago, but he seemed emphatic about it. And he was right. I hadn't imagined that anyone would want to invest that much money, and we weren't prepared for it. If Leif bought even ten thousand dollars' worth, he would send the price skyrocketing and create a mess out of the launch. We needed more trading liquidity.

I messaged Leeroy about the problem. He'd apparently already received a few similar messages from other potential investors. Even at this early stage, there was too much excitement about the launch for us to start off at such a low price with such limited funds for trading.

The original plan was to deposit 3 percent of the CRAFT supply, three million tokens, into the liquidity pool along with $30,000 of ETH to set the price at one cent. But if there was only thirty thousand dollars' worth of tokens to buy, then anyone who wanted to invest more than a thousand dollars or so could create a massive price swing. We'd end up with a super-volatile launch that would scare off big investors and could prompt everyone to dump their tokens. This was why teams often raised millions of dollars *before* launching their tokens. By seeding their liquidity pools with more money, they could reduce the volatility of the token at launch and create a better experience for anyone who wanted to buy in.

"What do we do?" asked Leeroy. The solution seemed obvious, but it felt absurd.

"What if we 10x the launch value and say we're worth $10,000,000?"

If people thought this would be the next Axie, buying tokens at a $10 million valuation would seem like a steal. The value of the underlying business didn't matter; what mattered was how much people could imagine it being worth.

"What would we have to change about the launch?" Leeroy asked.

"Well . . . the only thing we need to change is how much ETH we add to the liquidity pool."

"Okay, how much do we need?"

I bit my lip. He wasn't going to like this answer: "Three hundred thousand dollars."

"You want me to find $300,000 in two days?!"

I knew I was putting him in a tough spot. He'd either have to quickly raise some money from the people in Galt's group, or he'd have to put most of his personal funds at risk. It was a ridiculous amount of money.

Before I could reply, he started typing again. "Alright, yeah, you're right," said Leeroy. "This is the right move, let me work on it."

₿₿₿

Saturday afternoon, Leeroy sent me a message, and I noticed his profile picture had changed. The CryptoPunk was gone. Sure enough, he had sold it to get the money we needed for the new, higher-priced launch. If he was willing to part with his most valuable NFT, he must have believed in the project, and he must have thought my plan was strong. That could prove to be either the best, or worst, decision of his crypto career.

By Sunday afternoon, I was bouncing off the walls with anticipation. I couldn't wait to push the token live. We'd agreed to meet up at four p.m. to prepare everything. Tyrael was in charge of the community, so he would manage any questions coming in through the Discord. Excalibur was in charge of all the website- and game-related stuff, so he'd give me any help I needed to get the website live. Leeroy would lead the hype and excitement in the community.

Crypto projects use something called a *treasury* to manage their funds. It is a smart contract that allows the company to store ETH, USDC, and any other crypto assets but requires the approval of multiple authorized members to move those assets. CryptoCraft would be under public scrutiny once we launched the token, so we needed to make sure everything was done right. We couldn't use our personal wallets to move the funds around, it would look sketchy. They already had a treasury on Ethereum, but needed one on Polygon, too, since that's where the game would live. Leeroy set it up with Excalibur, Tyrael, and me as cosigners, so we could authorize all of the transactions needed to launch the token. I ran the code I had written to create the CRAFT tokens, then sent the tokens to the treasury address provided by Leeroy.

"Alright I'm gonna send in the $300k," Leeroy messaged. "Are you gonna send in the CRAFT?"

"What do you mean?" I messaged back. "I already sent it."

"Well it's not here, look for yourself."

I opened up the treasury and searched around. Sure enough, no tokens. Where were they?

I clicked around in the treasury interface to try to find them. Maybe it was just lagging; sometimes the visual user interface over a smart contract can be slow to respond. I went to look at the blockchain data directly to figure out what was going on. I found my transaction creating the tokens and the transaction sending them into the treasury. I sent them to the right address, so they should be there. I went back to the treasury and stared at it for a moment. Then I felt my heart lurch.

"Shit DON'T SEND THE MONEY!!!"

"Why what's up?"

I was already halfway through typing my next message: "Please please please tell me you didn't send the ETH yet."

"Not yet, I'm ready when you are though, why?"

I let out a sigh. That was way too close. Leeroy had the address for the treasury wrong. If he had sent the $300,000 to the address he had shared with me, it would be gone forever. The one he sent me was for the Ethereum treasury; the Polygon one had a different address. I had sent the tokens to a nonexistent address that no one could access. They were gone forever.

"Holy shit, wow," he messaged back after I explained what happened. "I literally had the confirmation window up to send all the money there."

Losing the CRAFT tokens didn't matter. I could create another version of them. But if Leeroy had sent all the ETH to the wrong address, we'd have been dead before launch.

I paused to let myself calm down. "You good?" I messaged.

"Yeah, I'm good, just rattled. Let's do this."

I recreated the tokens and sent them to the right address. Leeroy sent in a test deposit of $100. It arrived as expected, so he sent in the rest of the funds. We had everything we needed in place to launch the token.

"Leeroy," I said. "Is the announcement good to go?"

"Finishing it up now. Should be ready in a few."

"Is there anything else we need to do for launch?" Caleb asked.

"No, I have the transactions ready," I said. "When you guys are good, we can launch." My foot started bouncing under the table. This was the biggest moment of my crypto career so far, maybe the biggest moment of any work I'd ever done. I tried not to imagine the possibility that this could earn me tens or even hundreds of thousands of dollars. It was so faint, so unlikely. But it was possible.

It was all so strange, too. Here I was, working with five guys, most of whom I didn't know before a couple of weeks ago, and most of whose real names and faces I still didn't know. Now we were launching a digital currency people could use in a video game in the hope that they'd make money from playing. It was strange . . . and awesome. We hadn't even been on a *phone call* together.

"Alright, posted the announcement!" said Leeroy. "You boys ready?"

"Ready," we replied in turn.

"WAGMI," Leeroy said, and I saw the launch transaction start pending in our treasury. I'd never been more excited to see a loading wheel in my life.

Five seconds passed. Ten seconds. Fifteen. Then the explorer refreshed. The transaction was confirmed. Our tokens were live for trading.

"THEY'RE LIVE," someone I didn't recognize posted in the public chat. They must have been watching the treasury, too. "GO GO GO." They posted a link to where people could trade the CRAFT token.

The chat was suddenly flooded with excited emojis. It was impossible to follow everything that was being posted. People were going ballistic.

"Jesus . . ." I whispered under my breath as I started opening more browser windows to watch what was happening.

It was going to be a big night.

I opened the DEX where we had launched the token and navigated to their transaction explorer, where I could see the trades happening in real time. Players, speculators, and investors were buying and selling CRAFT tokens at a manic pace. The screen kept scrolling in front of me as new transactions came in, some for fractions of a dollar, others for hundreds, even thousands of dollars.

I checked the price and felt my heart lurch in my chest. It was over fifty cents. My million tokens were worth $500,000. The transaction feed froze for a moment, and then the price spiked to more than $1.50. My hands started sweating, and my heart started racing even faster. My tokens were worth more than a million dollars? That wasn't possible.

I messaged Leeroy and the team: "Are you SEEING THIS?!!"

"Yeah, don't get too excited," he replied. "It's mostly bots and early speculators, it'll flatten out."

I didn't want to believe him, but he was right. The other speculators and automated traders sold some of what they had bought, and the price dropped to seventy cents. Then it lurched back over a dollar again. Then down to fifty cents. It was bouncing around like a coked-up rabbit, with my net worth fluctuating by six figures every minute.

I took a moment to queue up a little gift for Johnny. He'd floated my name to Tyrael, which must have helped, along with Caleb's recommendation. Johnny had also sent me the Gutter Cat, which I'd never fully thanked him for, and it was worth 3 or 4 ETH now. So, I sent him 10,000 CRAFT and 100,000 GOLD. It was 1 percent of my total payment, and it might be worth a couple grand when things settled out.

"Hey, what's going on in the general chat?" Caleb sent to our group. I clicked over to where everyone was talking about the launch and saw what he was asking about.

"EVERYONE STOP BUYING THE TOKEN, IT'S A RUG," someone with a Bored Ape profile picture had posted in the chat. "THEY'RE SCAMMING US GET OUT GET OUT GET OUT." I started sweating again. If he had an ape, he might have some idea of what he was talking about. People with that kind of money didn't throw around these accusations lightly.

I messaged asking him to explain what he thought was happening, but he ignored me and kept typing: "THE TEAM IS MOVING TOKENS INTO THEIR OWN WALLETS TO DUMP ON US."

Now I was worried, too. I still didn't know who Leeroy or the other guys were. Could they have conned me into helping them execute an elaborate scam? From the outside, it would look like I was a willing conspirator. If this was a scam, I'd be on the hook. Caleb had promoted it heavily, and I had worked on it, and we weren't anonymous. If the community needed someone to go after in the event all their money was stolen, they'd go after us. If Leeroy and company signed a treasury transaction to transfer all the tokens to themselves, they could sell all of them on the market, take the money, and run. They'd make more than $1 million based on the current price, and there wouldn't be anything anyone could do about it.

I messaged the guy screaming in the chat again. "Hey, can you post a link to the transactions you're talking about?" He immediately posted a link. He wasn't bluffing. I felt my pulse pounding as I opened the link he shared.

Sure enough, there were two transactions sending 1 million CRAFT tokens from the treasury to other addresses, enough to drain most of the funds in the DEX and make off with everyone's money. It absolutely looked like we were sending tokens out to other wallets so we could dump them on people buying into the token.

But this guy didn't know how to read the transactions correctly, or he was being malicious, or he was trying to temporarily scare people into selling so he could buy in cheaper. The two addresses where the tokens were going were where the farming rewards were stored. If he had clicked through to the addresses, he would have been able to figure that out for himself. It was a lazy accusation.

I wrote up a quick explanation of what was going on. I showed that the addresses the tokens were going to were the same ones they were claiming CRAFT reward tokens from.

I sent the message and waited. The chat got quiet. Everyone else was waiting to see if he would agree with me that he was wrong, or if he would accuse me of lying, too. We could ban him from the chat, but that might only make things worse. When teams start aggressively banning people who ask questions from the chat, that's when you *know* they're scammers.

After an agonizingly long few seconds, he started typing again. "OKAY I WAS WRONG SORRY GUYS IT'S LEGIT BUY BUY BUY!!!"

I closed my eyes and exhaled. He wasn't trying to mess with us. He had been legitimately concerned. And now he was on our side. I'd seen people freak out over random transactions and accuse teams of scams before in other Discords, but this was the first time I'd had to deal with it myself. I might have to get used to it, though. It came with the territory.

The volatility slowed down, and the price was edging up to seventy cents, but the real test hadn't begun. Tyrael was almost finished executing the airdrop to send everyone their free tokens for having bought one of the CryptoCraft NFTs. In the original plan, the 667 CRAFT tokens per character would be worth $6.67. Then we changed the launch price to ten cents, and the airdrop became worth $66.67 per character. At the current price, though, we were sending everyone a free $466 per character. It was possible that everyone would immediately sell their tokens, take their free money, and run. That would crush the price, we would have wasted hundreds of thousands of dollars on the token launch, and the game would be dead in the water. The initial excitement had been nice, but this was where we would find out if we had succeeded or not.

Tyrael fired off the airdrop transaction. We announced it in the chat, and I opened up another set of tabs so I could watch what people did with all the free money they received.

One person deposited all their tokens. Then another did. Then someone added another $20,000 of liquidity. More tokens were deposited. People weren't selling. They were doubling down. Crypto people really *don't* pull their money out.

Within a few hours, the code I'd whipped together in a frenzy over the last couple of weeks was holding more than $1 million of other people's money. The token was stabilizing around fifty cents, which meant the game was valued at $50 million. That made no sense at all, but this was crypto. It didn't have to make sense. We'd given away more than $3 million to our community. The team had millions of dollars they could tap into to build the game. Twitter was blowing up talking about how successful and clean our token launch was compared to other projects. Nothing had broken. And my tokens were worth half a million dollars.

I sat back in my chair, a serene smile on my face, basking in the euphoria of success. Something had finally worked. It was all coming together. The months of grinding, learning programming and everything possible about crypto, it had finally paid off. I realized the guys at that fateful happy hour were right. Your big loss is the gauntlet that toughens you up for future success. Sometimes trying to "make it all back" is what bankrupts you. But sometimes it's what changes your life.

I clicked between the farms, the token price, and the community chat until I could barely keep my eyes open. I was exhausted. The last two weeks of manic focus had taken its toll on me. I couldn't fight it any longer. I desperately needed to get some real sleep. I closed out all my tabs and put my laptop away, then went upstairs to climb into bed next to Cosette.

I turned off my alarm and plugged in my phone, then rolled over in bed to finally rest. But as soon as my phone was gone, I felt my anxiety start to whisper in my ear. Nothing bad had happened . . . yet. But anything could happen while I was asleep. I hadn't taught anyone else how to manage the contracts. If there was a bug in the middle of the night, no one would be able to do anything about it. They would have to sit there and watch helplessly as our community lost millions of dollars, and it would be my fault.

I grabbed my phone and sent my number to the guys in the group. If something bad happened, and anyone was awake, they could call me, and I could hop on and, hopefully, fix it. I didn't want to have to sleep with the threat of waking up to a financial disaster looming over my head, but this would be my new reality for the foreseeable future. In all the excitement of the launch, I hadn't prepared for what life would be like on the other side. I'd seen some jokes on Twitter about how DeFi developers never get to sleep, and I guess this was why. Projects had run flawlessly for months and then were suddenly exploited in the blink of an eye. You never totally knew you were safe.

I tossed and turned, periodically checking my phone to make sure nothing was broken. I was stuck in a loop, the same mantra repeating in my mind over and over: "Please don't let it get hacked. Please don't let it get hacked. Please don't let it get hacked. Please don't let it get hacked. . . ."

TOKENOMICS 101: IS IT A GOOD BUY?

Half of my job for CryptoCraft was writing the code that birthed the tokens for the game and made them tradeable and farmable. The other half was designing the *tokenomics*: the logistics, economics, and game theory behind the token launch. That included everything from the pace at which the tokens would be released, to how many went to different parties, to how the CryptoCraft treasury could use its tokens, to how players could earn them. Tokenomics hadn't really existed as a skill before 2021, but by the end of that year, every team was looking for a tokenomics hire or advisor.

During the first bull market for Ethereum tokens in 2017 and '18, the tokenomics were simple: pick a price, put your token up for sale, and sell it. But now that farming was the main way of distributing tokens and you had to create liquidity on DEXes to make your tokens tradeable, teams would leave money on the table if they went with simple, 2018-style token sales. Understanding basic tokenomics can also help you make much smarter investing decisions. Every cryptocurrency or token worth buying publishes its tokenomics publicly, allowing easy evaluation.

The foundation of tokenomics goes back to high school economics: supply and demand. You need to know the supply of a token and how it will change, and you need to know if there is a good reason for people to want the token.

Starting with the supply side, you have to ask yourself: *Based on supply alone, should I expect this token to hold or increase its value, or will that value be inflated away by an increasing supply of the tokens?* The questions you want to ask are:

1. How many of these tokens exist right now?

2. How many will ever exist?

3. How quickly are new ones being released?

Bitcoin was created with a simple supply curve determining the rate at which all the bitcoins would be released over about 140 years. There will only ever be twenty-one million bitcoins, and they're released at a rate that gets cut in half every four years or so. Roughly nineteen million already exist, so there are only two million more to be released over the next 120 years. With 90 percent of the supply already in circulation, and only be 10.5 percent more bitcoins scheduled to be in circulation one hundred years from now, there shouldn't be any serious inflationary pressure bringing down the value of the coin. The annual inflation of Bitcoin was 1.77 percent in 2023, and after the next halving around April 2024, the annual inflation rate will be 0.885 percent.

Ethereum doesn't have a supply cap like Bitcoin. New ETH is regularly being released, and an infinite amount of ETH can exist on a long enough timeline. But when ETH is used to pay for transactions on the Ethereum network, some of that ETH is burned, destroyed forever. If enough people are using the network, more ETH is burned than created, making Ethereum net deflationary. That was the situation in May 2023, when Ethereum had an estimated –0.6 percent inflation rate. But that estimate changes daily based on network activity, so you need to check the most up-to-date number on a site like Ultra Sound Money.

Dogecoin also has no supply cap, but it is currently inflating at around 5 percent per year. So, of the three, we should expect inflationary tokenomics to erode the value of one DOGE the most, to very slightly erode the value of one BTC, and potentially increase the value of one ETH.

But supply is only half of the story. I could go into my backyard, break a few rocks, and then say they're the only rocks I'm ever going to break and put up for sale. I have a fixed supply of ten rocks and a zero-percent inflation rate. So they should be worth millions, right? Well, no, because no one wants my broken rocks. Having a fixed supply alone does not make something valuable. People also need to believe it has value, and that it will have value in the future. Which brings us to the other side of the equation: demand. For a crypto asset to have long-term value, there must be some reason for people to want it.

BTC can be used as a store of value, a medium of trade, and, yes, a speculative asset. It is a form of money. ETH can be used to pay for computing power on the Ethereum blockchain, whether that's to send someone some USDC or to mint a new NFT. And, of course, it can be a speculative asset.

What about the tokens for the applications on Ethereum, like Uniswap? Currently, the UNI token doesn't provide any utility, it's just a way to speculate on the future value of Uniswap. At some point, they'll turn on fee-sharing from the exchange to UNI holders, and then the token will have a yield attached to it. So, a reason to buy and hold it would be to earn a share of the fees generated on Uniswap. A share of the fees generated by the platform is the most common kind of yield you can get for holding a crypto token. Even Ethereum has a native yield, which pays holders a share of the fees generated by the network for staking their ETH. But if the yield is paid in the same token, you have to make sure that the yield offsets the inflation rate. If you're getting a 5-percent yield but the token is inflating by 10 percent, you're losing money.

And then there are the shitcoins. What exactly is the demand for

CumRocket or Dogelon Mars? It's to speculate, to play in the casino. They're going to zero, it's just a question of how quickly they'll get there and how high they'll go along the way. Sometimes people make life-changing money by gambling on shitcoins, but, 99 percent of the time, you'll be someone's exit liquidity. You gotta play to win, though, right?

14
The $20,000 Brunch

AUGUST 2021

I jolted awake the next morning, my fears from the previous night still fresh in my mind. I grabbed my phone to check the Discord and, to my relief, found nothing had broken.

One day without incident. I needed one of those factory-accident counters for my wall.

I pulled up the token price and saw we'd dropped to forty cents overnight. Still great, but I'd lost $100,000 since the previous afternoon. I'd have to get used to these kinds of swings; they might be a daily occurrence given how volatile crypto markets were.

I also had to try to stop thinking about all of that money as already being mine. I wasn't getting all of my tokens at once. I was on a contractor's vesting schedule by which I'd receive them over the course of the year, with a fraction of my million tokens unlocking every second. It came out to roughly 2,740 tokens per day. I could sell them each morning, pocket $1,096 a day, and I'd be making a huge passive income, but I felt like we were just getting started. I had already underestimated how much demand there would be for the launch. I could be underestimating how high it could go, too. If this was the next Axie, I didn't want to be the idiot who missed out on making millions because I was excited to make thousands.

So, I doubled down. I deposited some of my tokens back into the farm and turned some of them into liquidity. Cosette and I didn't need the money as urgently as we did at the beginning of the year thanks to her real estate work taking off. I could afford to leave my chips on the table.

I finished moving my new tokens around, cleared the few messages I'd gotten on Discord overnight, checked Twitter, and felt something I hadn't felt in weeks: I didn't know what to do. The launch was done.

I sent Leeroy a few messages asking about what I should work on next, but he was offline. Maybe now that the tokens were launched, he was going to ghost me. After all, he had enough money to hire a real engineer now. Or maybe he was celebrating the launch. The treasury had more money than they ever expected. He had been hoping to raise $500,000; instead, they had millions. He could thank me later.

I texted Johnny to see if he and Rose wanted to get brunch at a swanky spot downtown. I was feeling flush after the launch and wanted to celebrate, and I knew Johnny had been having a wild few weeks in the NFT world that I wanted to hear more about.

It was an unusually temperate day for August in Austin, so we sat outside by the street under the shade of an oak tree. I was trying to tamp down my smart-contract anxiety by not bringing my laptop everywhere, but Johnny set his up on the planter box next to our table.

"I just need to do this flip," he said. "Then I'll put it away." This explained why he wanted to meet for brunch at 11:50 instead of noon. If the launch was at noon, he needed to be ready.

Rose made an annoyed sound somewhere between a growl and a sigh. This clearly wasn't the first time this had happened.

I tried to relax and enjoy being outside, away from my computer, but I couldn't help myself. I asked Rose to switch seats with me so I could see what Johnny was doing.

The NFT game had shifted dramatically since the month before, when I bought my ape. It wasn't as simple as waiting for a launch, clicking buy, and then hoping you got something good. If you did that now, you would get wrecked by pros like Johnny. The problem was that *everyone* was trying to make money flipping NFTs. There had been one hundred million dollars' worth of NFT trades in May, when Johnny first got curious about them. That had tripled to $300 million in July, and now there had already been more than that in the first *week* of August. NFTs were taking off like a rocket ship, and everyone wanted to hitch a ride. Once again, the happy-hour guys were right.

"Alright, so, first, we have to go to the contract," Johnny said. Apparently you couldn't use the launch websites for the projects anymore. Websites were faulty and tended to crash during the surge in traffic that came with a launch. So, Johnny had learned to send commands to the NFTs' smart contracts directly, bypassing the websites to make sure his purchases went through. He pulled up the contract for the project that was launching at noon and showed me where the purchase command was. "If we try to do this right now, the transaction will fail, because it hasn't launched yet. But we can keep refreshing it until the contract unlocks and then race to get the buy in as quickly as possible."

"Do you need to pump up the gas price you offer to get the transaction through?" I knew some NFT speculators would jack up the transaction fee they were willing to pay to make sure their purchase happened as fast as possible. It was the best way to ensure you got an NFT. The downside was that you had to pay the gas fee even if your transaction failed, so it could be a risky gamble.

Johnny let out a nervous laugh. "Yeah, you could say that."

"How much are you gonna offer?"

"Oh, probably an ETH."

I was stunned. At one point, Johnny was down to a fraction of an ETH left in crypto. Now, he was paying one ETH, then worth $3,000, just to get a transaction through. He must have been doing way better than I knew.

"That's insane," I said. "How many are you buying?"

"Probably twenty, but you can only buy ten at once, so I'll have to do two transactions."

"You're going to spend $6,000 on gas fees?" That was probably more than Velocity made in a month.

Johnny shrugged. "I'll probably make at least $20,000 on this flip, so it's worth it. This is how it works now. If you don't jack up the gas, you don't get the NFTs. And you can immediately resell them for more than you spent, so it's worth it."

He refreshed the site again. Still nothing.

"Okay but what if you—"

"Wait! Here we go!" Johnny hunched forward like he was on his motorcycle. I peered over his shoulder. The site had refreshed to unlock the contract, and he was keying in the one ETH gas fee. "Got the first ten," he said. His first transaction had gone through. "Aaaand got the second."

He had spent $6,000 on transaction fees, plus $4,200 for the NFTs, all in a matter of thirty seconds. From across the table, Rose made a noise.

"Okay, okay," said Johnny. "I'm putting it away."

I shook my head. I still couldn't believe it.

As we left, he brought up OpenSea on his phone so he could check the floor price on the new NFTs he'd purchased. They were worth $1,500 each. Multiplied by twenty NFTs, and minus the $10,200 he'd spent on the launch, he had made almost $20,000. No wonder he was happy spending so much on gas.

I did some quick math in my head. "Hey, if you've been having a few wins like this, you should have enough to afford to shut down the shop now, right?"

Johnny's shoulders slumped. "I do, but I need more than that now."

"What? Why?"

"The espresso maker, our manufacturer screwed us. He never delivered them and ghosted me."

"WHAT?! You're kidding me. Can you sue him?"

Johnny shook his head glumly. "No, he's in China. There's nothing I can do about it. I hope he isn't selling the design to someone else."

"Fuck. How much money did he steal?"

"About $200,000. Almost everything I made from the preorders."

I stopped walking and stared at him. "Two hundred grand? Johnny, you *have* to do something about this."

Rose and Cosette stopped and turned back to look at us, but I waved them on ahead.

"What, you don't think I tried? What am I gonna do, fly over there and try to hunt him down? I checked. I asked people. There's nothing I can do. It's gone. So, I gotta cash out enough to refund everyone. And enough to finally shut down the shop."

"So, how much do you need now?"

Johnny smiled and let out a laugh. "Less now that this flip went so well!"

I shook my head. "I don't know how you're not more pissed about this."

"Oh, I was, but, like I said, there's nothing I can do now. Just gotta make it all back."

"Anything I can do to help?"

"Getting that CRAFT price up would be nice."

I laughed. "Alright, I'll see what I can do."

₿₿₿.

Returning home, I checked OpenSea to catch up on the NFT activity I had missed over the previous few weeks. When Johnny first showed me what he was doing, I had decided not to dive in, and that had been the smart move given how programming had worked out for me. But I couldn't shake the sense that I was missing out on something. Making tens of thousands of dollars in a matter of seconds was ludicrous, and he was doing it . . . repeatedly.

That was the difference between being late to the party and serving as exit liquidity, like we did with DeFi, and being early to the party and learning how it worked. Johnny had jumped into the NFT world when the only profile-picture projects were punks, apes, and a few other derivatives. Now there were more NFT projects than that launching every day, and each one had the potential to take off, at least temporarily.

NFT projects advertised all the benefits that came with holding one: You got to join a community. There might be future airdrops for holders. They were building a game. But everyone, or at least everyone smart, knew they were mostly a way to gamble. You bought them as early as possible hoping the demand outstripped the supply, and then you sold to the next person who thought it would go higher. Sometimes you would get it wrong and be stuck with a worthless NFT, but everyone knew that was the risk of playing the game. That's what made it exciting. How close could you get to the top and get out?

I hadn't played the NFT game like Johnny had, but buying an ape was quickly turning out to be one of the smartest things I could have done. I still had to decide when to sell, though. I couldn't use any normal investment rules. It's not like you do some smart rebalancing or portfolio diversification strategy with NFTs. It was somewhere between gambling and aggressive speculation. I just had to guess when the best time to sell it would be.

One bit of wisdom that I tried to keep in mind was that it's impossible to make the perfect investing decision. You can always find something you could have done better, whether that's buying earlier, selling later, or buying or selling more; it's impossible to make the exact right decision at the exact right time. You just have to do the best you can and set some rules for yourself, most importantly: don't go broke.

The second rule I tried to keep in mind was that if you own something but you wouldn't buy it for what it's worth today, then you should sell it. That's a way to combat our natural tendency to get excited and hold on too long when things are going up in value.

When I bought the ape, one ETH was around $2,000, and the ape had cost 3.8 ETH. Now, one ETH was around $3,000, and I could probably sell it for 18 ETH. Paying $7,600 for it felt a little reckless but justifiable. Would I buy it now for $54,000? No way. That was absurd.

The third guideline I was trying to follow was to understand how smart the money in the market was. With DeFi, I came in very late, and I was the unsophisticated exit liquidity for the investors who were early. I heard about the hype that had been going on for months, rushed in to get my piece of it, and ended up buying the top. If Iron hadn't gone so well at the end, I would have lost money. I'd been early to this era of NFTs, thanks to Johnny. Now, everyone else was suddenly excited about them and was rushing in to buy. OpenSea had doubled its volume last month and seemed like it was on track to do as much as ten times more this month. But it didn't feel like we'd hit peak stupidity yet. There were certainly some low-effort copycat projects launching, but that wasn't the majority of the projects just yet. When that happened, it would be a good sign that the mania was reaching its peak. When fewer and fewer good projects were launching, and they were being eclipsed by the flood of scams, that was when I'd know to get out.

I wished I could come up with a clearer time-to-sell sign, but this was the benefit of being plugged into the crypto world day in and day out, seeing everything on Twitter and Discord, and trading so actively in the space. I had developed a pulse, an intuition, for how crazy the mania was getting. I was starting to understand why I'd seen people on Twitter say you couldn't do crypto part time. You either hold Bitcoin and Ether and don't touch it, or you fully dive into the mania. Doing it halfway is how to lose money.

The rising fervor around NFTs presented a problem for CryptoCraft, though. Leeroy had said that he wanted to keep the game affordable for newcomers. But with how well our token launch went, and with the rising NFT market, a basic character to play the game cost upwards of $200,000. For a normal NFT project, rising prices were great; that was the main reason you bought an NFT. But for a video game where you needed an NFT to play, rising prices meant fewer people could play, both because of the affordability issue, and because people who were hoarding characters wouldn't sell them. Even if the prices weren't going up, there were only seventy-five hundred character NFTs, which meant only seventy-five hundred people could play. If Leeroy was serious about building it into a popular video game, it needed more characters.

Thankfully, there was already a solution: the NFT breeding pioneered by Axie. We could create a smart contract that allowed anyone with a CryptoCraft–character NFT to create a new character by paying some of our GOLD token. Then we could build in a delay for how often they could do it, to make sure we didn't flood the market too quickly.

It seemed like the perfect next project to work on, so I messaged Leeroy. "Hey, what if I worked on the recruiting contract next?" We'd talked a little bit about doing our own version of NFT breeding and had decided *recruiting* was a better term. A few moments later, he started typing.

"Actually, that could help. Excalibur has been too slammed with work to get to it. You'd save us a lot of time." Everyone else on the team had been working hard on making the game playable for the people who already had characters. If they got it done in time, there was a good chance CryptoCraft would be the first role-playing game based on NFTs. The game was very old-school looking, with eight-bit characters and minimal animations, but it could still be fun. And being the first to bring a new type of crypto project to market always made you stand out.

I asked Leeroy when he was hoping to go live.

"Maybe in two weeks?"

"Oookay, how far has Excalibur gotten on it?"

"He hasn't started it lol."

Of course.

I was starting to feel like Leeroy pulled these delivery dates out of his ass to push people to get things done sooner. Excalibur had been promising the first playable dungeon for weeks, and it kept getting delayed. Leeroy probably figured if he pushed for a very short deadline, it would at least get done sooner than if he gave a generous one.

"Great, alright, well, I can try to get it done in two weeks," I said. "It's a big contract, but it won't be impossible."

"Amazing, thank you!!!"

"Hey one thing though, payment. I assume there will be other smart-contract work after this, too. And I don't want to have to keep negotiating every time. How about you guys pay me thirty thousand CRAFT tokens a month via a smart contract, and I'll stay available to help with any smart contract or tokenomics stuff you need?" At the current price of seventy cents, I was asking for a $250,000-a-year retainer. It felt aggressive, but it wasn't out of line with what Solidity developers could charge. I wanted to get it locked down now before the token price went up any more, assuming it did. I could have asked for USDC or ETH, but I could afford to take tokens, and I knew the upside could be much higher if I did.

"Thirty thousand is kinda high."

"You know how much Solidity engineers charge. And I have the added benefit of knowing how to do the DeFi stuff."

"Yeah, but we're only paying ourselves $150,000."

"Sure, but that's cash. I'm asking for tokens. And you guys have millions of tokens on top of your salaries. Plus I'm not asking for benefits, or even employment. Just tokens."

"Thirty thousand is still a lot though. How about 25,000?"

"Deal."

Twenty-five thousand was the number I was aiming for, anyway. Thirty thousand would have been great, but I figured he wouldn't negotiate against himself again. Now, the total amount of tokens I would get over the next year was 1.3 million instead of 1 million. A daily harvest of 3,561 tokens, or $2,500 at the current prices, was almost $1 million per year. But it could be much more if the game took off, and the only way the game would take off was if more people could play it.

Two weeks was aggressive to get the recruiting contract done, especially while packing to move to the new house, but I'd figure it out.

THOUSAND-DOLLAR TRANSACTIONS

During the peak of NFT mania, what Johnny was doing was not uncommon. If you wanted to buy an NFT at launch, you had to pay a ridiculous transaction fee to make sure your purchase got through first.

Every time you submit a transaction to the Ethereum network (or another smart-contract network), you're making a bid for your transaction to be included. Your wallet automatically makes the best guess as to how much you will have to offer based on the current level of network congestion, but if you underbid, you might end up waiting hours for your transaction to be included or have to cancel it and try again. If you want to speed things up, you can manually increase the transaction fee you're willing to pay.

One reason you might do this is if you're worried about your transaction getting "front run" by other people on the network. When you submit a transaction, it sits in a queue where anyone can see what you're trying to do. If you are trying to make a huge transaction, like selling $10 million of ETH, someone could theoretically sell a ton of ETH first to decrease the price for your sale, then buy it back after your transaction goes through and pocket the difference. This was a common type of arbitrage people had written software to perform and was affectionately called a *sandwich attack*. If you wanted to avoid a sandwich attack on a large transaction, you needed to offer a high-enough transaction fee that your transaction would be processed before the attacker could react.

The most common reason people were willing to pay exorbitant transaction fees during this period was to get their share of an NFT launch. Most projects only launched with ten thousand NFTs, and speculators like Johnny might try to buy ten, twenty, or even a hundred of them as soon as they released. You might be competing with tens of thousands of people in a race in which only a few hundred of you would win, so you were stuck in a high-speed blind auction, but you were almost guaranteed to make a return on your investment if you were among those few hundred, even if you spent thousands of dollars getting the transaction through. The high transaction costs were just part of doing business. Many NFT speculators like Johnny ended up spending hundreds of thousands of dollars on transaction fees, but it didn't matter. Ultimately, they made much more than that.

15
Sell the News

The next two weeks were a blur of packing and coding. On my breaks, I rotated between token prices, NFT prices, and Twitter. The success of the CRAFT-token launch had earned me a bit of status. Every day, new people with NFT profile pictures and weird pseudonyms were following me by the dozens and interacting with anything crypto-related I posted. I didn't recognize most of them, but, gradually, some of the big names I had followed when I started out in the space were letting me into their circles. After one successful token launch, I must have seemed like a good potential source of alpha.

I suspected the Bored Ape profile picture helped, too. In the month since I'd bought it, they had turned into serious status symbols. Having one made people assume I knew what I was doing. It was a common mistake in crypto: people thought that if someone had a bunch of followers and an expensive profile picture, they were an expert and knew what the next big thing would be. It was an especially common mistake for newcomers, which is how the more malicious influencers were able to scam people so easily.

In most cases, people with tons of crypto money were either early to the party or lucky. Say you bought a thousand ETH back when it was only worth a few dollars, and you happened to hold it until now. You'd have nearly $3 million and would probably think you're a genius. If you then took a small portion of that $3 million and started day-trading with it, you could post charts on Twitter all day about all the trades you were making and show off how much money you had. But you didn't make money trading; you made it from being early. Trading was an effect of being rich, not the cause. But newcomers would come in and say, "Oh hey, this rich guy is doing lots of trading. I should do lots of trading, too!" You don't look at Jeff Bezos on his yacht and think, "Ahh . . . buying a yacht is how you become a billionaire!" But that is the exact logic most crypto newcomers were using. And, yes, I was one of those idiots six months earlier. Expensive lesson.

Along with my increasing number of followers came an increasing amount of outreach. More people were messaging me to ask if I knew of any launches coming up, and a few were asking if I could help with their token launches. In almost every case, people asking for token-launch help were doing the lowest-effort, most-derivative NFT or DeFi project imaginable, like Bored Dogs or CryptoDrunks. The people looking to get rich quick were starting to come out of the woodwork, as they realized the NFT mania was reaching a peak with people who missed out on punks, apes, and even Gutter Cats throwing money at everything in the hopes of finding the next 100x return on your investment.

I ignored almost all of these messages, but, towards the end of August, one message caught my eye. An entrepreneur/influencer on Twitter, someone not involved in crypto at all, had messaged me.

"Hey, Nat, have you done any NFT launches?"

I hadn't made the actual NFTs for CryptoCraft, but the token contract was close enough. I'd looked at the NFT code on OpenZeppelin, and it wasn't complicated.

"Sure, I know how to do it," I said. "What's up?"

We had interacted on Twitter but didn't know each other that well. He followed me for some non-crypto reason and must have noticed my new profile picture.

"I'm debating doing an NFT launch for my audience, just something fun and silly. Not a huge project." He wasn't the first. Influencers and celebrities were launching NFTs to try to cash in on their followers. Paris Hilton and Lindsay Lohan had launched art-based NFTs earlier in the year. Ashton Kutcher and Mila Kunis had launched an NFT project tied to a TV show called *Stoner Cats*. Even the lowest-effort new profile-picture projects were raking in millions from flippers hoping they could buy them at launch and sell them down the line.

"Like a profile-picture thing or what?"

"Yeah, exactly, I've already got the artwork. I just need the code."

It was tempting. He had hundreds of thousands of followers between Twitter and YouTube. Even a modest amount of marketing on an NFT launch usually meant it sold out. If he sold ten thousand NFTs at the standard 0.07 ETH launch price, that would be 700 ETH. Multiply that by the current ETH price of about $3,000, and you get $2.1 million in sales.

It was also an attractive gig as a programmer. You could charge a much higher percentage for an NFT launch, since the creator would earn so much money from secondary sales by taking a percentage of the transaction whenever any of the NFTs were traded on an exchange like OpenSea. If I charged 20 percent—not unreasonable for an NFT project—I'd make $420,000, another half a million dollars for a few days of work. And no one would even have to know I was involved with it; I could work in the background.

"I might be able to help," I said, not wanting to sound too eager. "Can you send me an example of the artwork?"

"Yeah, sure." He sent over the artwork, and I almost snorted out my coffee. It was awful, some of the worst profile-picture art I'd seen. He'd taken the CryptoPunk and Bored Ape template of a headshot with different attributes and applied it to coffee mugs. The artwork was *atrocious*. I couldn't believe he was willing to put his name on this. But it didn't matter how ugly they were. All that mattered was whether people thought they would go up in price. I told him I'd think about it and let him know tomorrow, and then I went back to programming.

Cosette came home an hour later, and I switched gears to packing with her. I filled her in on the opportunity and the conflict I was having over helping with such a low-effort project.

"Do you even have time to help him?" she asked. "I don't know how you'd have time for another project right now."

She had a point. Between the recruiting contract, moving house, baby prep, and following what was going on in crypto, I had already abandoned most of my hobbies and social life. My daily coffee consumption had increased to inhuman amounts.

"Mmmaybe?" I answered meekly.

Cosette raised an eyebrow. "Be honest. Are you still having fun?"

"What do you mean?"

"I don't know. When you and Johnny started doing this, it seemed like you were goofing off and having fun with it. I feel like it's changed. You guys don't even meet up anymore."

"We're talking online all the time."

"You know that's not the same."

"Look, maybe we don't meet up as much anymore," I said, getting frustrated, "but we're making money now."

"You don't have to get defensive. I'm just worried about you."

"I'm fine. It's fun. I'm having fun."

We packed in silence for a few minutes, filling boxes with books. Finally, Cosette asked me to tell her more about the project. I explained what he had told me he was working on, including my reservations about how low-effort it seemed.

"I thought you said not to buy stuff from influencers," she said, packing our couch blankets around the inside of another box of books. "Like, wasn't Mark Cuban getting involved in that project what made you guys sell?"

"I wouldn't buy it," I said. "Just help him launch it."

"So, who *would* buy it?"

I started to say "his audience" but caught myself. The honest answer was that dumb money would buy his NFTs, people who missed out on the start of the NFT mania and now wanted to get their slice of it and were willing to throw ETH at anything that came across their radar. It might make money, but it was also a sign of the end. With DeFi, the best projects were built quietly in the bear market, and the time to buy into them was back when no one cared about what was going on. By the time DeFi exploded in popularity, late followers were launching derivative junk left and right to try to cash in on the mania. Now, the exact same thing was happening in NFTs. The projects were getting worse and worse, but people were still throwing money at them. At least for now.

It seemed obvious now that Cosette had prompted me to think about it. When social-media influencers who were only lightly involved in crypto start launching projects, it's time to sell. Their audience is your exit liquidity. And if you weren't already invested in some area before the influencers started shilling it, you'd be an idiot to buy in. Otherwise, you're the exit liquidity.

"Shit," I said, put down the stack of books I was packing, and walked over to my laptop.

"What? What's wrong?"

"I gotta sell my ape."

"Why?"

"You're right. This is dumb. I gotta get out before the market tanks." I keyed in the passcode for my computer.

Cosette stared at me for a moment, then nodded. "Okay, do whatever you need to do," she said with a shrug and then went back to packing.

I checked the floor price on apes. They were selling for 18 to 20 ETH and still moving quickly. I didn't know when the NFT mania would end, but it was coming, and when the music stopped, I didn't want to have missed out on a massive return by being greedy. I put the ape up for sale at 23 ETH and went back to packing.

A few boxes of books later, my phone buzzed. It was another Twitter message, but not from someone trying to launch a project. It was from a friend who went by Ozzy on Twitter. He was one of the most NFT-savvy people I knew, and he ran an NFT-investing and -information group called the Shiny Object Social Club. "Hey you gotta delist your ape," was all the message said.

"What? Why?"

"Look at the floor man, it's lava. Yours is gonna get scooped and the price will blow right past it." I pulled up OpenSea, and he was right. I hadn't looked closely enough. Apes were on a tear. The floor had jumped from 18 to 21 ETH in the last few hours alone. Mine would definitely sell at 23 if I left it, but if the move kept going, I could get more for it.

"What do you think I should list it for?"

"I'm not sure, but make sure it sells before Saturday night."

"What's Saturday night?"

"The big Bored Ape announcement. I don't know what it is but that's why people are buying. They want whatever the airdrop is." I'd heard something was happening on Saturday but didn't realize it was an airdrop. That explained the sudden fervor. If holding an ape was going to get you something for free, people were willing to buy in at a premium now in the hope they would make their money back on the airdrop.

Ozzy explained that the prices on projects always run up before a big giveaway or announcement and then immediately plummet afterwards, sometimes as much as 50 percent. It had happened with Bored Apes a couple of months ago when they gave away dog companions for the apes. And it had happened with CryptoPunks when they gave away Meebits, 3D avatars with a Minecraft-like, blocky structure.

There's a phrase in investing: "Buy the rumor, sell the news." This was a perfect example. When the first murmurs were going around about the BAYC giving away something else to holders, that was the time to buy an ape. I had been ahead of that purely by luck. Now that everyone knew something was coming, the mania to jump in was intensifying. The best time to sell would be before the news broke.

It was impossible to know how high they would go, but apes were flying off the imaginary OpenSea shelves. There had been twenty million dollars' worth of sales in the previous twenty-four hours. That also meant Yuga

Labs, the creators of the BAYC, had made $500,000 in secondary trading royalties in that twenty-four hours. Most NFT projects, like BAYC, charged a small fee every time one was sold on the secondary market, usually 2.5 percent. So, every time an ape was sold, even after the initial sale, Yuga made money on it. Yuga didn't have to host or broker the sales at all, they all happened on OpenSea, and Yuga got a steady stream of ETH to their wallet for all the trading activity. It was an incredibly profitable business. They launched these ten thousand ape NFTs once upon a time, and they were making hundreds of thousands of dollars a day in residual trading fees.

CryptoCraft benefited from this, too, since their characters were also being bought and resold on the secondary market, which was earning them trading fees. That was how teams could make a ton of money by giving away free NFTs. You might airdrop the NFT for free, but if your community then goes out and sells them, you make a bunch of money anyway. It was a great new way to make money for artists, or whatever you call someone who makes ten thousand randomly generated primate headshots.

I logged into OpenSea to take Ozzy's advice and delisted my ape, but I had no idea what to relist it for. It was only Monday, and I had until Saturday, so I could take my time, finish moving tomorrow, and keep an eye on the price. During the move, I kept checking the floor price. It had shot up past the 23 ETH I had listed my ape at and was sitting at 25. It didn't feel like it was done, though. Sure enough, the next day it was at 34, and apes were bringing everything up with them. I forgot I had listed my Gutter Cat. It sold overnight for 5.99 ETH, nearly $20,000. I'd have to get Johnny a nice thank-you gift.

I was sitting in my new office, surrounded by boxes, trying to finish the recruiting contract, with a live feed of the ape sales on the screen next to me. They were hovering between 34 and 40 ETH, but we still had a few days. Johnny and I were texting about it constantly, trying to decide what the right move was. He had no idea, either, but we agreed that Friday night or Saturday morning would be the best time to sell, assuming the price didn't start dropping before then. The easiest way to guarantee it would sell would be to list it for the floor price right at the peak mania before the announcement. If I was too late, the value would likely drop substantially. But if I timed it right, I could get close to the maximum value possible.

Saturday morning came around, and the floor was above forty-five. By nine a.m., people were starting to spend 50 ETH on the cheapest apes. The announcement was coming that evening, so I was running out of time. I listed the ape for 59 ETH, an astronomical amount of money considering how much I'd spent on it, how much I'd lost in crypto so far, and how much I had hoped to make, but I figured I would probably get it.

By ten a.m., the floor was getting close to 59, and I started to doubt myself. Did I list it too low? Maybe I could get a little more out of it. I canceled the sale and relisted it for 61. Would it get that high?

I pulled myself away from my computer to go have coffee with Cosette. She knew I'd been trying to time this for the last few days but didn't know how high it had gotten.

"Do you think maybe you should lower it to make sure it sells?" she asked.

"No, no, it'll get there. I've got time."

"Yeah, but it's only, what, a couple ETH you might miss out on if you lower it, right? Isn't that better than risking it not selling?"

"Honey, I got it." I didn't mean that to be so snappy. I knew she wouldn't have bought an ape in the first place, so I couldn't take her advice on when to sell it. It would sell. I was sure.

We moved on to other topics, but my hand kept drifting back to my pocket to take out my phone and check the floor price. Getting through our twenty-minute coffee outing was excruciating, but it was nice to see what our new routine would be, and it was wild to think that our daughter would be on this walk with us in two months. I couldn't believe how fast that was coming up.

Back in our new home, I tried to continue making progress on the recruiting contract but could only focus for five or ten minutes at a time. I kept getting pulled back to OpenSea to watch the floor. It hit fifty-six, then fifty-eight. Someone listed for fifty-six again, and it was scooped up immediately. *Shit, was it about to go down?*

I set a timer for fifteen minutes before I could look again. I only lasted seven. Still stable. I could hear my heartbeat inside my head again.

I forced myself outside to go for a walk and try to calm down. *Should I lower it and get this over with?* No, it would work. I had to be patient.

In . . . out . . . in . . . out . . .

Halfway back to the house, my phone started buzzing with a flurry of notifications. There was a Twitter bot that published every Bored Ape sale, and it said mine had sold.

I stopped in the middle of the street and stared at my phone in disbelief.

61 ETH.

$198,000.

I sprinted back home and burst through the front door. "IT SOLD!!!" I yelled.

Cosette jumped in shock then sprang to her feet to hug me. We both couldn't stop laughing. I'd paid for almost a third of the house the day we moved in.

Everything was working out.

·₿₿₿·

People on Twitter who recognized the sale from my profile picture were commenting to congratulate me. Ozzy messaged me, too. He couldn't believe how high the floor had risen. Neither of us had expected it to get so ridiculous. Only two more apes had sold after mine, and they sold for about the same price. I had hit the absolute top of the pre-announcement market.

I tuned into the Bored Ape announcement later that evening to see if I'd made a good call or not. Ozzy had been right that there was an airdrop for ape holders, but it was so much more than we expected. The BAYC team had created a new collection of ape-themed NFTs: the Mutant Ape Yacht Club. Everyone who had an ape got one for free, but people could also buy one of an additional ten thousand they had created, priced at 3 ETH each. They sold out almost instantly, which meant the BAYC team, only three guys, as far as I knew, had made $96 million in a matter of minutes. It was the largest, wildest NFT sale I'd ever seen. And while spending 3 ETH on a brand-new, unproven NFT felt like a lot, within hours they were trading at 5 or 6 ETH. But the value of Bored Apes dropped from the pre-reveal peak of 60 ETH to 30. It was exactly what Ozzy said would happen.

As the mania from the reveal died down, I opened my crypto-portfolio tracker, called Zapper, and looked at everything in my wallet. I had more than two hundred thousand dollars' worth of ETH. My CRAFT tokens were worth another few hundred thousand. I had tens of thousands of dollars in other tokens I'd collected. My crypto net worth was nearly $800,000, more than ten times what I had started with a few months earlier, way beyond my initial goal. I could pull it all out now, and I'd have years of funds to support my family with.

But . . . was this the right time to quit? I had played Iron Finance perfectly. I had played the ape sale perfectly. Launching the CRAFT token could hardly have gone better.

The pulse of the market that I had dreamed of finding months ago, I had it now, and it was paying off more than I could have imagined. I had figured the crypto game out.

The one question I hadn't let myself entertain too seriously but had been hiding in the back of my mind since the start, was: *What if I never had to work again?* What if this was my opportunity to set my family up for the rest of our lives? What if I could "make it"?

In the early retirement and financial-independence communities, there are two guidelines for how much money you would need to never work again, called the 4 percent rule and the 2 percent rule. The idea is that if you have all of your money in index funds, they will probably grow by about 7 percent per year. If inflation is 3 percent, then you can spend 4 percent of your index-fund money each year, and you should be able to sustain that lifestyle indefinitely, because the growth will replace what you spent and what you lost to inflation each year. If you only spend 2 percent, then your investments will keep growing instead of staying flat. Plus, you'll be a little more protected from unexpected expensive events and spikes in inflation.

I opened a spreadsheet and started plugging in some numbers. I knew Cosette and I could live very comfortably, even with modest childcare costs, on $150,000 per year. So, how much money did I need to make to live on $150,000 per year passively? Well, if I divided that number by 2 percent, I got $7.5 million. That suddenly didn't seem like an unobtainable amount of money. I had gotten 10 percent of the way there in a few months. If I kept helping projects launch and got a share of their tokens and kept finding opportunities like BAYC, I could hit it.

I might not even have to do anything. If CRAFT got to $7.50, my tokens would be worth $7.5 million. That would have seemed absurd to imagine a month ago, but all we needed was for the right people to find it and start posting about it on Twitter. It wasn't impossible. I'd seen crazier things happen.

I knew Cosette wanted me to pull the money out, but I'd have to be an idiot to stop now. I could keep playing the crypto game, make my millions, and then retire to writing, playing with my daughter, and doing whatever else I wanted to do with my life.

The thought electrified and terrified me. I could be done working. Making it was on the table. I'd have to grind extremely hard and get a little lucky, but it was possible.

I was going to make it.

HOW TO BE A SHADY CRYPTO INFLUENCER

Crypto is full of bad actors who use their knowledge to take advantage of eager newcomers like you and me. It's only natural for new investors to want to find insiders who will share their secrets with them and make them rich. So, unsavory influencers establish themselves as beacons of knowledge using social media, and then use their influence to shill low-quality projects in which they have established positions, making themselves rich at their followers' expense. Here, roughly, is how to pull off this con:

First, search around for low-quality cryptocurrencies. A good example might have a silly or flashy name and a market capitalization, calculated by multiplying the number of coins in circulation by the price of one coin, of $100,000. For reference, Bitcoin's market capitalization, or market cap, in 2023 was around $500 billion. Find a dozen or so of these shitcoins and tweet out screenshots or make short videos talking about how you think they're going to go up. To be clear, you don't need to actually believe that.

Then, wait a few days. If any of them do start to take off, re-share your original posts about that currency or make more videos referencing the earlier prediction and bragging that you "called it." Then delete all the predictions that didn't come true. You can also tweet about "taking some profit here" or other such jargon suggesting you're making money off your predictions. Again, you don't need to have any real money on the line. If anyone asks for proof, you can block them or say you can't show your trades because of privacy concerns.

Keep doing that for a few weeks or months. Pretty soon, when someone looks at your profile, they'll see a social-media feed full of your prophetic predictions about where the market was going. Anyone who followed you along the way will have seen you whiff some of your bets, but anyone *new* finding you will look at your profile and think, *Wow, this person is a genius!*

As your following grows, more people will start to listen to your predictions and will buy things when you tweet or make videos about them. Once you hit that point, it's time to cash in. Find some more shitcoins and buy large amounts of them for yourself. Then, start tweeting and making videos about how they're definitely the next ones to take off. Your followers will rush in to buy, and then you can sell as they pump up the price. Some of them will buy the top and lose money, but they won't care, because they'll now have "proof" that you do indeed know what's going to move in the market. They'll think that they were too late this time but next time they'll do better. They'll turn on notifications for your posts so they know immediately when you mention something, and they'll keep buying anything you promote.

You can be even more aggressive by creating a paid membership for the people who want your *earliest* alpha. Then, you have people eagerly helping you run your pump-and-dump schemes. Once you establish your position in a shitcoin, tell the paid group about it. They'll all rush into it. Then, after a few days, tell the free group. They'll see the chart of the token taking off (thanks to the paid group), and they'll rush in to buy it. After a day or two, you and the paid group can start selling, using the free group as exit liquidity. Then, you can go on Twitter and show how early the paid group got into the coin and how much money they all made, and the free group won't even be mad; they'll want to sign up for the paid group so they can get earlier information. The paid-group

members will probably see how the scam is working, but they won't care since they're making so much money. And best of all, you're also making monthly membership fees on top of your pump-and-dump profits!

Remember, if someone *actually* knows how to make money in the market, they won't share those secrets publicly. Don't get tricked into being someone else's exit liquidity.

16

$100,000 a Day

SEPTEMBER 2021

The recruiting launch was coming up in a couple of days when I texted Leeroy, Caleb, Tyrael, and Excalibur to say that I thought we had an affordability problem. We had announced the recruitment event on Discord earlier in the week, and now we were starting to see a mini version of the same phenomenon that happened to Bored Apes. People knew that if they owned a CryptoCraft NFT, they would get to participate in the event and double the number of characters they had. So now, no one wanted to sell their characters, and the characters that were for sale kept climbing in price.

On top of that, we had already said that the currency used for the recruiting event would be our in-game currency, GOLD. Since we had listed GOLD for sale on an exchange, people were now hoarding GOLD to use for recruiting, so that price was getting pushed up, as well. Originally, we wanted recruitment to cost $50 to $100. But with the GOLD price climbing, the recruitment was getting closer to two or three hundred bucks.

"Yeah, I was wondering about the affordability too," Leeroy said. "Can we lower the cost?"

"Well, we could," I replied. "But then people would sell their extra GOLD and crush the price and we'd have to raise it again."

"Good point."

"I definitely want to make it cheaper though," I continued. "What if we decrease the price of GOLD instead? We have most of the GOLD tokens sitting in our treasury. If we start selling it, we'll bring the price down and we'll be making money, too."

"Can we sell our own token like that?" Tyrael asked.

"Normally, it looks bad," I said, "but if we tell the community we're selling more into the market to bring the price down and make recruiting more affordable, I can't imagine they would be too upset."

"I love it," Leeroy said. "I'll go post an announcement. Queue up the first sale."

I opened our treasury and queued the first sale. After Leeroy posted the announcement, he confirmed the sale, and $25,000 of USDC showed up in the treasury a few moments later. I felt a tingle of giddy excitement. We were making money. They had been making money off the NFT sales, and the token price had gone up substantially, but this was the first time USDC, as close as you could get to normal dollars in crypto, was actually showing up in our crypto-native bank account.

"Wow, that barely moved the GOLD price," said Tyrael. "Should we sell more?"

"Yeah why not." I queued up another $75,000. The price dropped a little, but still less than we had expected.

"Why don't we stop there and we can sell more tomorrow," said Leeroy. "One hundred thousand dollars isn't too bad of a first day's revenue."

Leeroy had said he expected to spend $50,000 a month on employees and tech to start building the game the way he imagined, so we had paid for two months of development for the game in one day. I couldn't help laughing. It was another absurd display of how much money was flying around in crypto and how much we had stumbled into. With the price of GOLD pushed down a bit from the sale, people were starting to buy it again. We might be able to make another $100,000 tomorrow. Best of all, the community was celebrating it. They were happy that we were maintaining the affordability we said we were aiming for. It was the best monetization strategy I'd ever seen.

Over the next few days, Tyrael and Leeroy kept selling chunks of GOLD to keep the price balanced, while I finished up and launched recruiting. It ran for a week, and, throughout the event, players kept buying more GOLD to recruit more characters. That kept driving the price higher, so we sold more to keep it lower. By the end of the week, the value of all the USDC in the treasury, combined with the ETH they'd already earned from the NFT sales, was more than $1 million.

It was one thing to have a token that was worth millions. It was another thing to have more than a million in ETH and USDC. In two weeks, CryptoCraft had gone from a bootstrapped startup with no monetization to having $1 million to deploy towards growing the game faster than before. It was an almost unbelievable achievement considering how hard it normally is to raise money for a startup. You might spend a year building a prototype and getting some early customers to prove you have a viable idea, then have to spend months begging investors to give you a few hundred grand. Or maybe you bootstrap for a year or two, then raise a couple million from a venture capitalist. But you'd need a product. You'd need customers, financials, pizzazz. You'd need smiling headshots on LinkedIn.

CryptoCraft had none of that. They had ten thousand NFTs of pixelated characters, a janky website, and a Discord. They had a couple thousand people playing the game, tops. They had a pseudonymous, questionably involved CEO who went by Leeroy Jenkins and a chief technology officer who went by Excalibur and used a picture of a sword as his headshot. Yet, they'd made more than $1 million from their community without having to give away any shares in their business, and they could now build this game for the foreseeable future.

As far as I knew, CryptoCraft didn't even have a bank account. They couldn't withdraw the money they had earned, because they had nowhere to put it, which meant it was all sitting in various tokens in the treasury.

I messaged Tyrael and Excalibur to ask if they wanted me to look into earning them some more money with their assets. It was all sitting there idle; they might as well make a little money from it.

Leeroy's estimated operating costs of $50,000 a month meant they would need $600,000 a year. If I could find a safe-enough, 5 percent yield on the USDC sitting in the treasury, they could earn that money passively if they had $12 million in the treasury. That was an absurd amount of money to imagine a small team like this having at its disposal, but they'd made more than $1 million in the last two months. It wasn't impossible.

I wanted to figure out what to do with my newfound crypto wealth, anyway.

₿₿₿

Quinn, Johnny, and I met up at Velocity for a throwback DeFi day. During the profile-picture mania, a host of new DeFi applications calling them-selves DeFi 2.0 had started launching, and it looked like that was where the speculative energy was going next.

One of those applications was the Terra Luna ecosystem I'd been hear-ing about since Leif first mentioned it at the happy hour. It had built its own blockchain using two assets: LUNA as the value coin, like Bitcoin or Ether, and a stablecoin called UST (TerraUSD). The setup was very similar to Iron Finance: the value of each UST was backed by LUNA tokens. If you had $50 of UST, you could trade that for fifty dollars' worth of LUNA. And if you wanted to create more UST, you had to deposit LUNA tokens, which were then destroyed to decrease the supply.

"Did either of you ever put anything into LUNA?" I asked.

"No, kicking myself though," Johnny said.

"I did," said Quinn. "But I put more into the fixed APR on Anchor."

The Terra blockchain had its own suite of DeFi applications, such as decentralized exchanges and lending-and-borrowing protocols, but the main application people used it for was Anchor. Anchor was like the lending-and-borrowing platforms on Ethereum, but if you deposited your UST into Anchor, you earned a fixed 19.45 percent APR.

It was the most lucrative stablecoin-farming option on the market. A fixed 19.45 percent APR for dollars was ridiculous. If the CryptoCraft treasury used Anchor, it would only need $3.15 million to earn $600,000 a year. They weren't too far off from being able to fund the whole business passively.

"Yeah, I'm looking at that, but I don't get it," I said. "They can't give away 20 percent on cash forever."

Quinn shrugged. "It's a marketing expense, like anything else. It'll go away eventually, and then we'll stop farming it."

"Yeah, I guess . . ."

The Terra ecosystem still felt weird. There was no USDC or anything besides LUNA backing UST. If something went wrong, the "stablecoin" could go to zero. It wouldn't get saved at seventy-five cents like IRON. Maybe everyone would move their money when the 19.45 percent went away, but maybe something worse would happen.

The founder of Terra, Do Kwon, was also concerning. It wasn't clear how Kwan got any work done. He seemed to spend most of his day on Twitter yelling at anyone who alleged that LUNA was a ponzi scheme or that it would crash. The minute he responded to someone, or quote-tweeted their criticism to his followers, tens and sometimes hundreds or even thousands of other LUNAtics (their name, not mine) would pile on calling you autistic or retarded (again, their language, not mine) for doubting LUNA.

LUNA was clearly off to the races, though. If I had bought it back when Leif mentioned it at the happy hour, I'd already be up by some multiple of my initial investment. I didn't want to miss out on another month of gains. "I think I'm just gonna buy some LUNA tokens. The whole Anchor thing seems weird," I said.

"Suit yourself," Quinn said. "You should grab some of the other DeFi 2.0 coins, too."

"Yeah, good idea," I said and bought a chunk of LUNA and a few other projects. As I finished buying my tokens, I asked Johnny what he was planning on doing.

"Nothing for now," he said.

"No? Why not?" I couldn't remember the last time he had passed on getting into a new narrative.

"Look," he said and spun his laptop around. He had his MetaMask wallet open showing his USDC balance. "I did it. Now I need to cash it out."

I stared at the balance and remembered our conversation in the car a couple of months ago. The couple hundred grand he needed for the espresso-machine preorders, the costs of shutting down the shop, enough to support him while he figured out the next steps: he'd done it. He'd hit his number.

I looked back up at him, and he had a huge, goofy grin on his face. "Holy shit," I said, "you did it." Then I paused as I realized what that meant. "So, you're shutting the café down? When?"

Johnny nodded. "Yeah, in a month or two. I don't want to surprise the employees, and we have a couple events scheduled. But after those, it'll be time." He stared back towards the entrance where more of the morning crowd was filing through the gate. The funds to build that gate had seemed so out of reach for him six months ago. Now, they were barely a rounding error.

"And then focus on crypto and getting the new espresso machine done?" I asked.

"You got it. It'll be nice to have more of my day back."

"I'm really happy for you," I said. "I'm sad to see it go, but I'm glad you found a way out."

"Me too," Johnny said and shut his laptop. "Me too."

WHEN TO SELL

When you start speculating in a volatile, fast-moving market like crypto, you have to be right twice: right when you buy and right when you sell. Most people focus on the first strategy, what and when to buy, but that part is often the easier of the two. The bigger challenge is knowing when to sell.

Books like *A Random Walk Down Wall Street* will tell you that more-active investors, those who are constantly buying and selling, tend to do worse than those who simply buy and hold index funds. That's true in the normal stock market, but if you approach crypto speculating with the mindset of a typical retirement investor, it will get you into trouble. If you treat shitcoins and NFTs like a Vanguard index fund and keep piling money into them and never sell them, you will be exit liquidity. Full stop. Very few projects have ever made it from one crypto hype cycle to the next. If you're speculating on new launches and not taking profits, you will lose money. It is true that you'll typically do better by holding BTC or ETH than trying to speculate on the hot new thing. But assuming you are trying to get rich quickly, you need to know when to sell even more than you need to know when to buy.

There is, of course, no hard-and-fast set of rules you can follow. You have to decide what rules make sense for you given your goals and your risk tolerance. But that is the first rule you need to follow: make rules, even though they can't be perfect. Whenever you buy something like DOGE or a Bored Ape, you need to know *in what situation you will sell it.* You need to have a rule on both ends: a rule for if it goes up and a rule for if it goes down.

Rules for when the asset goes up help protect you against being too optimistic. When the token you bought off a Twitter tip has quintupled its value in a month, you might start to believe it will increase another five- or tenfold. The sky's the limit, right? But you may already be at the peak, and all your paper gains will evaporate as it takes a nosedive over the next month. With a rule to sell on the way up, you'll make sure to lock in some profits.

Rules for when the asset goes down help protect you from the sunk-cost fallacy. The sunk-cost fallacy is a common failure in reasoning in which we overvalue something because of how much we spent on it. But the amount you spent is already gone, it's a sunk cost, and the token doesn't care what you spent on it. All that matters is where the price is now and whether it seems likely to turn around and go back up or keep dropping.

You can create a simple rule, like: *If it goes down 50 percent, sell; if it doubles, sell half to cover the initial investment.* Or you can create a rebalancing rule, like: *If this shitcoin becomes more than 10 percent of my total active-investing portfolio, sell half.* Other people use technical-analysis rules, which require tracking the price of the asset with fancy software to make decisions like: *If the price goes back above the average price over the last two hundred days, sell; when it drops below again, buy more.* Still others create specific price targets, like: *If this coin gets to $2, it will have a fully diluted value of $200 million, which makes it half the size of this other valuable coin, so that's a good place to sell.* I never created strict rules like that, and it burned me in the end. I did get quite good at buying intelligently, but I always held too long and didn't make good guidelines for when to sell.

One rule that I did follow, and the rule that helped me decide when to sell the ape, was what I called the money-pile rule. If you had all the money that this investment is now worth sitting right in front of you in a pile, would you put it back into this investment at this price? By asking that question, I would often realize that, no, I would be stupid to keep holding on to this asset. Even if it was way up and I thought it was going higher, it might already be worth more than I was comfortable losing. And if it was already down significantly and was going lower, the money-pile rule would help me find the willpower to cut my losses and get out of a bad investment.

17
What Does This Guy Know?

OCTOBER 2021

There's a local legend in Austin that jumping into Barton Springs Pool, a frosty, sixty-eight-degree swimming hole filled with water from natural springs, helps induce labor. Cosette jumped in on her due date, and, by that evening, contractions had started. Two days later, our daughter was here.

Sutton was perfectly healthy, and both she and Cosette endured the birth journey beautifully. By 7:30 that night, we had left the birth center, and by 8:30 we were all asleep, with Sutton swaddled up in her bassinet next to the bed.

The next morning, we drove to Velocity to grab coffee and so our friends could meet Sutton. We sat on the steps outside while Cosette told the birth story, and Johnny, Rose, and a few other friends listened in, circled around Sutton, who was bundled up in a koala-bear jacket. It felt completely surreal. My whole life for the last year had been fixated on getting ready for her. I'd started a new career, learned a new skillset, and become immersed in a new world that was stranger than I could have imagined. I had set my sights on that $7.5 million goal, but, now that she was here, did I still want to chase it?

I could think about it later. It was magical being with Sutton and Cosette. For now, I just wanted to spend time with them.

Eventually, the conversation started to drift off to other topics, and Johnny asked if I'd seen what was going on with CryptoCraft the last few days.

"No, I've been a little busy," I said. "Why, what's up?"

He pulled out his phone and brought up the price chart. CRAFT had been at eighty cents when the birth journey started, it had broken $1 on Sutton's birthday, and was now up to $1.26.

"Any idea what's going on?" he asked.

I shook my head no, but something must have been going on behind the scenes. A token doesn't randomly jump 50 percent in two days. It usually means a group of investors, or even one motivated individual, have found it and are trying to pump it up. It felt almost too spooky to be true.

"Welllll, maybe I'll buy a little more if it's taking off," Johnny said, smirking at me.

"Wait, I thought you were out of the game. Don't you need the money for the preorder refunds?"

Johnny flashed a huge grin. "I emailed everyone and explained the situation and told them I was working on a new espresso maker. Almost all of them said they don't want their money back. They're happy to wait."

"Let's *go!*" I said, stepping in to give him a hug. "I'm so happy for you. That's incredible."

"I know," said Johnny. "I couldn't believe it. And now I don't have to miss out on this next wave, too." He paused for a moment and looked back at the shop. "Oh, here." He walked inside and came back out with a bag of fresh roasted beans. "I figure you might need these with the newborn."

"Thanks, man. I'll let you know if I see any other gaming stuff taking off."

"Please do!"

When Cosette and I got home, Sutton went down for a nap, and Cosette decided to catch up on sleep, too. I was tired from the three and six a.m. diaper changes and wanted to lay down and rest with them, but I couldn't get the sudden price jump out of my head. I needed to know what was going on. There must be some news that came out, or an influencer pumping it. But to move the price this much, they had to buy *a lot* of CRAFT tokens. If nothing else, I should be able to track down the wallet or wallets that were buying.

I scanned through the on-chain transactions and, sure enough, a decent chunk of the buys were coming from one address. It had been buying small amounts every day for a while, but two days ago it had sped up. The mystery investor would buy a bit, pair it with ETH, and deposit it into the liquidity pool so they could farm the CRAFT-token rewards. I did some math on their purchases so far, and they had more than one hundred thousand dollars' worth of tokens. I was excited that someone had such a strong interest in the token all of a sudden, but it was scary, too. They were the biggest investor by a large margin. If they sold all their tokens at once, they would destroy the price.

The wallet didn't belong to anyone on the team, and no one was bragging about it on Discord, so I pinged Caleb to see if he had any idea who it was. Leeroy was missing in action again.

A few minutes later, Caleb responded. He'd noticed it too, done some sleuthing of his own, and managed to figure out who it was and get in touch with them. It was someone who went by Pegasus on Twitter, a successful crypto investor who worked with DeFiance Capital, a major, early-stage investment company with a focus on gaming. Leeroy had started raising a funding round for CryptoCraft, and apparently DeFiance was interested. So, maybe Pegasus was trying to establish a position and buy tokens before the fundraising became public knowledge. He could slowly buy tokens on the public market while the fundraiser was going on in the background. Then, once the fundraiser was announced, the broader public would likely rush in and buy the token now that it had the seal of approval from big-name investors. DeFiance wouldn't be able to sell its tokens, they would be locked up, but Pegasus's wouldn't be since he bought his separately. Pegasus could "sell the news" of his own firm's fundraising and make an incredible return.

If his firm was in the US, this would seem like insider trading, but DeFiance was based in Singapore. Presumably Pegasus was in Singapore, too, so he could do all the insider trading he wanted and there would likely be no consequences. Even if Pegasus was under SEC jurisdiction, it's not clear that this kind of behavior with tokens even counts as insider trading. Tokens were an undefined entity, they weren't explicitly a security, and no one had ever been sued for insider trading of crypto before. Especially if you were insider trading on smaller-market-cap tokens like CRAFT, you were unlikely to face any serious consequences. Pigs get fat, hogs get slaughtered.

I didn't know if that was what Pegasus was doing, but it certainly seemed like that could have been at play. It also wasn't *necessarily* nefarious. It made sense to personally invest in something you were pitching to your team. It showed that you truly believed in it. Assuming he intended to hold it for the long term and not immediately dump it as soon as the news came out.

He had put me in a strange position, though. I had more than two hundred thousand tokens locked in the farm, plus nearly $100,000 of my own in the liquidity pools thanks to how much he had pumped up the token price. Between my vesting tokens unlocking and the additional tokens I was earning from farming, I was getting more than four thousand tokens a day, which now meant a daily income of more than $5,000. So far, I was reinvesting everything. I'd barely taken any money out. But I couldn't do that forever, especially with such large amounts.

Selling more seemed like the obvious move, but there was one big downside. Well, aside from missing out on potential gains if the token went ballistic. If I started selling, someone would eventually notice and complain. It wasn't hard to figure out which wallet was mine, and people hate it when the people who work on a project sell their tokens. They interpret it as not believing in the project, or rugging the investors and community. It was a lose-lose situation: either keep everyone happy and risk losing all my gains, or start taking money off the table and risk getting attacked by the community.

I wasn't sure what to do, so I texted Leif to ask him for help. He and I had talked more since the happy hour and since he tipped me off to the need to increase the CRAFT liquidity, and he seemed like he would have the best answer to this question. We met up later that afternoon to take a walk around Austin's Lady Bird Lake.

"People will be mad if you start selling," Leif said, stepping to the side as a biker flew past us. "They don't want anyone to sell before they do."

"No," I said, "I think they don't like seeing that someone who worked on a project is selling tokens. It looks like they don't believe in it."

Leif laughed. "Yeah, sure, there's some of that, but the only reason people, smart people at least, are buying tokens is to sell them. And they want to sell them for a high price. If you're selling, you're pushing the price down. You're making it harder for them to get rich."

"Yeah, I guess—" I started to say.

"And it's worse when it's an investor or a team member, because there's no floor on what price you're willing to sell at."

I paused. I hadn't heard that idea before. "What do you mean?"

"Well, think about someone who bought the token right when you launched it. So, they had to pay, say, fifty cents. They really, really don't want to sell below fifty cents. They want to sell for five dollars. But for someone like you, or the other members of the team, you make money at any price. Even if your million tokens were only worth one cent a piece, you would still make ten grand. But every single other person would lose money at that price."

I watched a pack of runners skirt around us. Early token allocations were a massive advantage for anyone trying to make money in the space. If you were a builder or investor, and you got the prelaunch tokens for cheap, you were guaranteed to make money. But if you were buying the tokens on the public market, you were at a huge disadvantage. Early investors got to use the public as their exit liquidity.

That wasn't that different from what happened in traditional investing and public stock markets. The people who made the most money when a company went public were usually the ones who built the company or who invested very early. It was much harder to get the same kind of return on a company once it went public, if you got any return at all. Crypto had just sped the process up. A team could come up with an idea, raise some money, and launch a token in a matter of weeks or months. Then, the team and investors would slowly have their tokens unlocked, and the price at which they received them would be a fraction of the public token price. So, they could happily sell their tokens into the market at almost any price.

"You have to recognize," Leif said, "that you're in a game of chicken with the other big token holders. Right now, there's you, and there's this Pegasus guy, but there aren't any other big holders, right?"

"Well, there's the team."

"Yeah, but their tokens are locked up, right?"

"Yeah, until next year."

"Alright, well they don't count then. You're the only person who's getting tokens completely for free right now, who can sell them at any price and feel good about it. Pegasus could dump his tokens and crush the price, but even he has a purchase price that he wants to stay above. You'd be stupid to keep holding everything. You gotta start selling. Some people won't love it, sure, but the whole 'diamond hands' idea that you should never sell your coins no matter what is a way to turn you into exit liquidity."

"Well, should I wait until it gets higher?"

"No, there's not enough liquidity for you to wait. You gotta start selling some every day. Your market cap might be huge, but I guarantee you the liquidity isn't there to support someone selling a lot of tokens. If you wait until other people's tokens are unlocked, they'll dump on you, and you'll be kicking yourself for being greedy."

We kept walking in silence for a moment. "I don't know. This feels like the beginning."

Leif shrugged. "Look, I've seen how this goes down before. Entire venture capital firms are running this as a strategy by launching new projects on Solana and then dumping all their tokens on people. The minute other people's tokens unlock, they're going to stop caring about community and diamond hands and 'we're all gonna make it,' and they will sell as fast as they can, and you'll be left holding the bag."

"Alright," I said, "thanks for the warning. I'll think about it."

When I got home, I looked at how much money I had in CryptoCraft through a more sober lens. Leif was right, I was leaving too much money on the table. I couldn't keep reinvesting $5,000 a day. And I couldn't wait around for some specific number and try to time the perfect sale that way. I needed rules.

Rules were also important because I was in a weird informational position. I wasn't technically on the team, but I did have access to more information than most people. If I sold or bought a bunch of tokens when I knew some news was coming, that might be considered insider trading. The rules weren't very clear in crypto yet. If I sold a fixed amount every day, I'd both protect myself from acting emotionally, and, hopefully, avoid any insider-trading concerns, if that was even a thing. No one had ever been arrested for insider trading in crypto, and it was happening blatantly every day, but that didn't mean it was a good idea. There was no reason the SEC or some other regulatory body wouldn't come after people in the future. Traditional public companies put their executives on specific selling schedules for the same reason, to protect against the appearance of impropriety.

I decided to change my strategy from reinvesting everything to reinvesting 40 percent and selling the other 60. I'd pull out $3,000 a day while still staying heavily invested in the ecosystem, and if this did come crashing down, I'd be glad that I didn't overexpose myself. I wrote a script to automate the sale each day, wrote a few tests to make sure I didn't do anything stupid, then ran it for the first time. A few moments later, it confirmed that I had sold $3,000 of my daily tokens. I wanted to celebrate, but I still felt off about it. I had earned the tokens. They were mine to do what I wanted with. I could sell all of them if I felt like it. But the idea that you shouldn't sell anything from a project you believed in had its hooks in me, and I was scared about potential complaints from the community. I had to be the biggest seller in the market now, though. The core team didn't have any tokens unlocked, there weren't any investors, and, unless Pegasus started selling a ton of the tokens he was earning, I was probably selling more than anyone else.

I put away my laptop and went to help Cosette. If I was cashing out this much per day, I should enjoy my newfound freedom. I went downstairs and told Cosette to take a nap and I'd watch Sutton. I swaddled Sutton up and started bouncing around our living room with her, staring at her little eyes as her eyelids fluttered through whatever baby dream she was having. I slowed down my breathing to match hers, trying to enjoy a brief moment of calm, and remind myself that this was what I was working so hard for. These little moments were why I started down this crazy path in the first place.

As we rounded the living room, my phone lit up on the kitchen counter. Peering over, I saw it was a message on Discord from Tarot, one of the most active members of the CryptoCraft community and someone who surely had tens of thousands of dollars or more invested at this point.

"Hey man, I'd like to ask you an honest, well hearted question about some of your token selling activity if that is ok."

Shit, I thought. *Already?*

DIAMOND-HANDED FOOLS

One of the more harmful influences on casual speculators in crypto is the concept of *diamond hands* versus *paper hands*, the belief that, to make it to the eternal bliss of crypto-funded retirement, you needed to hold on to your coins with hands as strong as diamonds. Any weakness, any wavering in your conviction, and you'll sell too early and be one of those sad, pathetic, paper-handed fools who missed out on the generational wealth that could have been had by simply sitting around and waiting for deliverance.

In some ways, the crowd advocating for diamond hands has a point. Even if you had bought Bitcoin at the absolute peak of the market in 2017, let alone 2013, and held on to it as it dropped 80 to 90 percent from that high, you would have eventually made an incredible return as it recovered and surpassed those earlier peaks. The same was true for ETH. It dropped more than 90 percent after its 2017 peak, but now it was up about three times above that previous high. The diamond-handers won again. Well, if they sold at the top, which they didn't, of course, because remember: DIAMOND HANDS!

But outside of those two cryptocurrencies, and a few choice others, diamond-handers usually went broke. Following the typical buy-and-hold investment advice is an *awful* idea for 99 percent of cryptocurrencies. Most of the coins that took off in the 2013 and '17 manias did not hit new highs subsequently. If you had diamond-handed them, you would be slowly bleeding out. Even most of the cryptocurrencies that had taken off earlier in *this* cycle, in 2021, were slowly bleeding out to nothing. They would have one, maybe two big peaks, then never hit another one. And who was left holding the bag and being the exit liquidity? Everyone with diamond hands.

There's a concept in investing called the greater fool theory. It says that, in a bubble or an overheated market, you can justify buying something for almost any price because there will always be a greater fool you can sell it to. The vast majority of cryptocurrencies don't have any fundamental underlying value. You aren't buying stock in a company, and you usually aren't buying a cash-flowing asset. You are buying a speculative token in the hopes you can sell it for more later. A great way to make sure you can sell that asset for more later is to spread the gospel of diamond hands. It has a certain camaraderie embedded in it: if we all hold this together and don't sell, then the price has to go up! But everyone knows, on some level, that they only get rich by eventually selling it. What you want is for everyone *else* to have diamond hands to push the price up, so you can sell for a huge profit. And the best way to get everyone else to believe in diamond hands is to advocate for it yourself. It's another example of how much of crypto speculation is a game of chicken. Get in early while it's low, help contribute to the fervor to drive the price up, go along with the diamond-hands memes, and then sell at the peak of excitement.

Paper hands has to be demonized because it undermines the whole strategy. If you see someone selling, you start to wonder if maybe the seller knows something. Or worse: If they're selling, does that mean you're the fool? Demonizing selling as showing what a weak, cowardly, spineless speculator you are creates a powerful social pressure for everyone to continue participating in the game of chicken.

Anyone in crypto who stumbles into a huge win asks themselves before selling if they are having paper hands. The smart ones say *who cares* and sell anyway. The dumb ones double down on their diamond hands and ride their shitcoins back to zero.

18
Free at Last
OCTOBER 2021

I took a deep breath and stared at the message from Tarot. "Well hearted question about your token selling activity . . ." He must have already been following my wallet using some software and saw the sudden uptick in how many tokens I was selling.

"It appears," he continued, "you were initially granted 1,000,000 tokens and get some every day that you are selling. I have no concerns about you, your morals, or anything like that. But is that true? If so, I think the way it was explained, that the team has their tokens locked for two years, was misleading."

I let out a slow exhale. This was just a misunderstanding. He thought I was part of the team and that we'd lied about the vesting schedule. This was exactly what I was talking to Leif about; even active community members assumed I was an employee or cofounder or something.

"You're good," I said. "It's a fair question. I'm not officially part of the CryptoCraft team, I'm a contractor. For doing the contracts I charged 1%, vested over a year."

"Okay, I appreciate you clarifying. The item on you being a contractor vs. a team member makes a large difference."

"Totally. I deposited everything in the beginning and kept compounding, and now I have like half a million in the farm. Gotta diversify a bit."

"Understood, it's a lot of money, many people diversify and sell their vested equity and stuff and it isn't a signal of their interests/faith in the company. I'm just making sure nothing shadyish was going on."

"I hear you, they're fair questions."

"Appreciate it. Thanks for being honest and transparent. It's tough to have so much trust in an anonymous team with a CEO who's largely absent."

Interesting. So, the community knew Leeroy was absent, too. I had assumed it was only obvious to me because I was trying to work with him, but people on the public Discord must have noticed how rarely he posted. Most of the announcements came from Tyrael, Caleb, or me. No wonder Tarot thought I was one of the core members. They probably thought Caleb was, too.

Hopefully that was the end of this for now, but I couldn't shake feeling a little rattled, like my privacy had been violated. Someone I didn't know and had never met had basically gone through my bank account and said, *Hey, why did you spend money on this? Explain yourself!* It would be sociopathic, not to mention illegal, behavior in the normal financial world, but, in crypto, people felt entitled to do it.

Part of the problem was the tokens. When someone bought a token, they believed they could go on that team's Discord and pester them with endless questions because they were a "stakeholder." It made it impossible to get anything done. I would have preferred to say, *Fuck off, this isn't your business*, but doing that might have made me look like I was trying to hide something, which, if word spread through the community, could tank the token. My only "bosses" should have been Leeroy and Excalibur, but I had to respond to potentially thousands of other people, too. It wasn't anyone else's business what I was doing with my money. But I knew if one question came this quickly, it wouldn't be the last.

‑₿₿₿·

Johnny shut down Velocity on November 14. All the neighborhood friends who loved it came out for one last hurrah, and we bid farewell to our favorite local spot. As we reminisced about the last couple of years of sharing espressos and pastries, we knew we were saying goodbye to some of the people we saw there, too.

Johnny adored the community that congregated around the café every morning. He'd created a constant in so many people's lives; it was how he'd met many of his friends in Austin. Shutting it down wasn't an easy decision, but it had to be done. He couldn't keep bleeding time and money into it. His manic mastery of NFTs had bought him freedom from the shop and the funds he needed to build the espresso machine of his dreams.

The last visitors hugged Johnny goodbye, and I stayed behind to help him clean and close up the shop one last time. After a few moments of somber silence, punctuated by the hiss of steam escaping the espresso machines, he turned off the register for the last time. The Velocity journey was over.

As we finished cleaning up, I got a message from Leeroy saying that they were working on finishing the details for the fundraiser and wanted to go over some things. I told Johnny I needed to head home to get my laptop and gave him a long hug goodbye. I loved Velocity almost as much as he did. It had been my second home for the last year, and both our lives had forever changed while sitting at its picnic tables. I'd never forget what he had built.

When I got home, I took my laptop out to the backyard and clicked on the patio heater I'd placed over my desk. It wasn't too cold yet, but it was chilly enough to get into your bones after sitting outside for an hour. I brought up the chat and messaged Leeroy.

I knew they had been working on a fundraiser, but I hadn't heard any updates in a few weeks. Fundraising in crypto was extremely easy. Games were raising millions with far less validation than CryptoCraft had. And even though the token was doing great and there was nearly two million dollars' worth of stablecoins in the treasury, getting a few extra million to make sure they were safe for years was smart. They wanted to be certain they could continue game development even if the market crashed or people stopped wanting to pay to play for a while. Crypto had already had multiple "winters," in which almost no money was coming in and fundraising was nearly impossible. Even if they didn't need the money right then, they would be silly to pass on the chance to get it as insurance.

"I'm realizing," he messaged me, "that if we're going to do this fundraiser, we'll need to start taking things a little more seriously and professionally. So, I'm giving up the Leeroy pseudonym and will start telling people on the team who I really am. Starting with you."

This wasn't what I thought we were going to talk about at all. I'd wondered since the beginning who he was, but, with time, I had convinced myself it didn't matter. It's not like I would know his real name anyway. And at this point, even if Leeroy was perpetually absent, I felt confident enough that this wasn't some big scam. It also seemed odd that he would unmask himself now that the token was starting to take off. His desire for financial privacy would only get stronger as the game got more valuable, and he'd already created a trusted pseudonym. He would have to start over from scratch trying to build recognition with the community and the public. Maybe the investors he was talking to weren't comfortable with an anonymous team. That seemed like the only explanation that made sense given all the downsides. Either way, I didn't see why he was suddenly making a big deal about this.

"It's me, Caleb," he said. "Excalibur and Tyrael are my friends from college."

Of course.

I was so stupid for not figuring it out earlier. Leeroy knew a weird amount about me, and it had always seemed strange that Caleb supposedly told him so much about me. It also explained why Leeroy was never working, and Caleb was *always* working. He was trying to juggle two personalities, and it was easier to use his real one. And clearly part of why we'd never had a phone call was that I'd recognize his voice immediately. All the clues were there if I'd been paying attention. But as silly as I felt for missing it, I felt so much better about working with Leeroy now. He hadn't peaced out and gotten rich off my work. He'd been working extremely hard, as well. We laughed about it for a minute, but something else was clearly on his mind.

"I'm preparing for a meeting with investors tomorrow," he said. "I'm a little concerned because it looks like your wallet is selling off $5k+ of rewards per day."

There it was. I knew someone on the team would bring up me selling tokens eventually.

He continued, "That's over $1.5M you would cash out assuming everything stays where it is. I'm not sure if they will notice that or even look deeply, but it is possible. If we were all selling our rewards at that level it probably would be bad optics. So I want to hear from you on this."

The relief I'd felt moments before evaporated. They couldn't pay me what I'd asked to be paid, so I'd agreed to be paid in tokens. He had then offered to pay me more tokens than I'd asked for, which I'd partially refused. But now that I was making money from taking that deal, he wanted me to stop selling. What was I supposed to do, eat tokens? I could feel pins and needles starting to prick at my hands as my blood pressure rose. It didn't matter how much or how little he was paying himself. He was paying me *nothing*. If he didn't want to give me tokens for my work, then he should have paid me like I originally asked. I took a deep breath. I was overreacting. I needed to calm down.

"Caleb, I have over $600k invested in CryptoCraft right now, and considering I'm a contractor, 600k is a huge amount of my net worth to have here. I gotta take some off the table, especially since I'm going to have to pay taxes on all of this and I'm a little scared of what that's gonna look like." I sent him a screenshot of my deposits in the farms to prove it.

"I have no problem with you taking some money off the table. The issue to me is you're not positioned as a contractor to investors and the community, you're positioned as a core team member. So my concern is that if I found out the guy who built the tokenomics is cashing out at a $1.5m/yr run rate. If I was an investor, aware of this, I may not look at that positively."

I reread his message. Something about "you're not positioned as a contractor to investors" didn't make sense. I hadn't talked to any of the investors, and I hadn't worked on the pitch deck. Suddenly it all clicked. They might have been telling the investors I was more than a contractor. They didn't have any other Solidity engineers working with them, and to not have a Solidity engineer while trying to fundraise for a crypto project was a huge red flag. I wouldn't be surprised if they were acting like I was an employee, or even a *cofounder*, to be taken more seriously. And Caleb was right; if a cofounder was cashing out this many tokens, it would look bad.

Leif had been right, too. Even at the top in crypto, maybe especially at the top, you only get rich at someone else's expense. None of these crypto projects were paying out discounted cash flows. You bought and held a token to sell it for more later. When Caleb and I were riding the token pump and not cashing out, we had been on the same team. But now that I was cashing out, I was making money at his expense. His tokens were locked, he couldn't sell them.

But as annoyed as he might be, Caleb didn't have any leverage. My vesting tokens were allocated through a smart contract that Caleb couldn't revoke. If he ended my contract and kicked me out of the Discord, they'd be in a much worse position because they'd have no Solidity- or treasury-management support. And I'd still have all my tokens. He needed to keep me happy and involved. If he was misrepresenting me to the potential investors, that was his problem, not mine.

"I'm not going to stop selling, Caleb. If you need to remove me from the team because you're worried about optics, I understand."

"It's not about stopping selling, it's just having an understanding of what we think is an amount of selling that's not going to generate concerns," he said.

He clearly wanted to have his cake and eat it, too. He didn't want to pay me real money and also didn't want me to sell tokens. It was absurd. And the tax question was starting to scare me. If I locked all my tokens up and then had a six-figure tax bill next year, I wouldn't be able to pay it. Especially if the market tanked and my remaining investments were worth less than the bill. I did feel a little bad about the situation I had put him in. He was right that my selling habits might look questionable to an investor or a member of the community. But I also couldn't not sell just based on that concern. If he wanted me to hold my tokens for years and be fully committed to the project long term, he could have offered me a cofounder role, made me the first employee, or paid me *real money*.

"I know it's Sunday night," he continued, "we can revisit this convo another time!"

He knew he had no leverage. They probably needed to pretend I was a member of the team to raise money, which meant they needed to keep letting me do what I wanted to do. He'd made the decision to pay me like this, and, now that I was on track to make over $1 million, there was no way I was going to double down and leave all the money on the table. As exciting as the hype was, I had to be realistic. Most startups fail, their equity is worth nothing, and early employees never get a chance to sell their shares before the company dies. You'd be an idiot not to take money off the table if you could, especially since nearly every single crypto company that did well in 2017 was now dead. Maybe this time would be different, but probably not. When Pets.com and Webvan blew up in 2000 and '01, they didn't come back to life during the next tech bubble. They stayed dead, and Instacart, Chewy, and other businesses rose from their ashes. Most crypto projects were destined to die, too, regardless of whether or not you were working on them.

We kept talking about the fundraise, and Caleb shared that the leading firms interested in the investment were Three Arrows Capital, DeFiance, and Delphi Digital.

DeFiance was the firm Pegasus worked for, so he was certainly pushing it internally, since he must have had at least half a million dollars invested in us at this point. DeFiance was a major crypto venture capital firm, and if its investment in us was public, it would drive in a lot more capital and make Pegasus even more money, whether or not DeFiance ever made money on its investment.

Delphi was known for being a successful gaming VC, as well, and had put some of the first money into Axie Infinity. I'm sure they saw us as a potential next Axie and wanted to run the same playbook again. That wasn't surprising since they might have made nearly $1 billion off that first investment.

Three Arrows Capital, or 3AC, was the most interesting participant, to me. They were among the biggest winners in this crypto bull market so far, and their cofounders, Su Zhu and Kyle Davies, were notoriously ruthless traders who had amassed a multibillion-dollar fortune in crypto. They had been early investors in Avalanche and Luna, two of the three biggest projects so far this cycle, and had been early to Bitcoin and Ethereum when they launched, too. Beyond their trading history, Su was famous for his theory about how the bull run we were in was structurally different from the crypto hype cycles in previous years. He said we were in the *supercycle*.

Approximately every four years, the number of new bitcoins released to miners each day is cut in half. The first halving happened in 2012, then the next two happened in 2016 and 2020. Each time there was a halving, a bull market happened about a year later, first in 2013, then again in 2017, and now in 2021. It was almost considered scripture in crypto that each halving would usher in a bigger and better bull market. It made sense in a simple supply-and-demand kind of way. If the demand stayed constant, as the supply of new Bitcoin hitting the market went down, the price had to go up. Su's theory was that the 2021 cycle was when the crypto market would stop caring so much about the Bitcoin halving, and, instead of having the same peak and crash of the last two cycles, it would keep peaking, correcting, and reaching new peaks again, without the two- to three-year-long wait. He argued that there were so many more major cryptocurrencies besides Bitcoin now that it didn't make sense for Bitcoin's supply to drive the whole crypto market.

When Su first shared his idea of the supercycle, no one took it too seriously. He was known for spreading ideas he didn't necessarily believe in to try to move the market in one direction or another. But he kept talking about it, and it slowly built up a following.

When the market crashed in May, most people thought that was the end of crypto for this cycle. But Su didn't think so. He kept pushing the supercycle narrative. After the market bottomed out in July, it turned around and started grinding higher. Now, in November, it was on track to break through the pre-crash highs from May, and who knew how high it would go from there. Not only had Ethereum reached new highs, but the other tokens Su had invested in and promoted, like Avalanche and LUNA, were hitting breakout values, as well. This immediate correction and return to new highs was exactly the kind of supercycle Su had predicted, and he was starting to look like a crypto prophet. He had the Midas touch, with every project he was associated with turning to gold.

Since Su didn't get to invest in Axie, 3AC might have seen CryptoCraft as a way to make up for missing that opportunity. It was one of the best endorsements we could hope for. It also made me think twice about selling. Retail investors might flock to the token if the news came out that 3AC was investing. It was hard to imagine CRAFT hitting $100, or even $10, but the news of an investment from 3AC was the kind of thing that might get us there. But anything could happen. A conversation was far from an investment. I couldn't get too tempted by the big, imaginary dollar signs. And it might not matter anyway. Some of my other bets were starting to pay off.

WALLET WATCHING

One consequence of the way blockchains like Bitcoin and Ethereum are designed is that every transaction is public. Anytime someone sends money to someone else, you can see exactly which account sent how many coins to which other account. When someone uses a smart contract on Ethereum, you can see exactly how many tokens they swapped for how many other tokens using a DEX, or how much USDC they borrowed against how much ETH, and so on.

Making every financial transaction public results in a radically different world than the one we're used to. In some ways, it might be good. Imagine if we could see, for example, where every single dollar of government spending was going. You could create a perfect diagram of where each of your tax dollars goes at the state and federal level. It's hard to imagine how a little extra financial accountability for governments could be a bad thing.

On the personal level, it's weird. Once someone knows your wallet address, they can see exactly how much money you have in it and every transaction you make with it. Some websites even offer wallet-watching alerts, which notify you when a wallet you've flagged makes any kind of transaction. Even if you use multiple wallets, like one for savings and one for spending, it's trivial for others to track which wallets you're using most frequently. You might never want to send money to your friends, because, once you do, they'll know your wallet address and can poke their noses into all of your other financial activities. There are services that can launder your crypto for you by letting you send it to another address in an untraceable way, but using those services gets you onto a criminal watchlist in the US. So, even if the idea was to create some privacy for yourself, you're still drawing attention.

This is the big tradeoff that comes with using cryptocurrency. You get an always-running, decentralized, global, computing-and-finance system operating independent of any government or currency, but anything you do in it is completely public, and as soon as someone figures out your wallet address, they know *exactly* how much money you have and where you have it. For this reason, people who work on projects often end up not selling any of that project's tokens, because they are afraid of the backlash. In many cases, project founders got huge numbers of tokens but never sold any of them or made much money. The people who made money were the investors who bought in early and sold as it went up, who didn't care about everyone watching their activities. The public nature of crypto wallets is great when you're starting out and trying to learn, but once you have some money, the last thing you want is anyone on Discord being able to pester you with questions about your transaction activity. That's one reason that so many people in the crypto world use pseudonyms. Being anonymous or pseudonymous often isn't considered sketchy or suspicious in crypto. It is understood as a simple form of self-defense in a new world where your whole financial life is visible.

19
Out of the Fog
NOVEMBER 2021

id you see the Do Kwon tweet?" asked Johnny as he sat down at my kitchen island. We had moved our crypto hangouts to my house now that Velocity was being converted into a pho restaurant.

"No, what did he say?"

Johnny texted me a link. I opened it on my phone and shook my head. It was another of Kwon's public tirades, but this one was unhinged—even for him.

Someone who worked on the team for Anchor, the Luna application where you could deposit your stablecoins for a fixed, 20 percent APR, had proposed a number of improvements to the app for the next few months. Kwon had seen the proposal and responded in a series of tweets, saying, "January or February for something this simple? I will fire the entire Anchor engineering team if you don't give me something in half the time. Sprint or die. It's like a weekend job, just fucking do it."

"This guy has gotta be manic or something," I said to Johnny.

"Yeah . . . but the coin is up!"

"Way up."

When we bought LUNA in September, it was around $30 per coin. Now, it was passing $50, and it kept steadily climbing almost every day. Part of what was driving the adoption was the now billions of dollars invested in the stablecoin, UST, which people were creating to farm the 20 percent fixed APR. The only way to create UST was to destroy LUNA tokens, so the more that people used UST, the more LUNA was being bought and burned, cutting down the supply and driving the price up. It was a clever flywheel for driving more value to LUNA holders. However, the team behind LUNA knew there was the potential for a sudden bank run and hyperinflation, so they'd started buying *billions* of dollars' worth of Bitcoin to hold in reserve as an asset they could sell to backstop the price of LUNA in such an event. They already had three billion dollars' worth of Bitcoin and were planning to buy at least ten billion to have in reserve.

"NFTs are coming back, too," said Johnny. "Oh, are you going to put anything into the ConstitutionDAO thing?"

DAOs were one of the hot new trends in crypto. The acronym stood for Decentralized Autonomous Organization. They were supposed to be a more-democratic, software- and crypto-based way of organizing a company. Sometimes they worked—Ethereum itself was kind of a DAO—but they just as often fell apart from the lack of leadership and organization. The only copy of the US Constitution held in private hands was up for sale, and a DAO that had sprung up in the previous week wanted to buy it and donate it to a museum to show the power of crypto and decentralized organizations.

The organization had announced its intentions four days earlier, just seven days before the auction. The estimated value of the copy of the Constitution was $13 million, so the DAO needed to raise at least that much by that Wednesday if it wanted to have a shot at winning the auction. ConstitutionDAO started a fundraiser where, for every one ETH you donated, you would get one million of their PEOPLE tokens. The tokens didn't give you any rights or authorities. You didn't get to vote on what happened to the Constitution or have any chance of making money from it. The only benefit to donating, besides supporting the cause, was that if they succeeded, the museum plaque wherever they donated the Constitution would include your name as one of the contributors to the purchase.

"Yeah, I was going to put in 0.1787 ETH," I said.

"Why that number?"

"That's the year it was signed," I said.

Johnny laughed. "Okay, I'll do that too." He pulled up the fundraiser page and keyed in the donation amount. Then he paused and looked at his screen a moment longer. "Actually, I'm gonna toss in another 0.5 ETH. It's been a good month."

"Do you think they'll pull it off?"

"Well . . . they only expected to need $13 million, right? They're on track to blow past that."

"Yeah," I said. "I guess we'll have to wait and see."

₿₿₿

"Honey, can you change her?" Cosette said.

"Mmm, yeah, one sec." It was three a.m. and we were up for another change and feeding. When I turned off the alarm, a Discord notification caught my eye. There was some sort of new game launching that people were excited about. Maybe a competitor.

"No, *now*, put the phone down."

"One sec, one sec, I'm almost done."

Cosette made a growling noise and started to climb out of bed.

"Okay, okay, I'm going." I left Discord open next to the changing table so I could keep reading. From the bits I saw, it was another breeding game like Axie, but they didn't bother including any gameplay. I tucked Sutton back into her swaddle and placed her in the bassinet, then got back in bed.

Cosette rolled over to look at me. "I hate when you do that," she said. She sounded exhausted.

"Do what?"

"Your phone. It's like we barely exist once your phone is out, looking at prices or Discord or whatever." She broke eye contact and looked down at the foot of the bed. "I need help. I can't do this alone."

I felt a wave of guilt wash over me. "I'm sorry," I said. "I don't want you to feel alone."

"I know you don't. And I know you're not intentionally avoiding helping. It feels like you're not really here sometimes."

Sutton started stirring in her bassinet. "We can talk about this tomorrow," Cosette said. "Let's not wake her up."

"Alright."

In the morning, we went through our normal duties of feeding Sutton, changing her, getting dressed, letting the dogs out. We didn't talk about our conversation the night before. I tried my best to stay off my phone, though, as hard as it was. I felt guilty. I knew exactly what she meant about it feeling like I wasn't really there. I felt it, too. My eyes would start glazing over in a conversation as I thought about something going on in crypto-land. Every time I went to the bathroom, I checked token prices.

This day would be good for practicing being off my phone more. Thanksgiving was next week, so we were driving out to ROAM Ranch, a nine-hundred-acre regenerative farm an hour and a half outside Austin, to harvest our turkey. ROAM kept wild turkeys on the property. They would fly around, eat bugs out of bison poop, and help fertilize the land. They were huge, powerful birds, the kind that make you realize how dinosaur-like turkeys can be.

I turned off my notifications and tried to enjoy nature at the ranch. Bits of fog progressively lifted from my mind as the morning went on. Looking at something farther away than my hand and getting fresh air were pulling me into a headspace I hadn't been in for months. I couldn't remember the last thing I had done outside besides walking for coffee, or the last time I'd felt this present. When you're scraping the lung tissue of a turkey out through a hole in its butt, it's hard for your mind to be anywhere else.

After we finished processing our bird and bagged him up, we had some time to wander around the property. I had Sutton swaddled in a wrap against my chest and could feel her little breaths whenever we stopped moving. We walked a quarter mile to the bison pasture and saw the herd munching on grass, working their way across the restored farm.

I felt a deep respect for what the founders of ROAM, Katie and Taylor, had built. They had sold their first company and bought this huge ranch for them and their kids, built a beautiful house they could watch their ecosystem from, and now spent much of their time out there working on the land and doing what they were passionate about.

I had no illusions about being a gentleman farmer. I like having coffee shops within walking distance. But how long was I willing to live in this exhausting online world trying to get rich from it? Aside from Sutton's birth and moving, most of my memories since January took place behind a screen. I could hardly call them memories at all. It was like I wasn't there. I'd always looked down on people who turned into work zombies to make as much money as possible. Sacrificing your present life for some imaginary day when you'll slow down and enjoy the fruits of your labor seemed absurd. Religion might be on the decline, but we'd replaced it with a much more boring Heaven mythology: Be virtuous in this life so you can enjoy Paradise Retirement Home in the next.

I wasn't even sure what I was chasing. If grinding twelve to sixteen hours a day chasing this $7.5 million goal was costing me months of family memories, was it worth it? I could wake up, sell my tokens for the day, then go outside and do things. I didn't need to be constantly plugged in looking for the next win. I could find a better balance. I could have a life again.

The moment I got a taste of potential massive wealth, I lost myself, lost sight of what matters, and now the rest of my life—and, most importantly, my marriage—was suffering for it. I had dived into this world headlong because I was worried about money, but now Sutton was here, and I was still completely consumed by imaginary money, video-game tokens, and pseudonymous people spying on my financial activities.

I unwrapped Sutton and buckled her into her car seat. She was exhausted, barely stirring while I clipped her in, but also so calm and peaceful. Being out in the fresh air was good for all of us. I kissed her on the forehead and got in the car.

"Hey, you were right," I said to Cosette as I started driving. "About not being present. I got too sucked in."

"Why do you say that?"

"I noticed it walking around on the ranch. I haven't felt this normal in months. I think more from being outside than anything else." I felt embarassed as I said it, but it was true.

Cosette nodded. "I felt it too. I was so sucked into the real estate world this summer. I only noticed how disconnected I'd become once Sutton was born."

"Yeah, I should have taken a break then, too," I said. I'd hardly taken anything like a parental leave. I had worked a little less, but I was still grinding on, looking for token launches whenever Sutton or Cosette didn't need me. "I think Leif was right about it not being worth doing more work," I continued. "Especially not if it means being a crypto zombie."

"Don't you like doing the work though?"

"Yeah, but the psychological cost might be too high. I don't want to feel like I'm losing myself to it. If you could help pull me out if it feels like I'm getting sucked into it again, that would really help." It was like a drug, and I couldn't tell when I was in that headspace. This was the most lucid I'd felt in months, and I didn't want to give that up.

"I'll try," said Cosette. "But it can't be entirely on me. I need you to try too."

"I will."

$$\mathbf{B}\mathbf{B}\mathbf{B}$$

Back home, I cleared out as much noise as possible. I unsubscribed from the newsletters I was following and left many of the Discords. I unfollowed dozens of crypto Twitter accounts. I needed more in my life than token prices.

I hadn't read a book in months, and I was someone who had always been proud of the breadth of my reading. I hadn't even read a non-crypto article in months. What was I even interested in anymore besides crypto? I found some random other people to follow, like photographers and writers. I had to find my way back out of this rabbit hole I'd sprinted down.

Over the following week, I woke up each morning, sold my tokens, then went outside and enjoyed the day. I took walks with Sutton and friends, went to the gym, played with the dogs, watched Sutton sleep. I bought new plants for the house to replace the ones I'd let die over the last six months. I finally organized the garage. I cooked surprise dinners for Cosette. I felt alive. I hadn't realized how fogged-over I'd gotten. Finally, I was living the life I had been dreaming about at the start of the year. Passive income from magical internet money and ample free time to enjoy it. That one little trip to ROAM had snapped me out of the fog. There was no way I was going back.

SIGNS YOU HAVE A PROBLEM

If you ever choose to dive into the incredibly fast-paced, manic world that is a crypto hype cycle, or any kind of hype cycle, it's easy to lose yourself in it, like I did. Doing so is especially hard to resist since, unlike losing yourself in a video game or TV series, you can tell yourself that, by being obsessed, you will make life-changing money. You might even be *right*. But it can quickly become an unhealthy obsession, even an addiction. Here are some signs that it's happening to you:

You check prices every day. If you have an app like CoinGecko or CoinMarketCap on your phone, and you're constantly checking the prices of your investments, then you're probably basing too much of your emotional well-being on the prices of internet coins.

You abandon your other hobbies. When your casual interests start fading away and are replaced by hunting down alpha in Discord chats, and you find yourself reading new token white papers instead of books, you might be getting obsessed.

It's all your friends talk about. This is also a good sign that you're in a crypto bubble. If the only thing everyone around you talks about is crypto, then you're probably getting too obsessed, and the mania is probably reaching its peak.

You debate selling things to buy crypto. If you start opening your

Vanguard account and looking at your retirement funds, or you start thinking about how you don't *really* need the car you have right now and you'd rather buy something cheaper and invest the difference in whatever the ridiculous-sounding coin of the day is, then you definitely need to take a step back.

You believe that, with diamond hands, you'll "make it." When you start imagining the incredibly rich future you're going to have when your shitcoins go to the moon, and you start posting messages on Twitter or Discord about how much you believe in the team and the token, then you're not only addicted, you're in a cult.

You don't tell your partner how much money you're investing. If you have a girlfriend, husband, spiritually melded life partner, whatever, and you start hiding your investments and losses from them, that's a good indication that you know you have a problem.

You tell yourself you can "make it all back." If you've lost a bunch of money, and you keep plowing in more to try to make everything back on one good trade, you're likely digging your hole deeper and have a problem.

You stop following your rules. Despite making rules for yourself about how much to put into crypto, or when to pull money out, you start ignoring those rules because you think, *This is the one* or *I need to put a little more in.*

You don't think you have a problem. Even though you fit many of the criteria above, you shake your head and say, *Nat's being ridiculous. I don't have a problem. I'm being a smart, informed investor.* Yeah, that's what they all say.

You try to quit and get pulled back in. You delete all the crypto apps from your phone and unfollow everyone on social media but then *slow-wwlllllyyyyyy* find yourself getting sucked back into the crypto vortex.

Unfortunately, you and I both know that reading a list of symptoms like this won't pull your head out of the mania. After all, there's life-changing wealth on the line here. You can get your life back in order later. No, the only way you snap out of it is by having something truly terrifying happen to you.

20
Retired

DECEMBER 2021

I lasted a week.

My time away from crypto was lovely, like a warm bath for my mind. I started having thoughts about things besides imaginary internet money again. I wasn't picking up my phone every time there was a moment's silence or taking extra trips to the bathroom to catch up on Discord messages. But I hadn't quite turned the volume down enough.

Cosette, Sutton, and I were driving up to Dallas for our friends' daughter's Annaprashana, a Hindu rite of passage when an infant eats their first solid food. During a lull in conversation, I absentmindedly checked my phone, and a crypto tweet had found its way back into my feed. It wasn't from a crypto account, though. It didn't say much, just a simple question:

"So, what's going on with PEOPLE? Who's buying it?"

In the end, the ConstitutionDAO had come close to reaching their goal, but they were outbid by Ken Griffin, the CEO of Citadel, who spent

$43 million to buy the copy of the Constitution. When the fundraiser failed, ConstitutionDAO said you could trade in your PEOPLE tokens to get your ETH back, but the transaction fee was more expensive than the value of most people's tokens, so they hadn't bothered. There was nothing else you could do with PEOPLE tokens, though. The DAO wasn't going to do any-thing else with the money. You couldn't farm with the tokens. They had no utility whatsoever. If someone outside of crypto was asking "who's buying PEOPLE," something strange was going on.

The primary reason it was confusing was that there was no way to buy PEOPLE anymore. You could only get PEOPLE by trading ETH for it on the launch site, but that was closed. All you could do was redeem it. Constitu-tionDAO had said they weren't going to create any trading liquidity for the token, so you couldn't trade it on Uniswap. Unless someone else decided to create the liquidity.

I pulled up the crypto-tracking app CoinGecko, searched PEOPLE, and discovered that my hunch was right. Someone had created a trading pool on Uniswap for the coin, and there was more than ten million dol-lars' worth of PEOPLE and ETH in it. More than sixty million dollars' worth of trades had happened the day before, another $60 million in trad-ing volume had already happened today, and it showed no signs of slow-ing down.

I texted Johnny, "Hey are you seeing this PEOPLE action?" A few sec-onds later, he responded to say he hadn't noticed it, either. I checked some of the accounts I was following before, and there wasn't much mention of it on crypto Twitter until today.

That Tuesday, one PEOPLE had been worth four-tenths of a cent. On Wednesday, it rose to two cents, a five-time increase. On Thursday: three cents. The day before, it had hit eleven cents, and now it was at fifteen cents. The price on Tuesday was the rough redemption price, about one one-millionth the price of Ethereum. Now it was thirty-seven times higher than that, and no one had any idea who was buying it.

I reached into the back seat of our car and grabbed my laptop. I didn't need it for work, but I had thought to bring it anyway, like some part of my brain hadn't fully accepted that I was stepping back from crypto. Over my shoulder, I felt Cosette shoot me a concerned glance. "Everything's good," I said. "I'm just checking something."

I texted Johnny again. "Do you still have your PEOPLE tokens?"

"Yup, still have it," he texted back.

I finished connecting my laptop to my phone hotspot and checked my wallet. My mental math was right: my 178,700 tokens were worth $26,805; Johnny's 678,700 tokens were worth $101,000.

Cosette noticed me smirking. "What's going on?"

I told her about the surprise win.

"So . . . you're not disconnecting anymore?"

"No, I am," I said. "I didn't have to do anything for this. It just happened." She still looked annoyed. "Don't worry. I don't need to keep watching it."

I put my laptop away in the back seat and texted Johnny: "What are you going to do with yours?"

"I don't know, it hasn't dropped yet, I think I'll wait for that."

"Sounds good!"

While Cosette and I finished the drive to Dallas, I tried not to think about the price too much. In these hyper-volatile takeoffs, you never know if it's going to go up another tenfold or crash to zero, and it could all go south in a matter of hours.

By the time we got to the hotel, the price had peaked at sixteen cents and dropped to thirteen. I wanted to keep riding it out and see where the price went. I wasn't doing a very good job remembering that I was trying to take a step back.

I sent Johnny a text: "I'm selling here, this is probably a pump and dump."

He texted back: "same."

In between getting dressed and changing Sutton, I sold all my PEO-PLE, then told Cosette we'd made another $20,000 and I was done for the weekend. I'd be curious to know if I had timed it right, sure, but I was good at resisting the urge to punish myself by seeing if I sold too early.

The next morning, I had some downtime to do some research and try to figure out what had happened. Apparently, a bunch of YouTubers in China had started saying that PEOPLE was the first "truly fair launch" of a token. Anyone could buy it for a fixed price, and now there was a fixed supply that could only decrease. No inflation, no insider deals for VCs: the perfect digital money, even better than Bitcoin.

I doubted they actually believed that, though it was a great narrative to get people to buy the token. What most likely happened is that they added liquidity for the token over the previous few days to make the trading pools sufficiently deep, then started promoting it as the next big thing for people to buy into. They could start buying from their own liquidity to give the price the initial push it needed for their promotion to look legitimate, then everyone else would rush in and send it to the moon. It was a classic pump and dump. If that was what was going on, they'd already made millions.

On the drive back from Dallas the next day, I let myself peek at the price. It had dropped down to nine cents and hadn't gone back up. My timing had been great. Satisfied that I locked in a little extra win before going back to being offline, I deleted CoinGecko from my phone again and enjoyed the drive home.

$$\cdot ₿₿₿ \cdot$$

The next morning, Monday, I reinstalled CoinGecko on my phone. I had seen a tweet from a popular crypto and tech blogger with a cryptic screenshot of a farm that was paying 100,000 percent APY. I needed to know which one it was.

After a few minutes of digging through Twitter and trending coins on CoinGecko, I found it: Spartacus. It had launched on another Ethereum-like blockchain called Fantom, and it was advertising itself as the decentralized reserve currency of . . . *blah blah blah*. It didn't matter. It was just marketing talk for another copy-and-paste farm, like the ones on Polygon back in May. I put in $20,000. According to the dashboard, I would make more than $500 a day, even if the token price didn't go up. But it would. I was early. This was easy money.

₿₿₿

On Saturday, December 4, LUNA reached a new, all-time high of $75, up nearly double from when I bought it, putting it in the top-ten cryptocurrencies by market cap. It was worth just shy of $30 billion, a ridiculous amount for such a new blockchain. I had made around $30,000 so far, and it was gaining another few percentage points every day.

The founder, Do Kwon, was getting even more unhinged as Terra Luna gained popularity, but the Luna community ate it up. They were calling him the next Steve Jobs or Elon Musk, a visionary engineer with brutal expectations of his employees who was sure to make you rich if you followed him. Everyone in crypto wished they had bought Bitcoin when it launched, so they wanted to find the "next Bitcoin" or "next Ethereum" to compensate for not having done so. Could LUNA be the third major coin on the market? The price was certainly moving in that direction, but it wasn't just LUNA. Everything was going up.

₿₿₿

Spartacus had shot from a $28 million market cap to a $160 million one in a matter of days. It was declining a bit now, but the new tokens I was earning each day were offsetting their decreasing value. It was another five-figure win, yielding more than $1,000 a day. It would come back, too. The DeFi 2.0 narrative was just getting started. There's always a bit of a lull in faith as these things take off. The early people might be taking some profits, but everyone else will rush in and buy the dip.

·₿₿₿·

"Nat, can you strap her in so we can go?"

"Hmm?" [*screen-tapping noises*]

"Nat. *Sutton.* Car seat."

"Oh, yeah, yeah, one sec . . ."

·₿₿₿·

You only have to double your money ten times to turn $1 into $1,000, or to turn $10,000 into $10 million.

·₿₿₿·

"You made *how much* flipping Doodles?"

[*cackling laughter*]

"Good work. That's insane."

"Clarks?"

"Yeah, I could go for some champagne."

·₿₿₿·

LUNA was flying again. Once it broke past $75, it could easily go to $100 or $200. It might be one of the best bets I made all year. Thank God I doubled down with the ape and CRAFT money instead of pulling it out.

·₿₿₿·

"Nat, did you get more diaper pail bags?"

"Uh, what?"

"The diaper pail, you said you'd get more bags."

"Uhhhh . . ."

"Fine. I'll order them."

·₿₿₿·

Up, up, up.

Maybe take a few grand of profit here.

Did you know that you can buy a beautiful, restored Ford Bronco for just $150,000?

·₿₿₿·

Time to get out of Spartacus. It's been going down too long, probably not coming back. People will rotate to the next thing. Looks like some sort of snow-themed copycat on Avalanche. The APY doesn't even fit on the screen, it's so high. Who cares, money printer go *brrr*.

·₿₿₿·

Something is happening in gaming. DeFi Kingdoms, one of the Axie copycats, broke $500 million in market cap. They didn't even have a game, it was just a DeFi farm with extra steps. If CryptoCraft hit a $500 million market cap, that would be around $50 per CRAFT token. I'd have $50 million. Someone just had to notice CryptoCraft, think, *Hey, maybe that's the next DeFi Kingdom*, and start buying it, and we'd be off to the races.

·₿₿₿·

Here we go.

It wasn't clear who was buying it, but a number of wallets started making large purchases of CRAFT. It had been hovering in the $2 to $2.30 range for weeks. Then, on Tuesday, December 21, it shot up to $3. The

Discord chat started getting euphoric. This was our moment. People in the public chat started showing up in droves, excited about this new project they were starting to buy into following on the success of DFK.

₿₿₿

On Wednesday, CRAFT stayed above $3.

₿₿₿

Through Christmas, CRAFT hovered around $3.50. My 220,000 locked tokens were inching closer to being worth $1 million.

₿₿₿

On December 30, CRAFT broke $4. On the 31st, it jumped to $4.50. Then $6.00 the next day, $7.80, $8.50.

₿₿₿

On January 6, CRAFT hit $13. It was happening.

I clicked a few buttons on my laptop, and, in one day I had made $58,500. My locked tokens were worth $2.86 million. My unsold tokens were worth more than $1 million, and the remaining tokens I hadn't received yet were worth another $7.5 million. I had an eight-figure crypto net worth.

I messaged Caleb from my phone, "How does it feel to have a $1 billion company?"

With 100 million total tokens, at $13 per token, the fully diluted value of the token was $1.3 billion. I pulled up our treasury. Sure enough, it showed 90 million CRAFT tokens in the treasury, worth a total of $1.17 billion.

What was more unbelievable was the farms. The code I'd written had more than one hundred million dollars' worth of CRAFT, ETH, and USDC in them. Anyone who was involved in CryptoCraft from the beginning had come into life-changing money.

My $7.5 million goal suddenly seemed small. I'd blown past it. With ten, twenty, thirty million, I could live extremely comfortably without having to work. It would be generational wealth for me, my family, hell, even my kids' kids if we were smart about it.

I kept compounding what I wasn't selling back into the farms.

We were gonna fucking make it.

₿₿₿

I paid off our car.

₿₿₿

I paid $50,000 off the mortgage on the house.

₿₿₿

What do I even do with $40,000 a day? Is buying a Rolex stupid? It's half a day's salary. Fuck it, gotta celebrate the wins. I'll be responsible and get a Submariner. It's only $15,000. That's like 4 ETH. My ape was worth 4 times that. And, hey, watches are a store of value, too, right?

₿₿₿

"We made $30,000 today."

"Like, cash in our bank account?"

"Well, I left most of it in CRAFT and ETH."

"*Nat . . .*"

"We're still early, honey."

·₿₿₿·

I wonder how much Pegasus's tokens are worth. It must be in the mid-seven figures, too. They're probably worth more than DeFiance would even invest in CryptoCraft.

Are these crypto venture capital firms acting as loss leaders to make their founders secretly rich?

Weird that he hasn't sold any. What does he know?

·₿₿₿·

"Cheers to being done working," I said. We clinked glasses. CRAFT was still at $8. That meant $36,000 a day. My crypto net worth was fluctuating by over $1 million a day.

Rose shook her head. "I can't believe it, you guys are insane."

Johnny laughed. "Maybe, but it worked."

"Sure did," I said. We were shopping on Zillow between bites of sushi. Houses by the lake west of Austin big enough for a family of five were $2 to $5 million. Not so crazy anymore. We just moved, but we could afford to move again if this kept up.

"Hey, look. This has two houses on the lot. We could split it." Cosette turned her phone around to show everyone.

"Oooh, yeah, maybe we need to start a little commune," Johnny said.

"You have enough for the next prototype?"

"Yup, I have someone working on it right now. It'll be unlike anything else on the market."

"And you'll have some left over?"

"Enough for the down payment and to live off of while I get the machine into production."

"Incredible." I popped a piece of sushi in my mouth. "We did it."

"That we did," Johnny said.

"So . . . you guys are done? You're gonna take the money out?" Rose said, hopefully.

Johnny and I laughed. "I don't know about you," I said, nodding to Johnny, "but I'm not done yet. I think there's still more to come."

Cosette shook her head, and she and Rose locked eyes for a moment. They looked worried, or maybe frustrated, probably both, but didn't say anything.

"It's fine, honey. I know what I'm doing."

"I hope you're right," Cosette said.

I was. I would be. We were making it. Everything was coming together.

SIGNS OF THE END

I don't know when you're reading this. Maybe it's during a crypto winter, when the market is quiet and everyone is licking their wounds. Maybe you're in the peak of a mania, and there's some new narrative that's taking off, this era's version of ICOs or NFTs. Or maybe the market is heating up again, and you sense that this is your opportunity to make your riches, like I did.

The two easiest ways to miss out on making lots of money in a crypto speculative mania are by not participating and by holding your bets for too long. I don't suspect you'll commit the first error, since you're already deep into this book, but you very well might commit the second error.

So, when do you sell? How do you avoid holding on for too long and becoming exit liquidity?

I've already shared a few rules. My favorite is to sell something as soon as it's worth more than you would pay for it. If you're looking at the hundred thousand SHIBA tokens you bought for a hundred bucks that are now worth $10,000 and wondering if you should hold on, ask yourself if you would put $10,000 into it now. If you wouldn't, you should sell.

But sometimes you never get to that point. The specific mania you're participating in might blow up, like DeFi did after Iron. That's why it's even more important to know some Signs of the End, indications that the mania might be over, done, kaput, and you should take your winnings and leave.

Here are some of those signs, in no particular order:

When mainstream media starts talking about the narrative. When "normie" news outlets started covering DeFi and talking about the profile-picture NFTs, that was a good sign to quit. The mania was spreading to nonexperts who would soon rush in to get their part of it.

When your family starts asking about it. Mom and dad asking you to explain Bitcoin to them? It's time to sell. You can tell them to buy first, to help create your exit liquidity, depending on how much you like them.

When celebrities are promoting crypto projects. Mark Cuban talking about DeFi? Sell. Lindsay Lohan doing an NFT drop? Sell. Floyd Mayweather Jr. with a token handle on his fight gear? Sell, sell, sell.

When projects are launching faster than you can keep up with them. There are only so many good ideas out there. The faster projects are launching, the more likely any individual project is some low-effort, copy-and-paste cash grab. If you feel like you can't keep up with all the new projects launching, that's a sign of the end.

When price predictions get outrageous. If financial analysts are going on CNBC arguing that BTC could soon reach ten or one hundred times its current price, after it's already seen some massive gains in the last few months, that's a sign people are getting too greedy. Get out.

When leverage becomes the norm. If everyone is borrowing against their incredibly valuable assets to buy more assets, that leverage in the system is making it weaker and weaker, and the size of the drop necessary to unleash a cascade of liquidations is getting smaller and smaller. Even though the prices might be getting higher, you're actually getting closer to a catastrophic wipeout. When the leverage in the system starts getting higher, that's a strong sign to get out.

But there is one sign that trumps them all, one that you absolutely must listen to, even though it's the hardest to entertain, even though every part of your mind and body will fight against you, telling you this time it's different, that you're wrong, that it's not a sign of the end.

And that sign is:

When you think you've figured out the game and you're about to get insanely rich.

21
Wake Up
JANUARY 2022

I was flying out of my bedroom before I even finished reading the message. This couldn't be real. This guy was screwing with me.

Cosette called after me. "Honey . . . ?"

"Uh, it's fine. I just . . . gotta . . . fix . . . something . . ."

I could hardly form the words. My mouth wasn't working. My heart was hammering in my ears, and pins and needles burned my hands and feet. I squeezed my fists as hard as I could to get them to stop hurting as I stumbled into my office and fumbled through my laptop password, pulling up the message that had thrown me out of bed:

"Nat, someone found a way to hack us. It sounds bad. All of our funds might be at risk."

This was the absolute worst-case scenario. The one I'd pushed to the back of my mind. The one I'd pretended was impossible so I could sleep at night. I had always accepted the risk that I could lose all of my money. But if I lost $100 million of other people's money, too . . .

I couldn't let myself think about that.

"Does he seem trustworthy?"

I was running through every possible scenario in my head. Whoever was reaching out might be trying to scam us. They could be trying to trick us into doing something enabling them to hack us. Maybe they already hacked us and were holding our money ransom? Or maybe they were actually a trustworthy person and wanted to help us out.

Doubtful.

Just then, crying broke out in the next room. Cosette sighed. "I'll get her." I could hear the frustration in her steps to the nursery, but I couldn't think about that now. I put on my headphones and hunkered down.

Checking the code, everything seemed fine. Everyone's money was still there. Whatever the potential hack was, it hadn't happened yet. Maybe there was still time.

I looked at how much of my own money was at risk: just over $10 million. I desperately wanted to sell whatever I could. But this was crypto. Everything was public. Everyone could see what I was doing, and more than a few were already watching me. They'd notice if I pulled all of my money. They'd get scared and start asking questions. Or they'd assume I knew something was up and preemptively sell everything. A bank run would be almost as bad as a hack.

The hammering in my ears continued. My hands burned.

Caleb, who'd roused me out of bed, added me to a chat room with the hacker, Paul, who asked if I was the programmer in charge of the code.

"Yes, that's me. How can I help you?"

As Paul started typing his reply, I noticed a flurry of notifications coming from the public chat. *Fuck.* He'd sent a message to the entire community of thousands of people whose money was now at risk. People were starting to freak out and demand answers. What could I do? I tried to sound reassuring. I said everything was fine and we were on top of it. It's not like I was going to tell everyone they might be about to lose all of their money.

Meanwhile, I knew that whatever Paul was about to ask me to do could be part of a hack. The best way to get the gates of Troy open was to make us think he was trying to help us *prevent* a theft.

"If you could," he continued, "please send a small payment of a few cents from your account." He pasted what must have been his crypto address.

Sending a simple payment should be safe enough, but I wasn't an expert. I'd never dealt with a hacker, and there was no time to find or hire someone more experienced. If I played along and got us hacked, I'd be ruined. But if I didn't play along, and we got hacked, well, I'd be screwed, too. I dug my elbows into my desk and fell forward onto my hands, which were trying to rub the terror and fatigue out of my eyes.

When you work on a normal tech product, security holes are bad but rarely catastrophic. You find the bug, deploy a patch, and it's rare anyone ever notices. In crypto, security holes are a little different. One of the great strengths of crypto applications is their permanence. They can run forever independent of human management because they're deployed on the blockchain. The downside of this is that they're often unchangeable. Once they're deployed, their code is set in stone, and if there's a security issue, there's very little you can do about it.

When you hear about tens or hundreds of millions, even billions, of dollars being lost to crypto bugs or exploits, this is usually why. Someone finds a security flaw in a deployed smart contract, exploits the flaw, and steals everyone's money. And you can be sure that, once your contracts are live, other people will try to steal money from them. You could spend months testing your code trying to attack them from every conceivable angle and still miss a critical vulnerability. We, of course, hadn't done any of that. There was almost no testing, barely an audit, and I had always worried that there might be some lurking vulnerability we'd have to fix later. Now there was. And now that there was more than one hundred million dollars' worth of crypto stored in the contracts, that security flaw was a big fucking deal.

Paul, the mystery person who had joined our Discord looking for developers to talk to, wasn't sharing many details. He said there was a security vulnerability in the contracts, but he wouldn't say which contracts or what the vulnerability was, not until he had proof of who he was talking to.

While that sounds frustrating, this was the best practice in the space and a sign he had found something legitimate. A good white-hat hacker, who looks for vulnerabilities to help teams patch them, wouldn't say what the issue is until they knew they were talking to someone who was on the team. If they explained the vulnerability to the wrong person, that person might take advantage of it or share it with someone else who could.

"Hey, is everything alright?" I hadn't even heard Cosette come into the office.

"I hope so. I don't know. This is really bad."

"Are we okay?"

I turned my chair around and looked up at her. She was holding Sutton and giving me that worried look again. At least it was worried and not angry. "I . . . I don't know. I gotta fix it."

"You don't know? What do you mean you don't know?" She was trying not to raise her voice too much, but the tone said enough.

"Go for a walk or something. I'm going to fix it." I turned back around to my desk and stared at Paul's request. Cosette stormed out. I could apologize later. Once I'd saved our money. Hopefully.

I couldn't think of any risk to sending Paul the small amount he'd asked for as proof I owned the deploying wallet, so I did what he asked.

"I sent you the transaction," I messaged him. "Let me know when you receive it." The wait was excruciating. I was 99 percent sure that sending him a simple transaction like this wouldn't give him any special access to our code. But that 1 percent possibility was terrifying.

There was a tiny possibility that he wanted me to send him the bit of money so it looked like my wallet funded his wallet before it stole all the money. Then, if he hacked us with this wallet, the crypto paper trail would suggest that I was the one who did the hack, because I funded the wallet. That was the only potential risk I could think of, though.

"Confirmed," he said.

"Okay so what's going on here? What do you want?"

"I want to make sure everyone's safe. I work for RugDoc. We were doing a review of your smart contracts and noticed a potential security vulnerability. That's when I contacted you." RugDoc was an organization that investigated DeFi protocols. They would write reports on the safety and risks of any major new project that launched, and I'd often checked their site before putting money into a new farm back when I was farming more aggressively. That didn't make sense, though. We weren't a DeFi protocol. Why would he be investigating our code?

"Can I get some proof?"

"Certainly." He sent me a return transaction from the wallet I'd sent money to. The wallet had a few NFTs I could quickly verify were part of RugDoc, and the wallet's address was one of the verified RugDoc wallets on their website. He was telling the truth.

"Okay, thanks, don't you guys investigate DeFi protocols though? Why were you looking at our code?"

"Ah, yes," he replied. "We weren't investigating your farms for a report, we wanted to put money in them."

I snorted out a laugh. These security guys gambled as much as the rest of us. Hell, that was probably how they got into security in the first place. I almost considered it after Pounder stole Johnny's money.

"Ha, alright, so what did you find?" My fear was starting to ease a little bit. He at least *seemed* like a Good Samaritan. He wanted to help us. There was still a potential security hole to deal with, but at least these guys had found it first. If we fixed it before someone else found it, the money would be safe.

Paul explained that our contracts were vulnerable to a *flash-loan exploit*. Flash loans are a special kind of DeFi tool that allow you to borrow a ridiculously large amount of money, tens or hundreds of millions of dollars, with no collateral, as long as you pay the loan back almost immediately. The good news was that the exploit could only target the reward tokens, not the tokens users had deposited into the contracts. Those tokens were safe. So, we didn't need to make everyone withdraw their funds immediately. We just needed to reduce the number of tokens in the reward pool.

I could breathe a little easier. There wasn't $100 million of other people's money at risk. It was more like $2.4 million of CryptoCraft's money, plus whatever we lost from the token tanking when we alerted people to the exploit. Still, that meant I might lose most of the money I'd made if this went south.

I told Paul I'd get to work on a fix, and I emptied the rewards in the meantime to reduce the amount of money that could be stolen if someone else found the exploit. Hopefully no one was watching my transactions that day. If they were, they might notice that odd behavior and start digging.

Thanks to Paul's investigation, we knew where the vulnerability was. It was a simple fix. I only had to change one line of code, and the vulnerability would be gone . . . should be gone, anyway. That little bit of uncertainty was paralyzing. I knew this should fix it, but what if it didn't? What if, instead, we drew attention to a vulnerable contract without fixing the risk? And what if there was some new risk we hadn't caught that someone else then came in and exploited?

It was so easy writing these contracts when there was no money on the line, when we were goofing around on Discord wondering if anyone would put money into this thing. Now, it was a completely different game. People had made millions by being early to this project. The founders were about to close a fundraising round with some of the top venture capitalists in the space. Retail investors were pouring new money in every day. If I messed up a few months ago, it was no big deal. If I messed up now? It could destroy the reputation I'd managed to build the last few months.

But I couldn't focus on that. I needed to get the new contracts done.

The core problem only took a minute to fix, but I needed to test it as much as possible. It wasn't uncommon for teams to spend weeks or months coming up with tests to try to make sure a contract was secure. You'd come up with as many ways to attack it as you could, then ask your peers to come up with ways to attack it, then maybe hire an auditing firm to battle test the contract, as well, and see if they could find any weaknesses you hadn't thought of.

By dinner time, Paul and I were out of ideas for how else to test it. It would have to be good enough. It was getting late, so we decided to hold off on implementing the fix until the next day. At this point, if someone found the exploit, it wouldn't be the end of the world. We'd taken most of the reward tokens out of the contract, so the damage would be minimal.

Cosette walked by the office with Sutton to put her down for bed. "Hey, mind if I help?" I said and followed her into the nursery. As I changed Sutton's diaper and swaddled her up, the weight of the day slowly settled on me. I was beyond exhausted, physically and emotionally, and I could sense Cosette was, too. We turned off the lights, stepped outside, and shut the door. Finally, I looked at Cosette for the first time since this morning.

"I can't do this again," she said, her voice strained.

"Can't do what again?"

"This! This craziness, these mornings!"

"I know," I said quietly. "I don't want this either."

"No, Nat, you don't know. I don't understand what you're doing in there. You keep saying we're making so much money, but then something happens, and suddenly we're going to lose all of it. Time after time, you have to run and get your laptop and leave me with the baby. We were supposed to have a nice Sunday together, but you got sucked in the moment you woke up."

"Yeah but I had to—"

"I know, there's always something you *have* to do. There's all this money on the line. But you're not here, Nat. The moment your phone comes out, I lose you. You're looking at charts, or Discords, and you don't hear anything that's going on around you."

I felt the blood rushing to my head. "I'm doing this for us, though. We could be *done*. Like, do-whatever-we-want-with-the-rest-of-our-lives done."

"I don't care!" Cosette's voice cracked. "I'd rather have our old life and have you be here than whatever this is. When does this end? You said it was just until Sutton was born, and nothing has changed. Then you said you were going to slow down after Thanksgiving, but, if anything, you've gotten worse."

I paused and tried to take a breath. She was right.

"I know . . . I want to be better about it." My voice was barely above a whisper.

"Do you? Because you've said that before, and nothing's changed. You'll get better for a day or two, and then it's back into zombie mode." She took a breath and continued. "The grind was fine before Sutton was here. But she's here now." She looked up at me, eyes swollen, streaks running down her cheeks. "It's like we're your second family. Like you'd rather be on your phone or laptop than with us. Do you want her to grow up wondering if you care more about her or your work?"

She was right. I had turned into exactly what I was trying to escape. My shoulders heaved. I pulled her against me and buried my face in the side of her neck.

"I'm sorry. I'm so sorry."

We stood in the hallway, quietly sniffling, holding each other, and I felt the tension from the day pour out of me. I'd forgotten there was a world outside of crypto, a better world. In my blind obsession, I'd risked losing that better world, and I'd hurt the people I loved most.

I couldn't pretend to blame it on fear. The money problems were gone. We were fine. I was playing because I liked it. I was hooked on the thrill. I wanted more, always more. But I could see the cliff now. If I didn't pull back, truly pull back, there might not be a return.

We untangled and walked to our room, and I went to the bathroom to take a shower. I stared at myself in the mirror. I looked sick: dark bags under my sunken eyes, pale skin, oily hair, a layer of fat where there had been muscle. It wasn't worth it. I needed to get out.

I barely slept. I knew that when we announced the vulnerability the next day and told everyone to migrate, it might be the end of the party. People might flee to other projects. Caleb might want to fire me, but I didn't care anymore. Even if he didn't, I would find a way to ramp down my responsibilities.

I posted a message to everyone in the Discord letting them know about the security risk and the need to migrate their funds. After I hit send, I took a few minutes to pace around the kitchen while trying not to look at my phone, praying that everyone wouldn't immediately flee for other projects.

When I got back to my computer, seemingly nothing had happened.

There were a few dozen thumbs-up emojis attached to my message, and, most surprisingly, a slew of messages of appreciation in the discussion channels. No one was angry. They were thrilled we'd caught the issue before it was exploited. Pegasus reached out to us directly to say how smooth the process was.

I pulled up the contracts and watched the funds migrate over. Within a few hours, 80 percent of the liquidity had been transferred, tens of millions of dollars moved in a matter of hours by people all over the world. It was wild to watch, and not something I could imagine happening outside of crypto.

Lastly, we needed to settle up with RugDoc. They requested a bounty of 10 percent of the at-risk funds. Since the reward pools were the only funds at risk, there was only $2.4 million on the line, and they weren't asking for USDC or ETH, they were asking for CRAFT tokens. It was the best $240,000 we'd ever spent. We sent it over to their team wallet, and they ended up depositing their full share in various farms. They didn't sell any of it.

No other issues came up through the rest of the day. Despite my fears that this migration would tank the price, the price was up by the evening. Maybe more people were comfortable farming the token now that we'd caught a security bug. Either way, everything had turned out better than I could have expected. The crisis was over.

But now, I had a bigger problem to solve.

WHY DO CRYPTO PROJECTS GET HACKED SO OFTEN?

Almost everyone who has spent some time in crypto, assuming they're doing more than holding Bitcoin and Ethereum, has either been victim to some kind of hack or has been dangerously close to one. As I write this, in April 2023, the total losses on the Rekt.news leaderboard of the biggest crypto hacks, scams, and exploits amount to somewhere north of $5 billion.

One reason crypto projects are such a big target for hacks is the amount of money in crypto. Even if a clever hacker figured out how to hack the Chase Bank servers, they couldn't do very much because of the banking system's forms of security and controls. If you helped yourself to millions of dollars from Chase Bank, it would get reversed. Major crypto projects sometimes have hundreds of millions of dollars, even billions, in their smart contracts. And if you found an exploit, you might walk away with all of that money and no one could reverse it.

Another reason that hackers are drawn to crypto is the public nature of the code. You can't go read all the code Facebook uses to run its application in order to try to find a weak spot, but you can read all of the code behind any smart contract, which makes it much easier to find vulnerabilities.

And then a third reason is that there is often no recourse when crypto money gets stolen. If I write a smart contract that I put a bunch of ETH into, and you find a way to take that ETH out of it, there's nothing I can do once that ETH is gone. I can't ask someone at Ethereum to fix it, the blockchain is more or less unchangeable. Assuming you used an anonymous address to take the money, it would be extremely hard to track you down.

So, you have hundreds of millions of dollars being held by publicly readable code, with dramatically reduced consequences and risks for stealing it. *Of course* hackers would be drawn to this world.

One common way that hackers steal crypto funds is by exploiting a careless error in a smart contract. Let's say I meant to write my contract so that only my wallet could withdraw money from it. Then a hacker looks at the code and notices that I forgot to add that security check and *anyone* can withdraw money from it. All they have to do is run the withdrawal command, and, ta-da, the money is in their wallet. That might sound absurd, but it has happened.

Or maybe I was slightly less careless than that. Let's say I did add the security check, but there's another command in the contract that lets me change who can run the withdrawal command, and I forgot to put a security check on *that* function. A hacker notices that error, changes the owner of the contract from me to them, runs the withdrawal function, and now they have all the money. This, too, has happened.

These are fairly obvious errors, the kind that auditors would likely catch, but you could just as easily make a very subtle, non-obvious error that no one notices. For example, imagine a simple contract that allows you to deposit your ETH or USDC and earn interest on it. In the actual code, there would be functions like *deposit* for depositing funds and *withdraw* for withdrawing funds, but there might also be an *update balance* function for updating your balance after you deposit or withdraw money. If you didn't structure the contract correctly, an attacker might find a way to run the withdraw command without triggering the update-balance command. They could then deposit 100 ETH and make repeated withdrawals against that amount without updating their balance, so the contract thinks they still have 100 ETH deposited. As long as their balance shows 100 ETH, the contract will approve individual withdrawals up to that amount until everyone else's money is gone. Again, that seems ridiculous, but it has happened.

Carelessness in the real world is another common way projects get hacked. Every contract has a wallet, or set of wallets, that control it. If a hacker finds a way to steal the private key to a wallet that controls a major contract, they can sometimes drain that contract of its funds without ever having to find an issue in the contract itself. That's what happened to me when I accidentally published my private key online. The Ronin Network that powers Axie Infinity was exploited in this way, and the attacker stole a whopping $624 million.

Finally, sometimes the contracts are fine, and the wallets are fine, but the site hosting the contracts get hacked. Instead of an attacker going after the CryptoCraft contracts, they could have targeted the website where people interact with those contracts and changed which contracts the site used. That way, they could steal people's money by getting them to use malicious contracts the hackers themselves had written.

It's worth mentioning that the Ethereum blockchain *itself* never gets hacked, or at least hasn't yet. The same is true for Bitcoin. Hacks are usually caused by user error or poor smart-contract design.

22

The Bill

I hadn't lost everything to hackers, but I was still irresponsibly over-invested in CryptoCraft. So now the question was: How do I get my money out of the game, and how much could I realistically get out? On paper, I might have more than $10 million, but there was no way for me to turn most of that virtual wealth into dollars in my bank account.

The way market caps and valuations were calculated in crypto was a little absurd. Say I launched NatCoin with a million tokens. I then sell you 1 NatCoin for $100. If I have the other 999,999 tokens, do I have $99,999,900? Maybe on paper, but there's no way I could sell all of them for that price and collect all that money. The value is more imaginary than real.

This is why the net worths of famous entrepreneurs can be deceiving. Jeff Bezos owns around 17 percent of Amazon, so if Amazon's market cap is $1 trillion, Bezos is worth $170 billion. But if Jeff tried to sell all $170 billion of his Amazon stock on the market at once, he would destroy the price. It would crater from the sell pressure, and he might only get out a fraction of that amount. On a busy day in the market, Amazon might have $500 million of trading volume. If Jeff doubled that by selling $500 million of

Amazon stock every day, it would take him a year to exit his position, and who knows how low the price would go along the way.

Bezos's wealth is trapped in Amazon, and it seemed most crypto "wealth" is suffering from a worse version of the same problem. I'd joked with the team that the treasury was worth more than $1 billion. On paper, it was, but there was nowhere near $1 billion of liquidity for us to sell those tokens into. Even if we sold every single CRAFT token in the treasury, there was only $7.5 million of ETH in the exchange to trade the CRAFT for. The *most* we could get out was $7.5 million. Not quite $1 billion.

Meanwhile, I had an even bigger problem than the limited liquidity: taxes. I'd been amassing a staggeringly high tax bill over the last few months. I was afraid to calculate it, but it was only getting worse, and if I didn't address it soon, I might accidentally bankrupt myself.

I texted Johnny to ask if he wanted to pop by for a tax-prep party.

A few minutes later, he texted back: "Okay! I'll be there in twenty."

I rolled out of bed and threw on a pair of sweats. Today might be almost as painful as yesterday.

A quick thirty minutes later, Johnny arrived. We set up our laptops and connected our wallets to TokenTax, a popular crypto-tax software. After a few minutes, the results were in.

"Hoooooly shit . . ." I said under my breath as the screen refreshed. "I am so fucked."

Johnny's eyes had gone wide, and his fist was up against his mouth. "Ohhh man." He broke into nervous laughter. "Oh my god. There's no way."

We both sat there in silence for a moment, staring at our laptops in disbelief. My TokenTax report was showing $1.2 million in taxable gains. Johnny's was showing $2.3 million. Assuming a 35 percent tax rate, I owed $420,000, and he owed $805,000. Neither of us had anywhere close to that amount in cash.

"There's no way this is right," I said and started digging further into the report. If it were right, I had been dramatically underestimating the taxes on each transaction and would need to sell a huge portion of what I'd earned.

I combed through the transaction record and felt my pulse start to come down. There were mistakes. The program had double counted some of my largest transactions, including selling my ape. It thought I had made more money than I did. The mistakes on Johnny's report were much worse. The software was bad at tracking NFT sales, and he had tons of double- and triple-counted transactions that needed to be reconciled. We spent the next couple of hours sorting through our spreadsheets of data trying to make sense of it all. I had more than twenty-five hundred transactions to clean up. Johnny had closer to four thousand.

By the end, Johnny was feeling a little better, but I was still in trouble. My taxable earnings were closer to $900,000, which still meant I needed $315,000 in cash to send to the IRS. The only way I could get that was if I started selling more aggressively.

There was, of course, another option.

"How likely do you think it is that the IRS is going to look at this stuff?" I asked. We had spent hours reconciling thousands of obscure crypto transactions in a spreadsheet. It was challenging for us to parse, and we probably knew more about how this world worked than 99.99 percent of the people in the world.

"Yeahhhh . . ." Johnny let out a nervous laugh.

"I mean, this was a lot of work for us to figure out. Is some random analyst at the IRS going to comb through all these transactions with a fine-tooth comb like we did?"

"Probably not . . . I don't know, though. It's risky."

I looked back at my laptop and started chewing on my bottom lip. The last thing I wanted to do was send the IRS more than three hundred grand. I'd have to sell a huge chunk of what I still had farming, and that would incur *more* taxes that I'd also have to send. The total would be closer to $400,000, though at least I could send some of that the following year. That Rolex was feeling like a stupid purchase now.

I groaned. "We gotta do it. I want to be able to sleep at night."

"Yeah," Johnny said. "I think you're right."

The biggest problem with my earnings was that most of them came from claiming my CRAFT tokens from my one-year vesting contract. Every time I did that, it technically counted as income. So, if I collected ten thousand dollars' worth of CRAFT tokens, that was $10,000 of income I had to pay taxes on. If I then locked half of those tokens in the one-year farming contract, as I had been doing for a while, that was $5,000 I still had to pay taxes on but no longer had access to. If I had thought of this a few months ago, I could have made smarter decisions. It was stupid to lock up so many of my tokens.

This was a great problem to have, but it was turning into a massive headache very quickly. If I didn't start selling more aggressively, I might end up bankrupt from my tax bill. If I didn't pay my tax bill, I might end up with a huge fine or in jail. But if I *did* start selling aggressively to pay my taxes, I would have the usual social consequences from Caleb and the community from having paper hands and driving the price down.

The right choice was obvious: I had to ramp up my selling to make sure my taxes were covered. But I could only sell so much per day without drawing a huge amount of attention or tanking the market. The sooner I started the better.

Johnny headed out, and I started calculating what I needed to do to cover my taxes. I had two hundred thousand CRAFT tokens locked in the farming contract, so while those were collectively worth anywhere from $1 million to $1.6 million, depending on the day, I couldn't sell them until September. Who knew what the token would be worth then? I still had tons of tokens I had been holding on to, and I had the 3,561 tokens I was earning per day, but I could only sell so many of them without having a noticeable impact on the token price. I went to the DEX and checked what would happen if I traded different amounts of CRAFT tokens. It looked like I couldn't sell more than twenty thousand dollars' worth per day. It would take a minimum of twenty days of constant selling to pay my tax bill, assuming the token didn't drop any further.

Of course, I did have some of the money I had already pulled out, but I had converted most of the CRAFT I was selling to ETH, and that had been dropping like a rock since November. It was down nearly a third from when

I bought most of it. Despite that, I had more faith in ETH long term than CRAFT. I didn't want to sell my ETH unless I absolutely had to.

Five days later, CRAFT continued dropping. The twenty-day plan worked fine when it was at $6, but it was down to $4 now. Even if I sold every single token every day, I wouldn't get $20,000. And I couldn't sell every single token. Maybe I could sell 80 percent of them. That would get me to about $12,000 a day . . .

But now it would be another three weeks or so until I could pay my taxes . . .

And if it kept dropping . . .

After another week, CRAFT was down to $3.50. The liquidity was shrinking, too. The more people pulled their liquidity, the more my sales moved the price. I had to cut back more. This timeline to reaching my tax obligation just kept getting pushed out.

A few days later, Caleb messaged me: "Hey, have you had any problem taking money out of crypto?"

"No, why?"

"Well . . . one of my bank accounts got shut down," he said. I froze, staring at my phone. I had most of my tax money sitting in USDC in my wallet. I hadn't pulled it out. If I couldn't get it out, I couldn't pay my taxes.

"How much did you try to take out?"

"Twenty-five thousand dollars, I've heard of this happening to other people too . . . it's scary stuff."

"Okay, I better try, too," I said, then sent $25,000 USDC to Coinbase and converted it to dollars to send to my bank account.

It wouldn't be there for a few days, though. If it made it there at all.

₿₿₿

LUNA was getting so close to $100. I couldn't believe it was still going. And Anchor was somehow still paying nearly 20 percnt APR. How long could that go on for?

₿₿₿

A few days later, my money made it to my bank account.

I was selling as much as I could without destroying the token price, and I'd be able to get enough out to cover my tax bill as long as CRAFT didn't drop too much more. I was getting more messages from the community and Caleb. Everyone was pissed at me for selling so much, but I didn't know what else to do. Besides, if they believed in the token, they should have been happy they could buy it more cheaply, right?

₿₿₿

"You guys see the Axie hack?" Caleb said on Discord. I was already reading about it. Someone had tricked one member of the senior leadership at Axie's parent company, Sky Mavis, and managed to get the private key to one of the major wallets. Then, they'd stolen $600 million. It was the biggest hack ever . . . a new number one on the Rekt leaderboard.

"Who's going to recapitalize it?" I asked. A few weeks earlier, another project called Wormhole, which let you transfer your funds between blockchains, had been hacked for $326 million. The investors had to swoop in to fund it so that its collapse didn't destroy activity on the blockchains it was servicing. Would the same thing happen here?

"One of the investors will have to," said Caleb. "Hey, speaking of investors, I have good news, Nat. The fundraiser is happening. 3AC, Delphi, De-Fiance, they're all in. The news drops next week."

"Holy shit . . ."

Cosette looked up from her place on the couch.

"What's up?"

"The fundraiser, it's happening. CRAFT might be coming back."

"Are you going to sell this time?"

"Yes," I said, staring at Caleb's message. "Everything I can."

HELLO, YES, MR. IRS?

Not only was the looming need to pay taxes terrifying, but figuring out how much to pay was a massive nightmare in itself. There is little clarity as to how the government would classify the various cryptocurrencies we were buying and selling, and there are no clear rules on how to classify the various types of transactions we were doing, either. If you were an active trader, like Johnny and me, your decisions on some of those criteria could swing your tax bill hundreds of thousands of dollars in either direction.

The Commodities and Futures Trading Commission classified Bitcoin and Ethereum as commodities, but it hasn't made judgments on every other cryptocurrency, and certainly not on a little one like CRAFT. So, we had to assume the CFTC would treat the smaller coins like they treated Bitcoin and Ethereum, as commodities or as securities.

If you are buying and selling crypto, you have to know how much you paid for it, how much you sold it for, and report how much you gained or lost on the transaction. At the end of the year, if you are in the black, you pay taxes on your gains like you would for stocks or bonds. If you are trading crypto on Coinbase or any other exchange, the exchange handles the recordkeeping for you. It tracks your purchases and sales and reports them to you and the IRS at the end of the year. For those transactions, it's easy to figure out what you owe and no way to hide it.

But then there is everything in DeFi. If you swap between two tokens on Uniswap, no one is reporting that to the IRS. If you claim farming rewards from a project, the project isn't reporting that as part of your income. It's not like you have to put your Social Security number into HawkDex before you start farming. If you sold someone an NFT through OpenSea, OpenSea wasn't reporting your gain or loss. No one was tracking you, and no one was reporting what you were doing. You are on your own to do your best to be honest, but it isn't clear how to do that. Buying and selling tokens is fairly straightforward: there is a purchase price and a sale price. There are applications you could connect your wallet to which would generate a report of your transaction history to create your tax report for you. But once you did anything more complicated than swapping tokens, you ran into trouble.

Let's say you had one ETH and some USDC, and you wanted to add trading liquidity to Uniswap. When you deposit the ETH and USDC, you get a receipt token back from Uniswap, so it looks like you swapped ETH and USDC for this new receipt token. Does that mean you have to pay taxes on the change in price of ETH from when you bought it to when you deposited it? It doesn't seem like you should have to since you're just depositing it, as if in a bank, but will the IRS agree? What if you deposited your ETH into a lending platform like Aave to earn some interest on it? When you deposit in Aave, they give you a receipt token called aETH that represents your deposit. Does that count as a swap? It shouldn't, since it's also more like storing your money in a bank, but, again, will the IRS agree?

And then there were the gas fees you were constantly paying. If you bought your one ETH for $1,000 and had been using it to pay gas fees while ETH is at $4,000, do you have to pay capital gains on it as if you were selling it? Or can you write it off as an expense? What about interest-bearing tokens, which increase in quantity in your wallet over time. Do you have to treat every increment as income? Were farming re-wards a stock split, or income? Was an NFT a security or a collectible? What about the $35,000 that got stolen from me, could I write that off?

There aren't definitive answers, and every crypto-tax-calculating app that you hook your wallet up to will give you a different number for what you owe. If your goal is perfect honesty in your tax reporting, it's impossible. The IRS can barely keep up with the crypto innovations from five years ago, let alone all the weird DeFi and NFT stuff. Some people chose to not pay anything on their DeFi activities. But if you make mil-lions and try to cheat Uncle Sam out of his money, it almost certainly will come back to bite you, eventually.

23
Exit Liquidity
MARCH 2022

The fundraiser was a who's who of crypto-gaming investing. Three Arrows Capital was the lead investor, along with DeFiance, the firm that Pegasus worked for. The other lead was Delphi Digital, the firm that put some of the first money into Axie Infinity and Terra Luna. Those two deals, alone, had made them billions, at least on paper.

The deal was 10 million CRAFT tokens, 10 percent of the supply, for $5 million split across all of the investors. The investors were buying the tokens for fifty cents each, 85 percent cheaper than the current trading price. If the price held for a year and a half until their tokens started unlocking, they could sell them and make close to a tenfold return. Even if the price dropped 80 percent, they'd still double their money. With 3AC putting in $2.5 million, they might make another $2.5 million by sitting on their hands for a year and a half.

If it was such an incredible deal for investors, why did it make sense for the CryptoCraft team? Even though it was an 85 percent discount, there was no other good way to get $5 million from those 10 million CRAFT tokens. If Caleb tried to sell 1 million tokens at the current $5 price, the price wouldn't hold. You couldn't sell more than five or ten thousand dollars' worth without having a noticeable impact on the price.

Making a heavily discounted, over-the-counter trade was much better than destroying the token price and draining all the liquidity from the market. Especially once you considered how bad the optics would be if the treasury started selling tokens. The over-the-counter sale wouldn't directly affect the public market price, but we all assumed that, once the announcement broke, people would come rushing in. Hearing that Delphi or 3AC, let alone both, invested in a game was a strong signal it was something legitimate. Anyone in the space who hadn't yet heard of CryptoCraft would hear about it, and maybe more money would flood back into the token. I'd get the exit liquidity I needed to finish covering my tax bill, and then some.

₿₿₿

I rolled over in bed the next morning and grabbed my phone. The price had spiked from $3.00 to $4.20. I ran downstairs to grab my laptop and do my daily token sale. It hadn't been worth this much in weeks. Cosette came downstairs and gave me a funny look.

"It's coming back," I said.

She raised an eyebrow. "Already?"

"Yeah, the price jumped overnight." I turned around my laptop to show her the chart; more purchases were starting to happen as traders in the rest of the US woke up and saw the jump.

"Why, though? Did the fundraising news come out early?"

I turned the laptop back around and looked at the chart again. I hadn't thought about it yet, but she was right. There wasn't any obvious reason why the token should be taking off now. The news hadn't been released yet. Maybe someone had leaked it?

I made some coffee to start investigating, while Cosette played with Sutton in the living room. Someone out there must have found out about the fundraiser and was trying to get ahead of it. I started with the big crypto newsletters, but no one had mentioned anything. I searched through Twitter. Nothing there, either. I checked Caleb and the other team members' tweets. No one had teased anything. Then I started sifting through Discord groups. After checking through a few chats, I found a link to a YouTube video that was released by a crypto-research-tool company called Nansen. Their tools let you track what major wallets were doing in crypto, and, in their weekly demo video the day before, they happened to talk about CryptoCraft.

I opened the video and skipped ahead to the part that mentioned CRAFT. It showed that a few "smart money" wallets on Polygon were accumulating CRAFT tokens, but that still didn't answer the question of how those wallets knew to start buying them, only that it was just a few wallets making the purchases, not tons of smaller ones.

The video went on to show it was one wallet, in particular, that had been accumulating a huge number of tokens. As they explored the wallet's history in their tool, a name for it popped up, revealing who owned the wallet: Three Arrows Capital.

I stared at my laptop, confused. The investor tokens were locked for a year and a half. They weren't supposed to get them right away. If the CryptoCraft team sent them their tokens immediately, then they could sell them for $4 after having bought them for fifty cents. It would destroy the price. There's no way Caleb would have done that. This didn't make any sense.

I scrubbed through the video a little further, and Nansen showed that 3AC didn't just have the tokens, they'd been slowly accumulating them for months. They had more than 450,000 CRAFT tokens worth $1.9 million in their secret wallet.

Dread started to creep over me. There was only one reason they would have been buying tokens like that.

The $2.5 million 3AC had invested in the fundraiser bought them five million tokens, but they wouldn't start unlocking for eighteen months and wouldn't all be unlocked for three years. Who knew what the crypto market would be like at that point or what CRAFT would be worth? Those tokens would probably either be worth a huge multiple of what they bought them for, or they'd be worth zero. It was a high-risk, high-reward bet, the kind typical in early-stage crypto venture capital. But by making that bet, they got access to special knowledge about when the fundraiser would happen, who would be involved in it, the amount, and so on. They knew that there would be a big press release about the fundraiser the following week, which would get people excited about the project and bring in new money.

Three Arrows got to double dip on their investments by making a private investment, knowing when the news would come out, buying more tokens that weren't locked up leading up to the news, then selling them when the news broke. Smart investors with large pockets would assume Three Arrows knew something was coming, so they would buy alongside them, watch the news, and wait for a sign that whatever thing Three Arrows knew was happening had happened. Three Arrows would get the first-mover advantage, but anyone following them closely would profit, as well.

I sank back in my chair. I had miscalculated. CRAFT wasn't back. The fundraising announcement probably wasn't going to drive the price up. It would more likely tank it, because that would be when everyone sold the news. Three Arrows had been propping the price up for months with their buys going into the fundraiser. Once the news broke, they would stop buying, and the token price would drop like a rock. I needed to get out now. There were some other large holders, sure, but 3AC was one of the biggest, and they were about to use us all as exit liquidity.

I still had a bunch of tokens in my wallet from what I hadn't been able to sell over the previous couple months due to the limited liquidity. As long as I sold them all before Wednesday, I could get the maximum amount out before the dump. It would completely destroy the token price, but it was going to get destroyed anyway. Who cared if it was me or Three Arrows who did it.

$$\text{₿₿₿}$$

By Monday, CRAFT was above $5. I was still selling my normal amount, waiting. Early Wednesday would be my opportunity, slightly before the news broke, like with the Bored Ape. I just had to wait until then.

·₿₿₿·

Tuesday morning, it passed $6. One more day.

·₿₿₿·

I jumped out of bed Wednesday morning. It was time. I had been right to wait. The price was up to $7.20, the highest it had been since January. If I sold everything in a flurry of transactions now, I could get out hundreds of thousands of dollars—hundreds of thousands that might evaporate as soon as this news broke.

This was the perfect end of the cycle that had started the previous May. Everything was almost stolen from me by Pounder when I was gambling in DeFi. Then I had months of savings stolen by a hacker. I'd spent months grinding from the moment I woke up to the moment I fell asleep, trying to understand this world, trying to figure out how to make money in it.

Eventually, it had worked. We'd cleaned up on Iron. Johnny had made life-changing money on NFTs, and I'd made the best trade of my life on the ape. Then this opportunity had fallen in my lap. I had helped a video game launch its token and made more than I could have possibly imagined from it. What had Three Arrows or any of the other speculators done? Fucking nothing. They showed up and threw a bunch of money at the game so they could pump and dump it. Only one of us could get their money out, and there was no way it was going to be them. Fuck them.

My blood was rushing to my face, my chest tightening. I had been so stupid to get excited about them being involved. Everyone knew they were sharks and would do whatever they had to do to make money. The joke was on them, though. I knew their game. I was going to beat them at it.

I got to the kitchen and threw open my laptop, nearly ripping off the lid, and navigated to the DEX. I started queueing up the first sale of $100,000. The confirmation window popped up, and I hovered over the Submit button. My pulse was beating in my ears. I needed to sell. I needed to get out *now*. This was it.

I stared at my laptop with fury and dread for what felt like an eternity. The price kept updating as people kept buying. It kept slowly inching upwards. But I couldn't ignore the creeping sense of guilt over what I wanted to do. I, too, knew exactly when the fundraising announcement was coming out. I, too, had enough tokens to turn everyone else into exit liquidity. Pins and needles started climbing up my arm.

Fuck. What should I do?

I needed a walk.

I shut my laptop and went outside. I shook my hands until the tingling subsided. I wanted to get my money out so badly. I didn't care if people were pissed at me for selling. It was my money. I'd fucking earned it. I'd *won*. I wasn't going to watch all this money go to zero so Three Arrows and Pegasus and whoever else could get rich.

But this was also exactly who I was afraid of turning into. I could justify selling a share of my tokens every day on a schedule, but dumping everything based on secret knowledge that no one else had access to? That was the kind of thing mercenaries like Three Arrows did. Alpha was how you made money, but there were limits. If I started selling aggressively because I had secret knowledge about something that would tank the price, then I wasn't any better than Three Arrows. No better than the pump-and-dump schemers back in the DeFi mania days, regardless of how much it was going to cost me.

My pacing brought me back in front of our house. The only way I could get my head out of this screwed-up space it had been pulled into was if I let this money go. I didn't want to become like Three Arrows. That wasn't me.

I stood outside our front door and took a deep breath before walking inside. When I opened the door, Cosette was on the couch feeding Sutton.

"Everything alright?"

"Yeah," I said. "I'll explain on our walk. I love you."

"I love you too, honey. Come here." I sat down on the couch next to her and rested my head on her shoulder, looking down at Sutton. We sat in silence and watched her gurgle and fling her little arms around.

"Wanna go for that walk?" Cosette asked.

"Yeah, let me just do one thing first." I walked back into the kitchen, opened my laptop, and looked at the trade confirmation again. The CRAFT price was still going up, but I truly no longer cared. All of my rage had subsided into a somber acceptance. I deleted the sale I had typed in, ran my normal amount for the day, and closed my laptop.

"Let's go," I said.

₿₿₿

Later that morning, the news broke. The major crypto news outlet *CoinDesk* ran the story announcing the fundraise and all of the big names associated with it. The Discord was euphoric. No one in the community knew this was coming beyond some occasional hints that floated out from the team. Getting backing from investors of this caliber was a huge vote of confidence in the future of the game and community. People who had bought the top when CRAFT was over $10 were ecstatic to see it trending back up.

I kept watching the trading charts. Contrary to the excitement in the chat, there weren't big buy orders coming in. It was mostly sales. The price turned around as soon as the news broke, and, within a few days, it was back below $3.

It felt like the CryptoCraft party might be over. The NFT sales were slowing down, fewer people were playing the game, and, sure enough, without 3AC buying tokens to prop up the price, it kept sliding lower. I was still making a great amount of money, but it would never be the completely life-changing amount I thought it would be. On paper, I'd made a lot, but there wasn't enough trading liquidity to turn those tokens into dollars. Most of the money wasn't real.

I thought I'd figured out the game and won, but there were levels at which I couldn't compete. The Three Arrows guys and other big players like Sam Bankman-Fried and FTX were still using me as exit liquidity. Almost everything I had invested in since the hack scare had been going straight towards zero, too, probably for the same reason. Big investors got in early, waited for the tokens to be tradeable, then started dumping them on public investors chasing the hype. For the investors, it was an incredible way to make money. But I was tired. They could have their win. I didn't want to play anymore.

THE LIQUIDITY
PROBLEM

If you're fortunate enough to make some incredible trades, or launch a successful project, you might see your crypto net worth tip over into truly ludicrous numbers. Then you run into a new problem: liquidity. If you're holding shitcoins or other smaller tokens, there might not be anywhere near enough trading liquidity for you to exit your position.

One friend on a crypto journey briefly thought he was a millionaire. Then he realized this liquidity problem. He found a promising project which was similar to Polycat. Instead of playing it for a few days, he went all in. He kept claiming his rewards, re-depositing them, and doing everything he could to farm more tokens. He spent months building his position from $10,000 to more than a million dollars' worth of tokens. He was blown away by his good fortune. Until, that is, he tried to exit the position.

It turned out, the reason he was able to build his stack to $1 million was because there were so few tokens in the market, and so little liquidity for trading them, that very small purchases would send the price soaring. When he went to start selling his tokens, there was less than $20,000 of trading volume per day and less than $100,000 of liquidity. Even if he tried to sell ten thousand dollars' worth per day, he would destroy the price, and his tokens would soon be worthless. He knew he had to start selling anyway, and, in the end, he only pulled out $30,000. Only making $30,000 off a paper gain of $1 million was brutal, but it was my friend's only option. The same harsh reality has awaited investors in many similar tokens.

At the peak, the CryptoCraft liquidity pools had $7.5 million of ETH in them. By March 2022, that was down to $5 million and continuing to drop as people pulled their liquidity. And as the liquidity dropped, it was harder for anyone with a large amount of tokens to exit their position, and any token selling pushed the price down faster. This is the big down-side of giving people free tokens in return for providing liquidity. Once the rewards are no longer attractive, they can take away that liquidity and make your token worthless. When I was farming projects like HAWK and Polycat, I sometimes saw the trading liquidity for a token go from tens of millions of dollars to nearly nothing in a matter of days.

The worst part is that removing liquidity doesn't necessarily change the price of a token. If a DEX has $10 million of ETH and $10 million of CRAFT, the price of one CRAFT token would be $1. If someone removes $9 million of each, the price of the token would still be $1, but now there is 90 percent less ETH backing up the value of the token, so it is worth 90 percent less, even though you can't see that in the price.

This is a particularly acute problem for some NFT projects. If you have one hundred NFTs for a project with a floor price of 1 ETH, you might think you have 100 ETH. But odds are, if you listed all one hundred of your NFTs for sale, that would start pushing the floor down dramati-cally, and you might only end up with a fraction of what you thought they were worth.

It doesn't matter if you have $1 million on paper. If there are only a few hundred thousand dollars of ETH in the DEX to trade your token with, then that's all your token is *really* worth. Thus, when gambling on shitcoins and new launches, you always have to keep the liquidity in mind.

24

If It Seems Too Good to Be True

MAY 2022

A month after the fundraiser, Cosette and I took a trip to Italy with my family. This was the first time in more than a year that I had been able to enjoy a trip without constantly thinking about prices or worrying about being able to make a trade if something unexpected happened. It was the perfect time to clear my head and figure out what I wanted to do next.

As we boarded the flight home, I got a text from Johnny. "Are you watching this?"

"Watching what?"

"Something's up with LUNA. Get online."

I got to my seat and pulled up Twitter on my phone. The first tweet I saw was a screenshot of the price of the Terra stablecoin, UST. It should have been at $1, but it was at ninety-seven cents. That wasn't necessarily a huge deal. UST had broken its peg before, and when it did, people would use the redemption mechanism to bring it back to parity and make some arbitrage money in the process.

But that wasn't happening. I bought the airplane WiFi so I could keep refreshing throughout the flight, and I watched as the value of one UST dropped to ninety cents, then eighty cents, then into the seventies. By the time we landed, it had rebounded to ninety-two, but couldn't seem to get any higher.

It would never get above ninety-two again. By the end of the next day, Tuesday, it was dropping again, and, by Wednesday, it had hit thirty-five cents. UST and LUNA were stuck in a death spiral. People tried to redeem their UST for LUNA to take advantage of the arbitrage, but that was printing so much LUNA that the value of one LUNA was tanking as people sold it. Everyone who was holding LUNA was getting diluted, so they sold as quickly as possible, too, which drove the price down further. The price of one LUNA dropped from $60 on Monday to $1 on Wednesday. Once LUNA broke below $1, everyone panicked and rushed for the exits even faster. Two days later, UST was only worth ten cents, one tenth of what it should have been. One LUNA had dropped to one ten-thousandth of a cent, a 99.99999 percent drop in five days. It was exactly what had happened with Iron Finance in the previous June, but thirty-five times bigger. Iron had wiped out $2 billion. Luna had wiped out $70 billion.

I lost the $30,000 or so I still had in LUNA, but what had happened was far worse than crypto gamblers like me losing their money. UST had been touted as a safe savings account for casual investors to earn a steady 20 percent APR. A handful of companies, some backed by prestigious venture capitalists in Silicon Valley, had built apps to which you could connect your bank account, transfer your money, and they would put it all into UST for you. It wasn't just big investment firms and crypto natives who had lost money. Hundreds of thousands of people had their entire life savings wiped out. The number for the suicide hotline was the first thing you saw in the Luna community thread on Reddit.

In *The Black Swan* by Nassim Nicholas Taleb, he describes the life of a turkey on a farm leading up to Thanksgiving. Every day, the turkey wakes up and gets free food, is protected from predators, gets to run around the pasture, dig in the mud, and maybe make little chicks with the other tur-

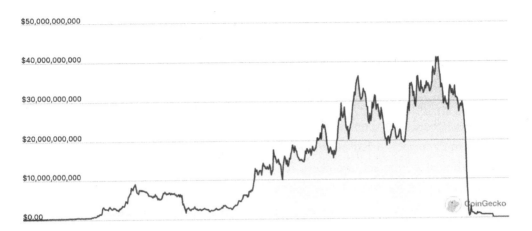

From a $30 billion market cap to zero in a few days

keys. Every day of its life, it gets more confident that it lives in a safe environment. Until, finally, the ax drops.

Every day for more than a year, LUNA and UST investors could wake up and feel like geniuses. If they had bought LUNA for $1 in January 2021, they would have been up 7,700 percent just before the crash. They were making 20 percent per year on the stablecoins sitting in Anchor protocol. Every day they got more and more confident that this was a safe, free-money machine. And then Thanksgiving happened.

The whole LUNA ecosystem had been built on faith and money printing, and the moment that faith wavered, the house of cards came crashing down. Giving away your own token was one thing. You could theoretically do that forever, and all you'd do is slowly devalue it. But printing dollars and giving those away? It was amazing Terra Luna lasted as long as it did.

₿₿₿

A few days after the LUNA crash, I drove out west towards Austin's Lake Travis to finally meet the CryptoCraft team in person. They had booked a palatial Airbnb on the water for a team retreat back when they were in the limelight and the treasury was earning hundreds of thousands of dollars a month. Those days were over, but they had already paid for the trip. They may as well enjoy it.

As I stepped through the colossal, double-door entrance, I had to laugh at how strange this all was. It was less than a year ago that I had direct-messaged Caleb, then going by Leeroy, asking if I could help on the NFT-video-game idea he had started. Now, he and his team had millions of dollars in the bank from selling tokens before the crash and from the fundraiser. At one point, the token I'd helped them launch had been worth more than $1 billion. Sorta. People had put $100 million into the farms. Again, sorta.

I dropped my backpack onto the banquet table by the pool. "Did you guys enjoy the fireworks?"

Caleb laughed. "LUNA? Hell, we stayed up all night drinking and gambling on it."

"Weren't you up by like $20,000 on it at one point?" Tyrael said, looking at Caleb.

"Yeah," Caleb said and smirked. "That was fun." I looked around the pool and saw the remnants of the festivities. The backyard patio was strewn with empty beer bottles, red Solo cups, and half-empty takeout boxes.

"I guess the party is over for a while now," I said.

"Probably," said Caleb. "I've got buddies who were completely wiped out this week. You know some venture capitalists were, too. It's only down from here."

We talked about the LUNA crash, what might happen from there, and everything that had already happened over the previous year. Eventually, I saw it was getting close to five p.m., and I knew I had to get home before the nanny left.

As I started packing my bag, Excalibur asked, "If the market's dead, do you think there's anything special we should do with the token?"

I paused and stared back at the three of them. The short answer was no. There wasn't anything worth doing, because CRAFT would probably go to zero along with everything else.

"I think you should focus on the game," I said. "You guys did it right.

You actually built something. People were playing the game and using the NFTs and tokens and everything. If you can build a truly great game by the time the next crypto cycle comes around, you'll be in an incredible position. Everyone else will be playing catchup."

Caleb looked at Excalibur, then nodded. "Yeah, that's what we've been talking about, too. Focus on making a good crypto game, and when the market comes back, we'll be ready."

Caleb and I locked eyes for a moment, and the unspoken message was clear. He didn't need me anymore. They had millions of dollars to build their dream game, and, as far as I knew, they didn't give up any equity in the company to get it. It was a dream situation for a startup company and an unimaginable one outside of crypto.

I didn't need him anymore, either. I'd made enough money selling my tokens to Pegasus, 3AC, and the other speculators who wanted to get rich off gambling on CryptoCraft. It was't the completely life-changing amount I thought it would be at that sushi dinner a few months earlier, but it was enough to quit this world and have the cushion I needed to support my family for a few years while I got my writing career off the ground. Whatever tokens I had left would probably soon be worthless though.

"I think that's smart," I said. "And I think you can pull it off."

They might not have had extensive experience building games, but they were obsessed. And they were early. If anyone from this cycle of crypto gaming was going to make it to the next one and come out with some kind of blockbuster, I earnestly believed they had a shot.

"I think so too," Caleb said, and we nodded at each other before I finished packing my bag and headed for the stairs.

As I reached the top and walked down the hall towards the entrance, Mark, a designer and the only person who had worked on CryptoCraft as long as I had, came out of one of the bedrooms wearing a swimsuit and nursing a beer.

"You're leaving already?"

"Yeah," I said, taking a moment to look back towards the team hanging out around the pool. "I think it's time for me to go."

CRYPTO ZOMBIELAND

Caleb did have another option. He could fire most of the team, do the minimal amount of work possible to avoid the appearance that the project had been abandoned, and the remaining team members could pay themselves huge salaries until they'd drained all the money in the treasury.

In traditional startups, when you run out of customers and no one wants to use your product anymore, you can shut down and move on to the next thing. But quitting isn't so easy in crypto. Launching a token isn't like selling stock or getting investors, but it *feels* similar, and if you abandon the project you launched, people might get upset. Sophisticated venture capitalists aren't bothered when something they put money into goes to zero, but retail speculators are.

So, instead of explicitly abandoning projects and inciting outrage in the community, many crypto founders take an easier path. They stop working on the project they launched but still share an update here or there to keep people happy. They wait for those people to get bored and move on. Then they put the project into *zombie mode* and hope that things go better the next time. It was one of the perverse incentives of being able to launch a token and have immediate liquidity for it. There weren't clear legal obligations attached to it. You couldn't take the money and run, that would get you into trouble, but you could crawl away slowly. That's exactly what many teams would do when crypto entered a bear market: slowly siphon off what cash they could, wait, and hope it went better next time.

As a result, at the end of each of the past crypto cycles, most of the money flooded out of the industry. Smaller projects, like CryptoCraft, bled out to near zero, never to come close to their previous highs. When the next cycle came around, people speculated on the shiny new things. Thus, teams that built something during one cycle were incentivized to launch something new the next time, rather than try to save their old token.

If an old crypto project has stopped tweeting, stopped posting announcements on Discord, and the founders are talking about other projects, it's a zombie. Don't put money into zombies.

25
Winter

SEVEN MONTHS LATER: DECEMBER 2022

You're going to fit the entire espresso machine into something this compact?" I said, staring in disbelief at the 3D-printed model Johnny was holding in front of me.

"Not just something this compact," said Johnny, "this shape specifi-cally." He handed me the machine, and I turned it around in my hands in awe. It was half the size of his original espresso maker. No one could com-plain about the backpack space it required anymore.

"That's insane," I said. "And people are still emailing about it?"

"Yup! Still tons of people who want to buy, and almost everyone who pre-ordered the original model is still happy to wait. Anyway, what can I make you?"

Around the time of the CryptoCraft fundraiser, Johnny had cashed ev-erything out of crypto. He and Rose bought a beautiful new home together using his NFT gains, and they were planning to start a family together soon. Velocity was gone, but Johnny had turned the bar area in their new house into a coffee aficionado's dream setup. He had a couple of his vin-tage espresso machines, the first model of his espresso maker, and a myriad of beans from around the world. The space to create this kind of home café was one of his favorite features of the house when they toured it a few months earlier.

I turned to Cosette. "Honey, what would you like?" Sutton was climbing all over her as she sat at the kitchen island with Rose.

"Mocha please!"

Johnny sidled up to the counter and measured out the espresso for Cosette. "So, this FTX stuff . . ."

Caleb had been right. The LUNA crash was only the beginning, and the crypto market had been imploding over the last six months.

When I tried to exit my CRAFT position, there were two routes I could have taken: sell it in the market, or borrow against it. I had chosen selling, since I didn't have access to a good debt market for it, but if I had been able to borrow against it, I might have done that, instead.

Apparently, that's what everyone did with their LUNA. Three Arrows Capital had $560 million worth of LUNA and UST, and they took out huge loans against it. When LUNA collapsed, their creditors tried to call in their debt, but 3AC couldn't pay. They had truly believed in the supercycle and had leveraged themselves to the max to take advantage of it. Now, their debtors had crippling holes in their balance sheets from putting their trust into 3AC. Firms like Genesis, Voyager, BlockFi, and more were suddenly insolvent, all because they, like me, had assumed the traders at 3AC were prophetic geniuses. Turns out, it's easy to look like a genius in a raging bull market.

Some of the firms blown up by Terra and 3AC were institutional investors, but others, like BlockFi, also held deposits from more casual investors. Once BlockFi had a massive hole in their balance sheet from 3AC's bad debt, they had to lock up customer funds and prevent withdrawals for a period.

Three Arrows wasn't the only major institution that was victim to LUNA's collapse, though. Celsius, another one of the "centralized DeFi" firms I'd considered parking stablecoins in, apparently had put customer money into risky strategies like the 20 percent yield on Anchor and hadn't gotten all of it out in time. When people started trying to withdraw their funds, the money wasn't there. Celsius had a billion-dollar hole in its balance sheet and couldn't give people back the money they thought was safely deposited there. Sure enough, when you can't explain exactly where the returns are coming from, they're probably coming from somewhere risky or shady.

Tens of billions of dollars were wiped out in the course of a couple of months. The total crypto market cap dropped from a peak of more than $3 trillion to less than $1 trillion. When people started asking how, the underlying answer was simple. It was the three things the massive run in the crypto market had been built on in the first place:

1. Printing money

2. Leverage

3. Farming

LUNA offered an extremely attractive stablecoin farm paying 20 percent. They funded that by printing money. Investors threw money in to farm it, and, as the value of LUNA rose, they borrowed against it to buy other assets. Or, they borrowed against their existing assets at low interest rates to farm the 20 percent APR. Either way, when LUNA collapsed, they couldn't repay their debts.

The big professional firms hadn't been much smarter than me and my friends, after all. They just had more money to throw around and got lucky for a time. Three Arrows kept farming LUNA and kept borrowing against it, and it ended up wiping them out. The same thing happened to Celsius, which was making risky bets with customer money to try to get that sweet 20 percent APR. Investors borrowed against everything else, too: their Bitcoin holdings, Ethereum holdings, anything they could take out debt against, they did. As the market ground lower, all of those debts were recalled, and individuals and firms were wiped out one by one.

The market would have continued cascading lower if one person hadn't stepped in to save it: Sam Bankman-Fried, the wunderkind founder of FTX. Instead of letting every victim of 3AC collapse, he started buying them and assuming their debts. He acquired Voyager, Genesis, and bought a large chunk of BlockFi, helping to recapitalize them and make their depositors whole. Bankman-Fried likely knew that if they all blew up, it would be awful for the crypto industry, and that saving them was in his, and everyone else's, best interest.

Unlike the rude, manic, bombastic Do Kwon of Terra, SBF seemed like a genuinely good guy. He was donating to political causes. He was speaking in front of Congress, helping to explain the positives of the industry. He came across as a nerdy, awkward, shy, but über-smart financier who'd figured out the game and won. He seemed like he deserved it. Turned out, we'd been fooled again.

It wasn't clear exactly what had happened, but we had an idea from the allegations that were flying around. When LUNA collapsed, FTX's sister company, the hedge fund Alameda, supposedly ended up with a multi-billion-dollar hole in its balance sheet. FTX apparently lent them customer funds to keep them solvent, and had only bought all those firms, like Voyager and Genesis, because if those firms went under, their debts would have destroyed Alameda. SBF must have thought he could trade himself out of the problem. He'd made billions of dollars before, why couldn't he do it again? If he made the money back, he could plug the hole, and no one would be the wiser. But his luck ran out. The hole kept getting bigger.

The demise of FTX wasn't all that different from the demise of Terra Luna. FTX had printed its own money, a token called FTT (FTX Token) backed by nothing. At one point, FTT reached a market cap of $10 billion. FTX and Alameda had then borrowed money against their FTT tokens and used those tokens for other investments and activities, apparently including some amount of investing in LUNA and farming the 20 percent yield on UST. When LUNA blew up, they blew up, too, but instead of calling it quits like everyone else, they tried to make it back. Print money, leverage it, use the debt to farm. Turns out they were the same as everyone else.

What did them in was some careful sleuthing by Changpeng Zhao, or

"CZ," the founder of the largest crypto exchange in the world, Binance. CZ figured out that Alameda and FTX were borrowing huge amounts of money against their FTT tokens, and Binance held a significant chunk of FTT tokens, so CZ didn't want his exchange to be exposed to the risk SBF was creating. He announced that Binance would start selling its FTT to reduce risk, and everyone else immediately started selling, too. As the price dropped, Alameda got margin called and couldn't cover the debt. Alameda blew up and took FTX down with it. Billions of dollars were lost in a matter of days.

"Feels good to be out of that crazy headspace," Johnny said.

"Seriously, I haven't looked at a price chart in days."

"How much is CRAFT worth now?"

"About six cents, last I checked."

Johnny let out a low whistle. "Jeez, from thirteen dollars to six cents. Brutal. Remember when we thought it was going to a hundred dollars?"

I groaned. "Don't remind me. You want to know the really crazy thing, though?"

"What's that?"

"I checked the wallets Three Arrows and Pegasus were buying with. They never sold. I don't know if they thought it was going to keep going higher or what, but everyone who followed them in ended up dumping on them."

Johnny laughed. "Well I'm not losing any sleep from taking Three Arrows' money."

"Me neither."

With the market down 80 percent from its highs, and with many of the big players bankrupt, it was clear the game was over for a while. There was no supercycle. Crypto was back in a new winter. In some ways, it was a relief. We had been worn down by our obsession. It was a fun ride, but not one we wanted to go on again anytime soon.

In the meantime, the same things would happen that had happened in every crypto winter. Traditional media outlets would call the whole thing a farce and focus exclusively on the bad aspects of the industry. Journalists would write books about crypto's "fall" and "death," and how it was one big scam all along. Everyone who missed their chance at life-changing wealth along the way would get to say *I told you so.*

But the people who had been around crypto for a while would nod their heads and say, "We'll see!" The critics love to focus on the bad aspects of the industry, but, in doing so, they completely miss what's being quietly built behind it. Crypto has this speculative, casino-like underbelly to it, but the technology making that possible has some fantastic uses. Bitcoin is slowly but successfully establishing itself as a store of value akin to digital gold. Ethereum is powering an increasing number of decentralized applications. Stablecoins are clearly the first major one, but many more are coming. Blockchain technology will keep getting faster, safer, cheaper, and less intimidating to newcomers. We will keep finding uses for it besides gambling on Dogecoin and Bored Apes. It'll start weaving its way into parts of our lives without us even knowing it's there. It will facilitate global computing and money transfers and perform whatever other uses we find for an always-on, unstoppable world computer and financial system.

And, yes, there will be other silly narratives and opportunities for people to try to get rich along the way. You can play in the casino if you want. Just be careful. Don't be someone else's exit liquidity. Take profits. Get some fresh air. Don't get tricked by the bombastic cult leaders who seem too smart to fail.

From its 2013 peak of $1,100, Bitcoin dropped to $171 in 2015. Then it came back. From Ethereum's 2018 high of $1,400, it dropped to $84. It came back, too. Maybe this time is different. Maybe this time crypto is done for good. But I doubt it.

I'll see you in the next bull run.

ACKNOWLEDGMENTS

I often see authors write some version of "it takes a village to write a book" in these acknowledgment sections. I get it now. It's true.

First, thank you to my wonderful wife, Cosette, for all of your love and support throughout both parts of this journey, living it and writing it. Thank you to Sutton for giving me the clarity I needed to step away from this world. And thank you to Kaia for bringing even more love into our family as I wrapped this up.

Johnny and Rose, I'm eternally grateful for our friendship and how this experience brought us together. Quinn, thank you for helping teach me about this world and sending me that first fateful alpha tip. We all had quite the ride.

Evan Armstrong, thank you for sending me that message back in 2021 saying that some of the crypto articles I was writing reminded you of story lines in *The Big Short*. You helped inspire this whole project.

In terms of turning this story into the book in your hands, there are two people I can't thank enough. Noah Schwartzberg, my amazing editor at Portfolio, thank you for giving such consistently helpful, spot-on, and detailed feedback on all the pages I sent you. It would not be half the book it is today without you. And thank you to my amazing agent, David Fugate. You saw the potential in this story, and in me, and helped change my life.

So many people read chapters or drafts of this book and gave feedback, and I appreciate all of you. In particular, thank you to Zach Bateer, Nathan Baugh, Anthony Gustin, my sister, Sonja, and my parents, Cherie and Randall, for reading full drafts and giving incredibly detailed feedback. Thank you to Dan Shipper for reading so many early chapters and gently telling me I needed to work on my storytelling.

Tiago Forte, Chris Guillebeau, and Zach Obront, thank you all for encouraging me to write this and for generously connecting me with people who could make it happen. And thank you again, Tiago, for being so generous with sharing everything you've learned about the publishing business since releasing your first book. Thank you, too, to Simone Stolzoff for being so generous in sharing your lessons on the publishing industry and for putting together the Portfolio group. Cece and Zoe, I can't wait for your books to come out, as well.

Finally, thank you for reading my book. I hope you learned something, had fun, and can see the good and bad in this wild industry a little better now.

GLOSSARY

Airdrop

Free tokens given away as a reward to early users of a crypto application. *Airdrop farming* is the process of using new crypto applications in the hopes of qualifying for airdrops in the future.

Centralized Exchange

A way to buy cryptocurrency similar to stock-trading applications. Centralized exchanges will usually obviate the need to deal with wallets and seed phrases, will hold all your cryptocurrency for you, and will let you buy and sell easily without having to worry about the more-technical aspects. They also typically make it much easier to buy crypto using fiat money, like USD, which you can transfer in from your bank account. But, since they hold your crypto, they can't be used to interact with other blockchain applications.

Decentralized Exchange

A type of smart-contract application, like Uniswap, that allows you to swap between cryptocurrencies entirely on the smart-contract network itself without needing to go to a centralized exchange, like Coinbase.

Decentralized Finance (DeFi)
A catch-all term for any kind of financial application built on top of a blockchain. Some examples of DeFi apps include stablecoins, lending protocols, and decentralized exchanges.

Diamond Hands
The philosophy that, to get rich in crypto, you need to hold on to your coins with hands as strong as diamonds. Never sell. Never spend. Never let them go. If you can do that, you'll be richer than you can possibly imagine. Or you'll be someone else's exit liquidity. Results may vary.

Floor Price
The cheapest price you can pay to buy one piece of an NFT collection. For example, the cheapest Bored Ape or the cheapest Beeple art piece.

Fully Diluted Valuation (FDV)
Another way to measure the value of a cryptocurrency, calculated by taking how many tokens will ever be in circulation and multiplying them by the current price of one token. Bitcoin will eventually have 21 million bitcoins in circulation, and the current price is $28,000 for one bitcoin, so Bitcoin's FDV is $588 billion.

Gas Fee
Another name for the transaction fee on a blockchain network.

Initial Coin Offering (ICO)
A way to launch cryptocurrencies that was popular during the 2017–18 mania. Typically, these launches were done on Ethereum, and startups would put their tokens up for sale for a fixed price denominated in ETH. There have been numerous lawsuits since then alleging that ICOs are unregistered securities sales, so their popularity has waned.

Layer 1 Blockchain
Any self-sufficient cryptocurrency network that doesn't need to rely on another network for its security, settlement, or other aspects. Bitcoin, Ethereum, Dogecoin, and Terra are all examples of layer 1 blockchains.

Layer 2 Blockchain

A blockchain built on top of a layer 1 blockchain which gives users access to some special benefit—like faster, cheaper transactions, or heightened anonymity—while still relying on the layer 1 blockchain for some of the functionality. Polygon, Base chain, Optimism, and Arbitrum are all examples of layer 2 blockchains.

Lending Protocol

A type of smart-contract application that allows you to deposit some cryptocurrency, like ETH, and borrow another cryptocurrency, like USDC, against it. Lending protocols were some of the first DeFi applications built, and some, like MakerDAO and Aave, have been running nearly flawlessly for many years.

Liquidity Tokens

A special type of crypto token representing your deposit into a decentralized exchange. When you add liquidity for a trading pair in a decentralized exchange, like supplying ETH and USDC, the exchange gives you back a *liquidity token* representing your deposit. At any time in the future, you can trade that liquidity token back into the exchange to get your share of the ETH and USDC back. However, the amounts you get back will be different from the amounts you put in based on how the balance in the pool has changed in the interim.

Market Capitalization (Market Cap)

One way to measure the value of a cryptocurrency, calculated by taking how many tokens are in circulation and multiplying them by the current price of one token. Bitcoin currently has 19.5 million bitcoins in circulation, and the price of one bitcoin is $28,000, so Bitcoin's market cap is $546 billion.

Non-Fungible Token (NFT)

A type of crypto asset for which each individual unit is unique in some way, like an individual painting or an individual seat at a concert. Popularized by artists like Beeple selling their digital art pieces and the profile-picture mania led by the Bored Ape Yacht Club.

Paper Hands

The opposite of *diamond hands*. A derogatory term used to refer to someone who sold their coins instead of holding on to them.

Private Keys

A string of letters and numbers that lets you control an account on a crypto network. A private key will typically look something like: ec072a30cda95d496350 86479bc517d0547c5bb29b85755f5c94cec98fe4c68a. By pasting that into a wallet, you can control whatever address it's associated with. If you lose your private key, or the associated seed phrase, there is no way to recover your wallet. It is gone forever.

Public Keys and Addresses

The public part of your blockchain account. It's used to create an *address*, which people can use to see your activities and send you cryptocurrency. You will typically never interact with your public key. You'll just share your address with people.

Seed Phrase

A string of twelve to sixteen words that gives you access to a theoretically unlimited number of accounts on a blockchain network. A seed phrase is usually used to create or restore a wallet, so if you lose your seed phrase, you lose access to all of the cryptocurrency stored in the associated wallet.

Shitcoin

A cryptocurrency with no meaningful use besides speculation.

Smart Contract

A blockchain-native piece of software that allows some process to run automatically on the blockchain network itself. Decentralized exchanges and lending protocols are smart contracts, as are NFTs and tokens.

Solidity

The most popular programming language for building applications on Ethereum and other blockchains.

Tokenomics

The economics behind a crypto token, including anything from how quickly the token is released, to how it's released, to what it's used for, to how it's initially priced. If you want to understand a cryptocurrency better, you can usually find a page or paper on its website explaining its tokenomics in detail.

Tokens vs. Coins vs. Cryptocurrencies

Cryptocurreny is the catch-all term for any fungible crypto asset, like BTC, ETH, or UNI (for Uniswap). *Coin* is, similarly, a catch-all term and is generally acceptable for any kind of fungible crypto asset. *Token* is typically used to refer to a cryptocurrency that is part of an application on a smart-contract blockchain, like the UNI token for Uniswap, but it's not a hard rule.

Wallet

A piece of software on your computer or phone that lets you interact more easily with blockchain applications and send and receive cryptocurrency. It stores your accounts, as well as your public and private keys, and is typically created or restored using a seed phrase.

We Are Gonna Make It (WAGMI)

A popular battle cry in crypto that we're all going to get rich together.

INDEX

ABOUT THE AUTHOR

Nathaniel Eliason was born in Washington, DC, and studied philosophy at Carnegie Mellon University. He is a writer and crypto insider with a wildly popular newsletter and podcast. He lives in Austin, Texas, with his wife and two daughters.